D1289564

LABOUR AND SOCIALISM

LABOUR AND SOCIALISM

A History of the British Labour Movement 1867-1974

JAMES HINTON

UNIVERSITY OF MASSACHUSETTS PRESS

Copyright © 1983 by James Hinton

All rights reserved

First published in the United States of America in 1983 by
THE UNIVERSITY OF MASSACHUSETTS PRESS
Amherst, Massachusetts
Printed in Great Britain

Library of Congress Cataloging in Publication Data
Hinton, James.
    Labour and socialism.

    Bibliography: p.
    Includes index.
    1. Trade-unions—Great Britain—Political activity—
History.   2. Labor and laboring classes—Great Britain
—Political activity—History.   3. Labour Party (Great
Britain)—History.   4. Socialism—Great Britain—History.
I. Title.
HD6667.H56   1983   322'.2'0941   82-21798
ISBN 0-87023-393-9

Contents

Abbreviations

AEU	Amalgamated Engineering Union
ASE	Amalgamated Society of Engineers
ASLEF	Associated Society of Locomotive Engineers and Firemen
BSP	British Socialist Party
CND	Campaign for Nuclear Disarmament
CP	Communist Party
ILP	Independent Labour Party
LRC	Labour Representation Committee
MFGB	Miners Federation of Great Britain
NAUL	National Amalgamated Union of Labour
NIRC	National Industrial Relations Court
NUGMW	National Union of General and Municiple Workers
NUM	National Union of Miners
NUR	National Union of Railwaymen
NUWM	National Unemployed Workers Movement
SDF	Social Democratic Party
SL	Socialist League
SLP	Socialist Labour Party
TGWU	Transport and General Workers Union
TUC	Trades Union Congress
TWF	Transport Workers Federation
UAB	Unemployment Assistance Board
UDC	Union of Democratic Control
WEWNC	War Emergency Workers National Committee
WSPU	Women's Social and Political Union
WTUL	Women's Trade Union League

Introduction

In writing this history of the British labour movement since mid-Victorian times, I have become increasingly aware of the limitations of my subject. This is not a history of the working class, a majority of which has usually been excluded for one reason or another from effective participation in the labour movement. It was not until the First World War that the proportion of the occupied population organised in trade unions exceeded one quarter, and the majority remained unorganised until 1974. For much of their history trade unions turned an excluding face towards the less skilled, the poor, women; and the movement as a whole was characteristically unresponsive to the needs of the more exploited sections of the working class. The Labour Party was rather more successful than the unions in winning the allegiance of the working class. Nevertheless, the proportion of the working-class electorate voting for the Labour Party has never exceeded two-thirds, and has recently tended to be a good deal lower. I have tried to situate the history of the labour movement within the wider context of the history of the working class as a whole. But this remains a history of the movement, not of the class.

Similarly, the impact of the labour movement on modern British society cannot be understood outside the context of its constantly renegotiated alliances with radical sections of the middle class. The achievement of a limited working-class franchise and of basic trade union rights in the 1860s and 1870s was only possible because the small trade union movement was able to construct alliances with more powerful middle-class political currents. Labour politics, as it took shape over the succeeding three decades, embodied complex tensions between independence and a continuing need to maintain good relations with Liberalism. The eventual establishment of a majority Labour Government in 1945 was itself the product of a momentary conversion of a substantial section of middle-class voters to the party of the working class. And within the leadership of the movement itself, alliances between professional trade unionists and members of the middle-class intellegentsia have often played a central role: as, on the socialist left, have organisations combining the most politically radical members of both classes. I have indicated the importance of middle-class radicalism in its various forms to my theme – whether these radicals appear on the scene as voters or as vanguards, and whether the alliance is one in which labour dominates or is dominated. But it is the standpoint of the working-class adherents of these alliances that remains centre stage.

The central concern of this history is with the relationship between working-class organisation and the idea of a socialist transformation of society. That relationship has always been problematic. Pervading the self-awareness of the labour movement was the image of the two 'wings' – the political and the industrial, the Labour Party and the trade unions. This curious dualism reflects the way in which the movement acted to negotiate a place for the working class within the framework of a capitalist democracy: the unions bargaining, the party reforming, neither seeking – nor, by their division, able – to challenge the fundamentals of bourgeois society. Beneath these 'wings', a section of the working class was able to construct a way of life which nurtured the values of solidarity and mutualism within the larger, competitive social environment. Individualism, selfishness and the pursuit of sectional interests were never absent from this world of labour: but neither were they its organising principles. What constituted labour as a *movement* was the belief that each struggle was, or could be, linked into a larger social purpose. Embodied in the network of working-class institutions and practices was a sense of class identity and interest, of membership of an oppositional culture whose common objective was the creation, bit by bit, of a fairer and a more co-operative social order.

The relationship between the institutions, structured by the day-to-day processes of accommodation with the existing social order, and the project of social transformation which gave those institutions coherence as a movement, was necessarily an ambiguous one. The history of labour is a history of acceptance of the rules of an accommodative game compatible with the bourgeois social order. But it is also a history of recurrent revolt against those rules, against the established terms of working-class subordination. The ambiguity was embodied in conflicts between those (often the established leaders) who placed short-term institutional interests first, and those (often a new generation of rank-and-file activists) who perceived new opportunities to reopen the negotiation with bourgeois society on which those institutions were premised. It was in these conflicts that the balance between institutional stability and oppositional movement was defined and redefined. But the very recurrence of the conflict points towards impasse. If it was the dream of a new social order that made labour a movement, it was the reality of a social order structured by capitalism that ensured that each new transforming impulse would eventually be contained and subordinated.

There is one final limitation to my subject. When I first thought about writing such a history ten years ago there was reason to believe that the labour movement, after a period of crisis, was poised on the brink of a great leap forward similar to the explosions of 1889–90, 1910–20 or the Second World War. This no longer seems the right perspective. In the spring of 1982 the difficulties experienced by the labour movement since its high point in 1945 appear to mark, not a temporary interruption to the forward march of labour, but the disintegration of a particular pattern of working-class institutions and ideology which had previously given substance to the very conception of a 'forward march'. The steady decline of the Labour vote since 1951, the extreme tensions between the trade unions and Labour governments in the 1960s and 1970s, and the palpable decline of any popular conception of an alternative social order to capitalism since the 1940s — all these developments point to the conclusion that what we had thought of as the 'labour movement' has itself entered a terminal crisis. Whatever alternative instrument for the construction of a new social order emerges over the coming years, it is unlikely to bear very much resemblance to the particular institutional and ideological structures whose emergence and consolidation over the last century constitute the central themes of this book. Consequently, this history is not intended as an account of the foundations on which mass socialist politics can be rebuilt. Such an account would have to pay as much attention to the recent history of the women's movement, the environmental and peace movements, the fragmented but vigorous world of community politics, the complex cross-currents of socialist and libertarian ideas over the last twenty years, as to the labour movement itself. The process of rebuilding a socialist political movement will involve the discovery of new ways of putting together the traditional institutions of the labour movement with other oppositional forces in British society. In the meantime I offer this book as a respectful description of certain familar ghosts which will continue to haunt the minds of those who seek to transform society for some time to come.

1

Working-class organisation in mid-Victorian Britain

By the 1870s most of the characteristic institutions of the modern British labour movement were already in existence. The granting of the vote to a section of the urban working class in the Reform Act of 1867 symbolised the emergence of an arena of political and social freedom within which a small elite of working men could claim citizenship and corporate status. The claim was staked out partly in the language and politics of popular Liberalism, partly in the intricate expanding network of working-class organisation – co-operatives, friendly societies, clubs and, above all, trade unions. The previous quarter century had seen the widespread establishment of local Trades Councils and, in 1868, the TUC. Modern unions in the engineering, building and other craft industries are the direct ancestors of national organisations first established between 1850 and the 1870s. In cotton, coal and iron stable trade unionism and collective bargaining first developed in these years. And it was in the early 1870s that the unions, for the first time, secured a satisfactory legal status. What sort of people inhabited this emergent 'world of labour'? What were their beliefs and aspirations? And how did they negotiate a place for themselves and their institutions within the larger structures of inequality, exploitation, poverty and oppression which characterised the social order of mid-Victorian Britain?

I

The mid-Victorian economy presented an anarchic mixture of the old and the new. Steam power and the factory had revolutionised the division of labour in the textile industry. But the dream of the 1840s, of the self-acting machine which would finally liberate capital from its dependence on the skills of intractable human beings, proved elusive. Even in the textile factories skilled labour was not eliminated. Often, steam power worked to increase, rather than reduce, the demand for both skilled craft labour and brute muscle power.

The coal that powered the steam engines was dug by armies of men with pick and shovel, just as it was navvies with wheelbarrows, not mechanical excavators, who networked Britain with railway tracks during the middle years of the nineteenth century. The building workers who constructed the factories and the sprawling towns worked by methods relatively untouched by the industrial revolution. At the forefront of technological change, in the machine-building workshops, the personal skill and cunning of the engineering craftsmen remained crucial to production. There was no mid-Victorian equivalent to the long-drawn out immiseration of the hand loom weavers, which holds such a central role in the history of the working-class protest during the first half of the nineteenth century. But, piecemeal, the competition between factory and hand technologies continued. The older forms proved surprisingly resilient. In some cases the artisans survived, producing for a luxury market. More commonly, steam power was held at bay by the exploitation of men, women and children working at minutely subdivided tasks in dark, insanitary workshops, or the home.

This was a very diverse workforce, and only a small proportion of it belonged to trade unions. In the language of contemporary social commentary 'skilled' and 'organised' were often used as synonomous terms, with the mass of the workers being seen as both unskilled and unorganisable. In reality the divisions within the working-class were far more complex than this simple bi-polar model can encompass. Because different sections of the Victorian economy were organised in such very different ways there was no uniformity in the methods by which workers in particular sections of industry were able to mark themselves off as higher paid, skilled and organised. But those who achieved skilled status did have something in common.

Particular groups of workers acquired skilled status to the extent that they succeeded in convincing the world at large that other people could not do their jobs. In the 1860s the Amalgamated Society of Engineers (ASE) declared: 'It is our duty to exercise that same care and watchfulness over that in which we have a vested interest – i.e. our skill – as the physician does who holds a diploma.'[1] As with the medical profession, part of the engineer's protection lay in the cultivation of an aura of mystery – 'craft' – around his activities.

A 'skilled' worker was one whose skills were mysterious. In the absence of any scientific analysis and understanding of the labour process in which he was engaged, his skill could not be transmitted by formal instruction. It could only be picked up through experience – as knacks, as tricks of the trade. A miner was skilled when he knew the difference between an innocent rumble in the rock, and one which presaged disaster. A turner was skilled when he had acquired sufficient experience to know which tool to use and at what speed for a particular job, and how best to prepare the tool. None of this knowledge was systematised or written down: consequently it could remain the property of the workers, rather than the employers.

Skilled work involved the worker in conceiving the task as well as in executing it, in making decisions about the operative details of the job, and in a working day punctuated by such decisions and by the performance of ancillary tasks – preparing tools, setting-up machines, shoring-up the roof of the mine. It followed that the skilled worker exercised a measure of control over the pace of his work, that he was not overlooked and bossed every minute of the day.

Trade unionism had as much to do with the preservation of job autonomy, usually by exercising informal sanctions rather than by any formal agreements with employers, as it did with the direct defence of living standards. In fact, the ability of a mid-Victorian union to maintain privileged wages scales for its members depended, as the engineers well understood, on its ability to protect 'that in which we have a vested interest' – skilled status.

The largest group of mid-Victorian trade unions operated in craft industries – industries in which the labour process had not been changed beyond recognition by the industrial revolution. Building and printing are obvious examples. But even in engineering the pre-industrial division of labour between an artisan who actually made something and a labourer who fetched and carried for him remained the predominant form. Before the late nineteenth century the semi-skilled machine minder was only a threat on the horizon to the engineering craftsmen.

In the craft industries skilled workers were traditionally recruited through a system of apprenticeship, and the defining characteristic of craft unionism was the attempt to restrict entry into the trade by limiting the number of boys admitted to apprenticeships. They were seldom entirely successful. Faced with rapid and unpredictable expansion in the demand for skilled labour, the Engineers were forced to open their doors to men who, though never having done an apprenticeship, had spent a qualifying period in the trade and could earn a craftsman's wage. The Typographical Association was able to insist on maintaining strict apprenticeship quotas only at the expense of abandoning whole sections of the printing industry to non-unionism.

Attempts to control the supply of labour were supplemented by attempts to control its distribution. The payment of tramping and removal benefits, to encourage workers to migrate from areas of depressed trade to areas where jobs were plentiful, was one of the oldest techniques of craft unionism. Though still commonplace after 1850, tramping tended to decline as the growing integration of the national economy brought good or bad trade to all areas simultaneously. Other friendly benefits, covering unemployment, accident, sickness, old age and funeral expenses, served partly to provide a measure of economic security to individual members and to bind them to the union. But they were also intended to remove from the labour market workers who might be tempted to work below the craft rate. Not all craft unions paid the full range of benefits: in the 1850s and 1860s, for example, the Typographical Association paid only strike and tramping benefit. But most craft unions aspired to do so.

In so far as union benefits were used to restrict the supply of labour this could be done without encroaching directly on the authority of employers. But other methods of restriction – limitation of apprentices, and, its necessary corollary, the attempt to confine traditionally skilled work to men recognised as skilled by the union – involved direct conflict. So did efforts to restrict overtime, establish standard hours of work and minimum wages, and generally to control the pace and conditions of work. The unions' demands were laid down in their rule books, and it was normally the responsibility of the branches to enforce these rules, together with those 'customs of the trade' that remained unwritten. To this end organisation and pressure within the workshops was supplemented, when necessary, by the branch withdrawing members from shops not observing union rules, and supporting them on unemployment benefit. This technique of the 'strike-in-detail' was explained by the Flint Glass Makers in 1850: 'As man after man leaves, and no one (comes) to supply their place, then it is that the proud and haughty spirit of the oppressor is brought down, and he feels the power he cannot see.'[2] In most cases local regulation was rather less unilateral, and involved more contact and bargaining with employers, than this quotation suggests. Agreements on working rules, and sometimes on disputes procedures, with federations of local employers were increasingly a feature of industrial relations in building from the 1860s and in engineering from the 1870s. But the primary strength of these unions remained in the pervasive informal mutualism of the craft community, reinforced by union friendly benefits, rather than in the formal processes of collective bargaining. Membership of the union represented a formalisation of membership of a pre-existing collectivity of 'the trade' – a formality that many tradesmen did not bother to observe, though they might well be prepared to support the union in a strike, or even, like the non-union engineers who dominated the Tyneside Nine Hours League in 1871, to take the initiative themselves in militant action.

In the craft industries trade unionism was an outgrowth of the informal community of the trade. In other sectors, where the mystery of the worker's skill was less well protected, skilled status was more commonly a product of trade union organisation, rather than the precondition of it. This was particularly true in cotton, where the remorseless motion of the steam engine left little scope for the kind of on-the-job autonomy characteristic of an engineering workshop. The ability of the cotton spinners to command high wages and status owed little to any intrinsic difficulty in the jobs they performed. Spinners minded machines and were paid according to output. They worked alongside two or more hourly-paid piecers, whose work they supervised. So long as the industry was expanding most of the piecers could hope eventually to become spinners. In constructing their skilled status the spinners' main problem was to prevent employers using the piecers, who quickly picked up the skill, to do their work at lower rates. They did this by struggling to regulate piecer promotion according to seniority. In effect the seniority system tied both piecer and spinner to working for a particular employer. Piecers could not move around without losing their place in the queue. And spinners found it difficult to move since any employer taking on a spinner from outside risked provoking a strike by his own piecers who were queuing for the vacant spinner's job. Unlike the craft unionist, then, the spinner was not free to move around and could not easily develop techniques for playing off one employer against another. The skilled status of the spinner was peculiarly dependent on employer goodwill. Employers accepted it because it enabled them to use the spinners as a supervisory elite with a vested interest (because they were paid by the piece) in intensifying the labour of the low-paid and unorganised piecers.

The other main group of cotton trade unionists were the weavers.

Exceptionally, among mid-Victorian unions, weavers' trade unionism did not rest upon any systematic restriction of entry to the job,
nor did the weavers, many of whom were women, acquire the status
of 'skilled' workers. The key to their success in organising stable
trade unions lay in quantity rather than quality, in organisational
strength, and in the development of a complex process of collective
bargaining with the employers. In all this they anticipated the new
unionism of less-skilled workers which developed in many industries
from the later 1880s.

The miners also put a premium on collective bargaining, though in
many respects the hewers who formed the backbone of mining trade
unionism had more in common with craftsmen than with factory
operatives. Because of the physical conditions of mining the hewers
exercised an exceptional degree of control over their immediate
work situation. Close supervision was a geological impossibility.
The rudimentary form of miners' trade unionism was restriction of
output intended to push up coal prices, and with them wages, by
restricting the supply of coal. 'Overtoil', declared the Miners
National Association in 1863, 'produces over-supply; low prices and
low wages follow. . . . The evil of overtoil . . . is therefore a fair and
proper subject of regulation.'[3] In Scotland hewers traditionally met
reductions in wages by reducing their output – the 'wee darg'. In
Lancashire the pace of work was controlled by the putter's custom of
removing filled tubs from the hewers he served in strict rotation.
Each hewer therefore had to work at the pace of the slowest man, or
the man with the most difficult place. In the North East the hewers
controlled the allocation of good and bad places at the face by the
practice of 'cavilling'. Four times a year they met to draw lots for the
places available. This deprived managers of the power to use the
allocation of places as a disciplinary weapon. Given this degree of
job control, why did the hewers find it more difficult to construct
stable trade unionism and skilled status than, for example, the
spinners who were certainly less 'skilled' in any objective sense of the
word? Mining concerns tended to be large, and employers' organisation at district level relatively well developed. In an isolated mining
community the power of the owner was all pervasive. There was
little alternative employment for the vicitimised miner. Where the
owner was also the landlord, strikers were evicted from their houses,
often permanently, to make room for imported blacklegs. The owners' power was further enhanced by company sick clubs, doctors,
schools, often financed by compulsory deductions from wages. The

establishment of union friendly benefits, or independent benefit societies controlled by the men, was thus a question not only of welfare, but also of power. Similarly the growth of co-operative stores helped to make striking miners independent of shopkeepers who would refuse credit at the behest of the owners. But these lines of defence were as yet weakly developed, and the miners' control of their own communities belongs to a later period.

Miners were also subject to blacklegging on a large scale. Not only were their strikes undermined by the importation of miners from less well-organised coalfields, their attempts at organisations were periodically placed in jeopardy by waves of impoverished immigrants from the countryside and from Ireland. The susceptibility of the hewer to the blackleg did not occur because inexperienced miners could cut as much coal as the skilled men. Rather it reflected the fact that wages represented an exceptionally high proportion of the coal owners' outlay – around 50 per cent. In the factories, where wage costs were small in relation to the value of the plant, machinery and raw materials, the fall in production caused by replacing skilled workers with green labour would not easily be compensated by a lower wages bill. In mining, on the other hand, employers were often prepared to accept a period of reduced output as the price of reducing their wage costs.

Beyond the struggle around the frontier of control in the pit, the miners used two main techniques in their attempts to improve their position. Firstly, they organised to secure protective legislation from Parliament. Apart from measures concerned with child labour and safety, the miners also won some statutory regulation of their payment. Owners were required to allow a full-time representative of the men to check the weight of coal brought to the surface – the 'checkweighman' – and forbidden to pay by volume rather than by weight. Secondly, the miners relied on collective bargaining at district level, developed extensively during the boom years of the late 1860s and early 1870s.

II

The organisation of trade unions in the mid-Victorian period usually rested upon systematic attempts by small groups of relatively privileged workers to defend their status against any encroachments by the mass of the labouring poor. Trade union growth was associated with widening wage differentials, and with the crystallisation of a structural divide within the working class in many areas between labour aristocrats and others. The source of the division was in the workplace, but it tended to spill over into the community as skilled workers used their higher earnings to mark themselves off socially from the rest of the working class. Able to afford better housing, artisans attempted to segregate themselves from the dirt, discomfort and immorality of the inner city slums. They participated in a formidable range of voluntary organisations – co-operatives, adult education institutes, the temperance movement, nonconformist chapels – cutting themselves off from the street and pub culture of the poor. Even in the mining villages, where trade unionism was less systematically exclusive than in the crafts, the unionists used the financial walls of the co-operative store (no credit, no cheap adulterated food) and the friendly society, and the spiritual walls of the chapel to mark themselves off from 'the drunkards, the pigeon-flyers and dog-runners'.[4]

The self-conscious differentiation of a respectable section of the working class from the unruly poor appears to have been an integral part of the formation of a stable trade union movement. A number of other factors reinforced the organised workman's sense of belonging to an intermediate social stratum. Despite the growth of large-scale production in some industries, small units persisted and, with them, the possibility for the skilled worker of becoming a small master or setting up as an independent tradesman – as, for example, 5 per cent of the members of the plumbers' union did during the 1860s. The labour aristocrat often felt more social and political identity with the small master, the shopkeeper, publican and tradesman than he did with the unskilled worker. More prosperous workmen had long been accustomed to use their power as consumers to influence the voting of shopkeepers, thus staking their claim to a political status whose official recognition they campaigned for in 1867. In the more affluent friendly societies, and in many other voluntary organisations, skilled workmen freely shared local democratic management with the shopocracy and their kind.

It would however be a mistake to view the mid-Victorian labour aristocracy as having assimilated itself to the aspirations and lifestyle of the lower middle class. Read superficially their language often suggests embourgeoisment – 'respectability', 'self-help', 'manly independence' – all these were keywords within the labour aristocratic culture. But the meaning of words is coloured by the social context within which they are used. The elite of organised working men remained an elite *within* the working class. 'Self-help' was embraced, but not in the individualistic spirit of the self-made man. Only as a member of the collective could most working men hope to advance themselves. However moderately it might be expressed, the mutualism of the trade union ethic remained profoundly at odds with the individualistic ethic of bourgeois society. Even the pursuit of 'a fair day's work for a fair day's pay' – the most seemingly accommodating slogan of mid-Victorian trade unionism – involved the systematic operation of restrictive practices which orthodox political economy found deeply obnoxious. Behind the respectable face which trade union leaders liked to turn towards the established order, lay the day-to-day cultivation of an ethic of solidarity and the mutualism of the workshop community. Solidarity, and the sacrifices it demanded for the good of the collective, was no less real for being restricted to an organised elite of the working class. What the labour aristocracy sought was not escape from its class situation, but rather the establishment of an acknowledged status for itself within the existing social order.

The revolutionary aspirations associated with the popular unrest of the 1830s and 1840s had not altogether vanished. Respectable mid-Victorian working men might well have agreed with the philosopher of liberalism, John Stuart Mill, that the capitalist organisation of production would eventually give way to co-operation. *
What was absent in the later period was the sense that the co-operative commonwealth was an immediately realisable objective. Before the mid-century it had been possible for important groups of working-class activists to view large-scale capitalism as an aberration, and to believe that an alternative social order could be constructed through the free co-operation of small-scale producers. By the 1860s and 1870s there was no mistaking the fact that the alliance of capital and the steam engine had become the organising principle of the social order. There was no route open any more for 'the people' to organise the production of the necessities of life in their own egalitarian way. Experiments in co-operative production continued throughout these years, but they no longer appeared as the

---

* J.S. Mill, widely read and admired among educated working men, predicted that 'the form of association . . . which, if mankind continue to improve, must be expected in the end to predominate, is not that which can exist between a capitalist as chief, and workpeople without a voice in the management, but the association of the labourers themselves on terms of equality, collectively owning the capital with which they carry on their operations, and working under managers elected and removable by themselves.'[5]

cutting edge of a revolutionary programme. Capitalists held the means of production and any change in this arrangement would require a frontal assault on capitalist power. Many mid-Victorian trade unionists believed that capitalism was an unjust and exploitative system. The aristocratic Boilermakers were not alone in asserting that the 'capitalists, like prowling wolves, snatch eagerly at . . . every shadow of a chance to grind us to the earth. . . .'[6] But few, if any, believed that the working class possessed sufficient organised strength to confront the wolves head on. Perhaps one day they would. But in the meantime the priority had to be given to finding some way of living with capitalism.

III

One key to that accommodation was the long and complex process of negotiating a political alliance between organised labour and an insurgent section of the middle class. The sporadic efforts of middle-class radicals and moderate working-class leaders to build a political alliance of the two classes had constituted an important, but subordinate, theme in the history of Chartism. From the late 1850s, however, such efforts occupied the forefront of working-class politics, ensuring the containment of workers' political aspirations within a structure of popular politics organised around the conflict between 'the people' and an establishment dominated by landed wealth, rather than between labour and capital.

A number of factors underlay the increased dynamism of reform politics from the late 1850s. The growth of a cheap provincial press gave a voice to the grievances of local businessmen and professionals excluded from the magic circle of financial and landed wealth that dominated establishment politics in London. Members of the nonconformist churches moved into politics to campaign against religious discrimination and for non-denominational education and the disestablishment of the Church of England. Sympathy with what appeared to be an international tide of liberation in the early 1860s – the American Civil War, the Italian Risorgimento – brought the leaders of middle-class radicalism, notably John Bright, into close working relationships with representative trade union leaders of the post-Chartist generation. The Reform League – the key organisation of working-class politics in the 1860s – emerged out of these internationalist campaigns.

In February 1866 Russell and Gladstone, the leaders of Parliamentary Liberalism, introduced a Bill designed to make a very modest extension to the existing franchise. It was the rejection of this Bill, and the defeat of the Liberal Government by a combination of Tories and Whig dissidents, that precipitated the mass agitation for reform. At the peak of its strength the Reform Leage had about 65,000 members organised in 600 branches, 100 of them in London. The membership was overwhelmingly working class, and the demand was 'manhood suffrage'. More than half the League's income came, not from its members, but from the deeper pockets of middle-class Radicals who saw the League as a useful supplement to their own campaign (co-ordinated by the Reform Union) for the more modest goal of 'household' suffrage. John Bright's immense prestige rested on his ability to straddle the League and the Union, holding the agitation and the cash together in at least a rhetorical unity.

The fall of the Liberal Government in June 1866 was greeted by a series of huge demonstrations. In July the League, pressed from the left, decided to challenge a government ban on political assemblies in the parks. When Edmund Beales, a lawyer and President of the Reform League, was denied access to Hyde Park by the police, he obediently marched his column off to Trafalgar Square. But the bulk of the demonstrators tore down the railings and invaded the park. Three days and nights of rioting followed in the West End, until the Home Secretary, Spencer Walpole, tearfully accepted Beales' offer to return to the park and restore order. These events electrified the Reform agitation throughout the country. Through the autumn Bright addressed huge working-class meetings in most provincial cities.

It is customary to ascribe the Hyde Park riots to such elemental forces as the fury of the East End mob lured 'up West' by the prospect of a shindig. But some credit must also go to the deliberate political action of the League's left wing. In April 1866 Benjamin Lucraft, an ex-Chartist, had initiated outdoor meetings on Clerkenwell Green, preaching the cause of Reform to a class of workmen not usually found at the League's branch meetings. Some of the 'scum' in the Park had no doubt attended these meetings, and knew very well what they were about. Subsequently George Potter, who through his paper the *Beehive* and the London Working Men's Association advocated a more militant policy than that of the dominant trade union leaders, took the initiative in organising the first Trades Reform demonstration, forcing the League and the London Trades Council to follow suit. If Bright and the moderate League leaders felt, with a mixture of fear and exhilaration, that they were being swept along on an unexpected wave of spontaneous militancy, there were others in the League who saw that militancy as the reward of their deliberate efforts.

A bad harvest, a hard winter, rising unemployment and a cholera epidemic deepened discontent, and the agitation continued to grow. Soon after the Parliamentary session began in 1867 Disraeli's Conservative cabinet introduced a new Reform Bill. Within the League, the left seized the initiative, threatening an indefinite 'universal cecession from labour' until the suffrage was granted. George Potter, at that time involved in organising a national trade union conference and in close touch with the leaders of the Northern trade unions, took up the cry at a meeting in Trafalgar Square. These may have been empty threats, but the use of physical force to assert the right of assembly in Hyde Park was known to be well within the League's capabilities. The confrontation came in May. Against the advice of its best known leaders the League resolved on a new rally in Hyde Park. The government, anxious to demonstrate its independence from outside pressure, banned the meeting. Neither side could back down without humiliation. At about 6 p.m. on Monday 6 May, led by the Clerkenwell branch bearing a red flag surmounted by the cap of liberty, about 150,000 people marched into the Park, held an orderly, if triumphant meeting, and peacefully dispersed. No attempt was made to interfere with the demonstration. The government had capitulated.

Two weeks later Disraeli accepted a Radical amendment which quadrupled the numbers enfranchised by the Bill. The connections between the events of 6 May and Disraeli's move have been much debated by historians. Two points are important here. Firstly, the new franchise continued to exclude all the rural workers and most of the urban poor. The League was not unduly distressed by this: it had always qualified its demand for manhood suffrage by the phrase 'registered and residential'. It was the respectable working class that the League represented and whose enfranchisement it sought. Nor did the League press for a major redistribution of parliamentary seats towards the populous urban areas. The core of Conservative political power in the countryside survived intact – a fact which Disraeli had not overlooked in his readiness to outbid Gladstone in accepting Radical proposals to extend the franchise in urban constituencies which were in any case already largely controlled by the Liberals. The lack of interest shown by the League in the question of redistribution indicates a desire for the vote more as a symbol of status than as a lever of power. Respectable working men sought recognition as earnest and morally responsible citizens; they did not seek to enter electoral politics at the head of an avenging army of the dispossessed.

Secondly, the tensions within the League showed that if the citizenship offered by popular Liberalism were to be denied, then a different and altogether more menacing prospect might open up for working-class politics. Whether that calculation – that it was safe to concede, but dangerous to resist – was the key to the Parliamentary decision to extend the franchise is debatable. What is clear, however, is that it would indeed have been dangerous to resist. The accommodation achieved by organised labour within mid-Victorian society rested upon an alliance with middle-class radicalism, not a complete suppression of separate political identity. More class-conscious definitions of politics were available to these respectable working men. When their aspirations to a secure place within the existing social order appeared to be frustrated, they showed a readiness to reach out towards forms of political activity which would have threatened their middle-class allies as much as it threatened the existing political establishment.

IV

The achievement of a secure legal status for the trade unions also involved a struggle which, at times, threatened to carry the mid-Victorian labour movement beyond the politics of accommodation. Trade unions were still only semi-legal organisations in the 1860s. The Master and Servant Act made it a criminal offence for workers to leave their employment in breach of contract. This was frequently used against strikers, and had long been a subject of Parliamentary agitation by the unions. Moreover under common law the unions were defined as societies 'in restraint of trade'. This prevented them from taking action in the courts to protect their funds against dishonest officials. This problem had, apparently, been solved when in 1855, as a result of agitation by the London trades, trade unions were allowed to register under the Friendly Societies Act. Several major unions took advantage of this. In January 1867, however, in the case of *Hornby* v *Close*, the judges undermined their new found security by ruling that the United Society of Boilermakers, a registered union, was unable to prosecute an official who had embezzled union funds.

A few weeks earlier a Royal Commission on Trade Unions had been set up in response to the outcry occasioned by violent sanctions used against non-unionists in the Sheffield metal trades. Anxious to disassociate their unions from such tactics and to secure legal protection for their funds, the London-based leaders of some of the major craft unions joined with two of the more sympathetic members of the Royal Commission to manipulate the trade union evidence. These officials, who the Webbs later called 'the Junta', had been working closely together for some time. Their primary concern, beyond the establishment of strong, wealthy craft societies, was to make trade unionism respectable in middle-class eyes and thus to win for it, and for themselves, a recognised and secure position within the existing social order. That this would involve important changes in that order, in the direction of greater social and political equality, they were well aware, but they believed that these changes could best be achieved by persuasion rather than by militancy.

The Junta presented the Commission with a deliberately misleading picture of trade union activity which made scant reference to strikes, restrictive practices or the every day realities of industrial conflict. The tactic appeared to succeed. The majority report was far less anti-union than had been feared, while the Junta's evidence provided the basis for a minority report which urged full legal protection for the welfare activities of the respectable trade societies. Particularly valuable was the evidence of enlightened employers, like the Nottingham hosiery manufacturer A.J. Mundella, who could testify to the beneficial effect of recognising 'responsible' trade union leaders on his profits.

The General Election of 1868 returned a Liberal Government led by William Gladstone. Although this election was fought on the new franchise, organised labour made little independent impact. George Howell, secretary of the Reform League, used the League's organisation to enforce a secret deal with the Liberal Whips designed to minimise the danger to Liberalism from any independent working-class candidates. In return middle-class radicals like Sam Morley – Engels called him 'the commanding general of (the) sham labour general staff' – continued to finance the League's activities, and to line Howell's own pocket.*

* Howell made over £120 out of the 1868 election, and bought a house. Later he added a row of slum cottages as well. Howell was more concerned to use his experiences in the labour movement to feather his own nest than were most labour leaders – though the fact that he preserved his very frank diary may have led historians to exaggerate the degree to which he differed in this respect from others.

These manoeuvres effectively destroyed the Reform League. In its place the Junta established a Labour Representation League which worked closely with the Liberals with the object of securing the return of some 'qualified workmen' to Parliament. On one occasion, in a Scottish by-election in 1870, the new League put up a candidate against both parties. The Tory won. Despite this show of independence there was no attempt to reconstruct the local organisational basis for independent labour politics that had briefly existed in the Reform League.

In 1871 the recommendations of the Minority Report of the Royal Commission on Trade Unions were finally translated into law by the Liberal Government. By excluding trade unions from the common law category of 'combinations in restraint of trade', Parliament gave legal protection to their funds. But this measure was accompanied by a Criminal Law Amendment Act which, endorsing recent judicial decisions, made picketing illegal. The Junta's own moderation had betrayed them. They had presented their organisations as friendly societies rather than trade unions. Now Gladstone gave them what they had asked for — more literally than they had anticipated.

By 1871, however, a more militant temper had emerged in the labour movement. To some degree this was a product of the submerged tradition of unbending Chartist radicalism which had briefly shown its face at the height of the Reform Bill agitation. Established in the autumn of 1869, the Land and Labour League drew together proletarian radicals involved in agitations against repression in Ireland and unemployment in London. The League stressed the evils of landlords and bankers, but was vague in its analysis of capitalism. 'The Land for the People' was a slogan which had, and long continued to have, a secure purchase in working-class politics, particularly among the urban unemployed. Whether the land, once nationalised, was to be let to smallholders, to co-operatives, or to be farmed by state administered collectives, was a matter of debate within the League. The nationalisation of slum property and a public housing programme were also discussed. These were distant goals. Meanwhile the League was emphatic in its opposition to those who had sold the Reform League to 'that ghastliness, that knavery called Liberalism', and it insisted, in strict Chartist fashion, that 'he who is not for (the full programme) is against you'.[8] The League was closely associated with Karl Marx's First International. Since its establishment in 1864 the International had won the affiliation of a large section of the English trade unions, primarily because of its successes in preventing blacklegging by foreign workers during strikes. Those of its supporters whose desire to develop the International as a political organisation in England independently of the trade union leaders had been frustrated by Marx's somewhat elitist tactics,* threw themselves wholeheartedly into the Land and Labour League.

Following the defeat of Napoleon III at Sedan in September 1870 working-class opinion rallied to the new French Republic with an intensity reminiscent of that engendered by the American Civil War. The international issue – recognition of the Republic by the Liberal Government – was linked to a domestic one – Republicanism. Anti-monarchist agitation reached unprecedented heights during 1871. Republican clubs were founded in over fifty towns, and 'Mrs Brown' (Queen Victoria) was heartily reviled. But the Paris Commune (March–May 1871) exposed the breach between the meritocratic goals of middle-class republicans and the social republic of the proletarian left. Many labour aristocrats preferred the former, believing that Communism 'would make the skilful and thrifty workmen suffer for those who were neither'.[9] From the summer of 1871 the left splintered into a host of sectarian currents. The International itself did not long survive the defeat of the Commune. By 1872 it had lost most of its English trade union support, and Marx, in despair at the failure of the long-awaited European revolution, preferred to kill the International by transferring its headquarters to New York than to allow it to be captured by Bakunin and the anarchists. By 1872 the political initiatives of the proletarian left were in disarray. Meanwhile, however, their concern to expand the labour movement beyond the ranks of the labour aristocracy had played a role – albeit a minor one – in stimulating the growth of trade union organisation during the early 1870s.

V

In 1851 Mayhew, a sensitive and well-informed observer, remarked that the London poor were 'as unpolitical as footmen'. Far from 'entertaining violent democratic opinions, they appear to have no political opinions whatever'.[10] Historians have been fond of this

---

* Marx, dependent on the support of the English trade union leaders in his battle against French Proudhonism in the International, and sceptical of the possibility of building a socialist movement in England, preferred to wait for the anticipated European revolutionary crisis to radicalise the British situation before attempting direct involvement in British politics. The crisis arrived in 1871 – but its immediate impact on the British left was, as we shall see, more disruptive than positive.

quotation. However the inertness of the mid-Victorian poor can be exaggerated. They appeared – tumultuous, violent and not altogether ignorant of their interest – at election hustings. Bad harvests still caused bread riots in the towns – by no means an entirely irrational form of collective action. Sabbatarian attempts to restrict shopping and drinking on Sundays led to a major and successful series of riots in Hyde Park in 1855, and fifteen years later Liberal licensing legislation provoked enormous demonstrations of the unashamed and some rioting from the unrespectable. Not only miners but also other dispossessed groups – builders' labourers, navvies, dockers – attempted trade union organisation and, more frequently, struck during the 1850s and 1860s. It was above all in the boom years of 1871 to 1874 when unemployment fell lower than at any time before the First World War that important sections of the poorest and most oppressed workers asserted their presence, anticipating the better known events of the 'new unionism' nearly twenty years later.

The strike wave of the early years of the 1870s was sparked off by the successful five-month strike of engineering and shipbuilding workers in the North East for the Nine Hour Day. Traditionally a very badly organised district, the North-East strike was led, not by the unions – whose national executives were sour about the whole business – but by a Nine Hours League representing ten times as many non-unionists, including labourers, as union members. Local Nine Hours Leagues spread the movement to other areas and other industries. Even shop assistants struck on the Tyne. Meanwhile, urged on by members of the Land and Labour League, the London dockers were organising against wage cuts, and in December 1871, inspired by the victory on the Tyne, they established a Labour Protection League. Casually employed on a day-to-day basis; sectionalised by the existence of numerous local labour markets and by the complex sub-division of dock work; subjected to seasonal unemployment and chronic underemployment the London dockers were desperately hard to organise. The dockers were cut off from the respectable London labour movement not only by their poverty, but also by their religion. Most were Irish and Catholic: a social disadvantage from which, however, they could draw some cohesion. A series of small strikes won wage rises during the next few months, and within a year the League had 30,000 members, including, as well as dockers, a sprinkling of engineering labourers, dustmen, slopmen and scavengers. Most of this membership was rapidly lost, and following a costly lockout of corn porters in 1876, the Labour Protection League retained only 2,000 members by the end of the decade. The most permanent result of the activity of 1871 to 1872 was the establishment of a stable sectional organisation of the relatively skilled stevedores, which was to play a central role in the revival of mass unionism on the waterfront in 1889.

From the early months of 1872, in the arable counties of Southern England where wages were lowest and farming most labour intensive, agricultural labourers began to organise. Since the Swing Riots of 1830 rural workers had been among the most downtrodden of the poor – an agricultural labourer could double his income of 8–12/- a week by blacklegging on a docker. To the urban craftsmen his condition appeared little better than that of a Negro slave:

> In intellect he is a child, in position a helot, in condition a squalid outcast, he knows nothing of the past; his knowledge of the future is limited to the field he works in. . . . The squire is his king, the parson his deity, the taproom his highest conception of earthly bliss.[1]

By the spring of 1872 Joseph Arch had organised a National Agricultural Labourers Union from his base in Warwickshire though many other unions, particularly in Kent and East Anglia, remained independent of the 'National'. During the next eighteen months small local strikes against selected farmers succeeded in pushing up wages by 20–30 per cent. The systematic promotion of migration to better-paid districts, and of emigration to the colonies, whose agents were ubiquitous in the villages, also had some effect on wage levels. Around 150,000 labourers flocked into the unions, whose leadership was predominantly in the hands of men independent of the tyranny of squire, farmer and parson – rural and small town craftsmen, journalists, tradesmen and the like. The farmers organised Defence Associations, and the Eastern Counties lockout of 1874, following closely on the Conservative election victory of that year, halted union expansion. The appalling harvests of the late 1870s, the influx of foreign grain, the switch from arable to less labour intensive pastoral farming, and the increasing mechanisation of agriculture all militated against revival. By the mid-1880s agricultural unionism was largely extinct, and earnings had fallen back to the level of the late 1860s.

Agricultural unionism grew in the context of Church–Chapel conflict. 'Now my dear friends,' said a leader of the Dorsetshire labourers, 'I entreat you keep away from the drink, and abandon the smoke; and then, with the help of the Union, and with the blessing of God, you will become freemen.'[12] As in the mines Primitive Methodists predominated among the leadership: and, with few exceptions, the parson aligned himself with the farmer. The curate of Bishop's Tachbrook was not untypical. He preached on the text 'lay not up for yourselves treasures on earth', deducing that: 'It was very wicked to agitate for more than 12/- a week as the income of a labourer's family.'[13] 'Freedom from Priestcraft' ranked equally with freedom from landlord and farmer in the objectives of the *Labourers Union Chronicle*.

Hostility to the established church meshed with hostility to aristocratic power in securing middle-class radical support for the revolt of the rural poor. Chamberlain's 'Free Land' and the programme of John Stuart Mill's Land Tenure Reform Association – which, in search of urban working-class support went as far as it could without endorsing the goals of the Land and Labour League – provided a workable basis for the Radical alliance with urban workers in support of agricultural unionism. The Radical press spread word of the movement from village to village, and Radical money helped to sustain strikes and union organisers. In return Radical political needs were well served by the leaders of agricultural unionism who, as the union declined in the later 1870s, devoted more and more of their time to Liberal politics.

One of the favoured routes of escape from the land was to go to work on the railways. This option was open only to the more deferential or crafty labourer who could secure the necessary recommendation from a local man of property. The railways offered secure, if dangerous, employment, and the chance of promotion to a skilled grade. In return the companies demanded complete subordination: 'Not an instance of intoxication, singing, whistling or levity, while on duty, will be overlooked, and besides being dismissed the offender will be liable to punishment.'[14] No doubt the more innocent whistlers were overlooked, but not those troublesome characters who also organised petitions, or trade unions. Nevertheless trade unionism made some headway, chiefly among footplatemen, in the 1860s, and in 1871 the first all-grades union, the Amalgamated Society of Railway Servants, was established. Long hours of work were the chief grievance. Strike action secured shorter hours and wage advances from a number of companies, though it was generally disowned by a squabbling leadership which preferred to look to their middle-class patrons – notably M.T. Bass, the brewer and Liberal MP for Derby – to put pressure on the railway executives. Membership reached a peak of 17,000 at the end of 1872. There were 275,000 railwaymen at this time. Ten years later it was down to 6,000, less than 2 per cent of the workforce, and the drivers had split off to form the Associated Society of Locomotive Enginemen and Firemen.

The early 1870s also saw rapid expansion of organisation in the coalfields. The existing Miners National Association, led by Alexander MacDonald, concentrated exclusively on Parliamentary lobbying and made no attempt to co-ordinate industrial action between the coalfields. This suited its two main supporters, the district unions in Northumberland and in Durham, which were well enough organised to secure recognition by their own efforts and had no wish to commit their funds to supporting strikes in the poorer and less well-organised districts. In 1869 a rival national organisation was established, the Amalgamated Association of Miners. Neither in Lancashire, which took the initiative and dominated the Association's executive, nor in South Wales, its other main base, was it possible to build centralised district unions with any staying power. In Lancashire the systematic use of blacklegs, imported particularly from Wales and Staffordshire, had restricted union growth in the 1860s, though Thomas Halliday was able to establish a loosely federated district union. For a few years the Amalgamated Association, which he founded and led, was successful in developing a centralised wages strategy for its constituent unions. While the coal trade boomed in the summer of 1871, Halliday held back his Lancashire miners from strike action and concentrated the whole resources of the Amalgamation on the South Wales owners who were paying wages 20–30 per cent below the English average. A three-month strike in South Wales was financed by levies in Lancashire and protected from the usual blacklegging by a vigorous campaign among the Staffordshire miners. Victory in Wales was followed by the concession of wage advances throughout Lancashire with little need for strike action. At its peak, in the spring of 1874, the Amalgamated Association had 100,000 members, almost as many as were claimed by MacDonald's Association, whose figures were probably inflated. But it was already in trouble. As prices fell and wage cuts were imposed the Executive found it increasingly difficult to maintain unity. The centralised strategy depended on persuading men to stay at work and levy themselves in support of strikes elsewhere. This proved even more difficult when miners everywhere faced wage reductions than it had in the years of rising prices. One district after another seceded, often reaffiliating to the National Association which cost little and made no attempt to limit their autonomy. In August 1874 the Amalgamated dissolved into the National.

VI

The resolution of the question of trade union legal status took place in a context created by the trade union explosion of the early 1870s. In 1871 a Trade Union Congress assembled to discuss the Liberal Government's trade union legislation. This was the third meeting of the TUC, which had been founded on the initiative of the Manchester and Salford Trades Council in 1868. Unlike earlier attempts at a general trades union federation, including one made in 1866, the TUC never intended to involve itself in strikes or lockouts. Rather it defined itself as a forum of debate and a voice for the trade union cause. The 1871 Congress, the first which could claim to be representative of the trade union movement as a whole, demanded total repeal of the Criminal Law Amendment Act, which had outlawed picketing, and appointed a Parliamentary Committee to co-ordinate the campaign.

At first the Parliamentary Committee showed hardly more political independence than the Junta had done. The Committee was dominated by two men — George Howell, the Junta's nominee, and Alexander MacDonald, the miners' leader, who was even more remote from the grass roots struggles of his members than were the Junta officials. Howell and MacDonald, agreeing that the way forward was via 'legislation not agitation', made a private deal with sympathetic Liberal MPs to promote an amendment excluding some of the more objectionable clauses in the Act. Exposure of this manoeuvre led to a fearsome row which the government used as an excuse for doing nothing at all.

Meanwhile the Act was being vigorously used by the courts, especially against the less well-organised sections of the working class. Seven women in South Wales were imprisoned for saying 'bah' to a blackleg. In 1872 the stokers at the Becton gas works in Woolwich struck, dimming the lights of London's West End, and revealing that Hyde Park rioters were not the only danger to the comfort of its affluent inhabitants. Mr Justice Brett, on behalf of the latter, reacted ferociously, jailing six of the leaders for conspiracy. In the course of his judgement he defined almost any trade union activity as illegal, since it implied a 'molestation' of the employer: 'an unjustifiable annoyance and interference with the masters in the conduct of their business.'[15]

These events made it certain that nothing less than total repeal would content the TUC. Agitation grew, led partly by a Gas Stokers Defence Committee operating independently of the TUC. In the 1874 election the TUC ran a concerted campaign for repeal, issuing a list of questions embodying Labour's legislative demands which was put to all candidates. Trade unionists were urged to vote only for those who gave satisfactory answers. Both the Labour Representation League and the miners put up independent candidates. As a result Disraeli, returned at the head of a Conservative Government, was more or less pledged to repeal. After a decorous delay during which further prosecutions reaffirmed that peaceful picketing was a crime, the Conservatives introduced two Bills which repealed the Master and Servant Act; abolished imprisonment for breach of contract; expressly excluded trades disputes from the law of conspiracy; and underwrote the right of peaceful picketing. Nothing is ever final in the law, but the 1875 Acts settled the legal status of trade unions for a generation.

At the 1875 Congress of the TUC, the delegates celebrated their victory with fulsome praise both of the Conservative Government and of their Liberal allies in the House. As the trade union explosion of the early 1870s gave way to defeat and demoralisation in the ranks, the leadership became just as respectable and accommodating as the Junta had ever been. Nevertheless the campaign for legal status, like the Reform struggle of 1866–7, had shown that the accommodation which the mid-Victorian labour movement sought could not be achieved without major struggles. These conflicts exposed a more threatening side to working-class aspirations than the sweet reasonableness customarily projected by the leadership. The achievement of citizenship and corporate status by an elite of working men owed something to the accommodating style of their leaders. But it also reflected the continuing danger that a denial of the modest demands of the labour aristocracy would force them into a revolutionary alliance with the mass of the oppressed. The radical political currents which gave rise to this danger at moments of crisis did not subsequently disappear. Behind the facade of a satisfied Lib-Lab leadership in the decade following the 1875 Trade Union Act, the possibility of a new socialist politics was taking shape.

Notes

1 ASE *Rules*, 1864. Quoted in S. and B. Webb, *Industrial Democracy*, London 1901, pp. 469–70.

2 S. and B. Webb, *The History of Trade Unionism*, London 1902, pp. 199–200.

3 B. McCormick and J.E. Williams, 'The Miners and the Eight Hour Day, 1863–1910', *Economic History Review*, 2nd series, vol. xii, 1959, p. 223.

4 J.E. Williams, *The Derbyshire Miners*, London 1962, pp. 120, 134.

5 J.S. Mill, *Principles of Political Economy*, 1848, Pelican ed., 1970, p. 133.

6 Statement by executive of United Society of Boilermakers, 1865. Quoted in J.E. Mortimer, *History of the Boilermakers' Society*, vol. 1, London 1973, p. 65.

7 F. Engels, 'The English Elections', 1874. Reproduced in K. Marx and F. Engels, *On Britain*, Moscow 1962, p. 507.

8 'Address of the Land and Labour League to the Working Men and Women of Great Britain and Ireland'. Quoted in R. Harrison, *Before the Socialists*, London 1965, pp. 246–50.

9 Harrison, *op.cit.*, p. 233

10 H. Mayhew, *London Labour and the London Poor*, vol. iii, London 1851, p. 233.

11 Lloyd Jones, article in *The Beehive*, January 1872.

12 J.P.D. Dunbabin, ' "The Revolt of the field": The Agricultural Labourers' Movement in the 1870s', *Past and Present*, 26, 1963, p. 69.

13 Pamela Horn, *Joseph Arch 1826—1919. The Farm Workers' Leader*, Kineton 1971, p. 71.

14 Rules of the Taff Vale Railway Company, 1855. Quoted in P.W. Kingsford, *Victorian Railwaymen. The Emergence and Growth of Railway Labour, 1830—1870*, London 1970, p. 20.

15 K.W. Wedderburn, *The Worker and the Law*, Harmondsworth, 1971, p. 331.

2

Society, politics and the labour movement, 1875–1914

Between the 1870s and the First World War a mass labour movement was formed in Britain. Trade union membership grew from about half a million in the mid-1870s to over four million by 1914. By 1914 nearly a quarter of the occupied population belonged to trade unions, compared with a mere 4 per cent in 1880. Membership of the co-operative movement grew, in line with the unions, from about 600,000 in 1880 to over three million by 1914. Trades Councils, previously confined mainly to the larger industrial towns, spread rapidly over the whole country, reflecting a growing identification among working-class activists with a national movement, broader and more political than mere sectional trade unionism. The formation of the Labour Party in 1900 gave further expression to this sense of a working-class movement. By 1912 more than half the total trade union membership was affiliated to the Labour Party, though the co-operative movement as a whole remained aloof. The growth was impressive, but it should not be exaggerated. At one moment, in 1889–90, it had seemed possible that an alliance between socialist politics and the poorer sections of the workers who were exploding into trade union organisation, could remake the whole working-class movement. In fact the promise of New Unionism was not fulfilled. The formation of the Labour Party at the turn of the century represented, not a victory for the socialists, but the effective containment of the socialist impulse within older labourist traditions. Within the unions sectional division and conflict remained endemic. And organised labour, for all its growth, remained a minority of the working class. Paradoxically, its very expansion involved the consolidation of certain patterns of organisation and of ideology – in the approach to women, for example, or the poor – which tended to confine the movement within its minority position.

During the last quarter of the nineteenth century Britain lost its supremacy as the workshop of the world. While the rate of growth of

British manufacturing industry slowed down, rapid industrialisation in other parts of the world reduced the British share of world industrial production from over 30 per cent in 1870 to under 15 per cent by 1913. British capitalism responded to the challenge of the new industrial economies largely along traditional lines, storing up problems for the future. Manufacturers, facing stiffer foreign competition in the more industrialised areas of the world, turned increasingly towards the Empire and developing countries to sell the textiles, iron and steel, railway rolling stock and basic machinery which German and American capitalism no longer needed to import from Britain. At the same time the relative weakness of Britain's export performance was compensated by a huge expansion of the income from overseas investment. Between 1870 and 1914 capital export was the fastest growing sector of the British economy. Increasingly funds went, not to Europe and the United States, but to the Empire and other developing countries. This contributed to the expansion of markets on which British exporters relied, while at the same time it yielded an influx of dividend and interest payments to sustain the British balance of payments. By thus retreating from the most dynamic sectors of the world economy, British capitalism was able to remain viable with a manufacturing base geared to producing the textiles and heavy capital goods characteristic of the first industrial revolution, and to evade the necessity to modernise industry in line with the more advanced technology emerging in Germany and the United States. Before 1914 the relative backwardness of British industry, although becoming increasingly apparent, had not yet reached crisis proportions.

The adjustment of British capitalism to the rise of competing industrial economies was, in the short term, successful. But it did not occur without tensions which made their mark on the politics of late Victorian Britain. Increased foreign competition and a general fall in the world price level, both of which tended to squeeze profit margins, undermined middle-class faith in the sacred cows of mid-Victorian liberalism. Free trade was challenged by some manufacturers demanding protective tariffs in order to shore up their home markets. Their demands were given political weight by the New Imperialist currents at the turn of the century. Attitudes to the unrestrained operation of market forces began to change. Where free trade Liberals, reflecting Britain's unchallenged economic supremacy, had seen the promise of a millenium of international peace and prosperity, New Imperialists, anxious about the strategic implications of Britain's declining weight in the world economy, stressed the unpatriotic machinations of cosmopolitan finance and trade. Imperialist reactions against liberal capitalism on the right were matched by socialist reactions on the left. Exceptionally severe slumps in the late 1870s and mid-1880s undermined faith in the inevitability of economic progress, creating a receptive audience for those who argued that capitalism might not hold the key to the elimination of poverty. High unemployment levels, affecting skilled as well as unskilled workers, undermined some of the basic assumptions of Lib–Lab politics in the labour movement, helping to create the preconditions for the emergence of socialism from the 1880s.

The ability of British capitalism to find a (temporarily) viable role within the new international division of labour limited the appeal of both protectionist and socialist ideas. The British political elite fought off the lure of protectionist imperialism until after the First World War. Similarly socialism failed to capture the labour movement. Part of the explanation for the subordination of socialism within the emergent mass labour movement is suggested by the fact that, despite higher unemployment levels, the working class as a whole substantially improved its material position from the 1870s. Falling prices, which worried manufacturers, contributed to a general rise in working-class living standards by 30 to 50 per cent between 1870 and 1900. But statistical phenomena as abstracted from real social life as aggregate wage and price indices can tell us little about the links between economic change, the growth of a mass labour movement and the limited appeal of socialism. To uncover those links we must move a good deal closer to the ways in which workers actually experienced the processes of economic change.

Underpinning the emergence of a mass labour movement in the last quarter of the nineteenth century was the growing predominance of regular industrial wage-earners, concentrated in substantial work units, within the working-class population. The proportion of the occupied population involved in agriculture was halved, falling from 15 per cent in 1871 to 7.5 per cent in 1901. The mass of rural immigrants went, not into manufacturing industry, but into the most rapidly expanding sectors of the domestic economy, transport and mining. This involved a major shift from worse to better paid jobs, from less to more regular employment. By 1911 there were nearly one and a quarter million miners, providing a powerful and relatively prosperous bedrock for the labour movement. In transport, casual labour persisted on the waterfront and in road transport, but it was the steady work on the railways that grew fastest.

Manufacturing industry remained constant at about 40 per cent of the occupied population, the relative decline of textiles and clothing being balanced by a rapid growth of metal working and food processing industries. It was during this period that the factory became the predominant form of organisation in almost all industries, at the expense of outwork and petty workshop production. During the 1890s the factory very largely superseded outwork in provincial shoe-making. A similar shift occurred in clothing, hosiery, furniture and the light metal trades. By 1911 women were less likely to go into domestic service, or to take in work at home; more likely to find employment in the new food processing, metal working and chemical factories.* The number of washerwomen declined in face of the factory laundry. Overall, by 1913 four and a half million people were employed in factories (average size 40–50), slightly more than half a million in workshops (average size 4–5). In 1907 less than 3 per cent of the manufacturing workforce were outworkers.

The growth of the mines, railways and factories swelled the intermediate strata of the working class, and these strata were the chief beneficiaries of the great price fall between 1873 and 1896. The expansion of the co-operative movement, and of food, clothing and footwear chain stores is an indication of the trend. Better fed, better clothed, better shod, even, after the building boom of the 1890s, a little better housed, the prospect of a richer and more varied life outside work itself opened up to large numbers of workers and their families. Other changes pushed in the same direction. By the early twentieth century the average working week was probably around 56 to 57 hours, compared with between 60 and 72 hours in the mid-Victorian years. Some of this gain was consumed by increasing time spent travelling to work as towns grew in size, but some remained to be devoted to domestic life and recreation.

With more leisure and more money to spend working-class people could construct a new family and consumption-centred culture. For the higher paid, pianos, gramophones, bicycles became the means to a richer family life, as well as symbols of status within the neighbourhood. As new populations settled down after the upheavals of

---

* There was, however, no overall increase in the proportion of women workers, except in white-collar work, because the relative decline of textiles, which employed the largest percentage of women, masked their advance in other manufacturing industries, and because they were virtually excluded from the most rapidly expanding sectors, mining and transport.

industrialisation, kinship and neighbourhood networks could be consolidated, sheltering working-class people against the harshness of the urban environment. For most working-class people the possibilities of recreation broadened. Music Hall peaked after 1890, and the cinema was well-established in working-class areas before 1914. Every conceivable working-class institution had its own brass band. Football spread as a participant and spectator sport, aided by the emergence of the Saturday half-holiday which enabled sportsmen to circumvent the killjoy prohibitions of sabbatarian local authorities. Meanwhile cheap railway excursions opened up the seaside to the working class and made it easier to spend Sunday in the country or visiting relatives.

It was in the last decades of the nineteenth century that the main features were created of a working-class culture that, by the 1950s, had come to be seen as 'traditional'. This culture embodied real gains for a large section of the working class. Rising living standards, and a more established, settled, less hand-to-mouth existence, contributed to the strengthening of the labour movement. Larger workplaces and steadier employment made it easier to maintain trade union organisation. Higher real wages released cash to finance union activity. For a small, but significant section increased leisure time could be devoted to adult education, trade union and political activism.

It would however be easy to exaggerate the degree to which a socially and culturally homogenous working class had emerged by 1914. Profound divisions persisted within the working class, and these continued to set limits to the expansion of the labour movement until after the First World War. The growth of the intermediate strata of the working class did not mean the disappearance of a labour aristocratic elite. The superior status of the labour aristocracy was eroded by the rapid growth of white-collar employment, particularly where salaried clerical, technical and managerial staff interposed themselves between skilled workers and their employers. Similarly, rising standards of living among the mass of respectable workers immediately below the aristocrats in the social hierarchy tended to diminish the starkness of their privilege by closing the gap beneath them.

In most expanding occupations, food manufacture and transport for example, status divisions among the workforce were less extreme than in the craft sectors – although on the railways engine drivers retained separate organisation and a position of exceptional privilege. The spread of mechanisation and the factory undermined the position of handicraft artisans. Nevertheless, craftsmen in the shipyards, in engineering and foundry work, in printing and building, spinners in cotton mills, rollers and puddlers in iron and steel, hewers in the pits – all continued to lord it over their less skilled helpers. Craftsmen resisted the encroachments of the less skilled, often, as in engineering, maintaining their monopoly of work whose real skill content had been reduced by technological change. One result of the relative technological backwardness of British capitalism before 1914 was to prolong the viability of craft unionism, enabling skilled workers to resist novel doctrines of all-grades, industrial unionism. Where skill hierarchies were secure within an unchanging technology – as in some of the lesser shipbuilding crafts for example – relations within the workgroup were often cordial, if scarcely egalitarian. But where skilled workers had reason to fear the encroachments of their helpers, New Unionsim often appeared as a direct challenge to aristocratic privilege. The early 1890s saw a rash of bitter conflicts between skilled and less skilled trade unionists – spinners and their piecers, platers and their holders-up, hewers in the North East and their putters. Robert Knight, the boilermakers' leader, expressed a common attitude to signs of independence on the part of the less skilled when he declared in 1893: 'The helper ought to be subservient, and do as the mechanic tells him.'[1] Twenty years later engineering craftsmen still viewed the organisation of their less skilled workmates with alarm – effectively preventing the opening up of the ASE to semi-skilled workers, and reacting to the success of the Workers Union among these grades with undisguised hostility.

While the exclusiveness of the aristocracy remained an important factor in the working-class movement, it was the hopelessness of the poor which presented the movement with its most critical problems. Despite the general rise in living standards, in 1900 'the poor' constituted up to 40 per cent of the working-class, families living on an income of 21/- a week or less. Poverty was endemic among the unemployed, casual and seasonal workers, or simply low-paid regular wage earners. In the absence of any system of social security, apart from the Poor Law, ill-health or accident could deny even a subsistence income to a respectable worker and his family, unless trade union benefits could tide him over. The largest concentrations of poverty were to be found in London and the other great port towns where casual labour prevailed. Other black spots included the sweated workshop and outwork trades of the West Midlands, Leeds and Manchester, the Yorkshire wool and Scottish jute industries, the building trades and the food processing factories generally. The old suffered worst, and women and children. While a casual labourer might get sufficient food to maintain physical efficiency, his wife and children would go without. Although infant mortality fell substantially, as late as 1913 one in every four funerals was the funeral of a child under five years old. The effects of undernourishment on those who lived were revealed in 1917 when little more than a third of the young men medically examined for military service were without 'marked' or 'partial' disabilities.

The problem posed by poverty for the labour movement was an intractible one. Despite the new unionism of 1889–90, and despite occasional spasms of revolt, the great mass of the urban poor remained impermeable to working-class organisation. They were intensely parochial. Dependent on kin and friends for help in times of crisis, needing to be known locally in order to get credit from shopkeepers and jobs from employers, unable to pay the transport costs involved in living at a distance from the workplace, their lives were narrowly circumscribed by the immediate locality. Denied status or power in the wider society, and ignorant of the world outside the slum, the poor could retain their self-respect only by limiting their horizons to those in the same situation as themselves. Hence the indignation – so well recorded by Robert Tressell in *The Ragged Trousered Philanthropists* – against those idealists who threatened to bring them up against the larger parameters of their deprivation. Since experience taught that nothing could be achieved by collective action, the missionaries of the labour movement tended to be seen as either naive or self-seeking.

Strict limits were set for the development of working-class politics in Britain by this continuing structural divide within the working class. The central concern of British socialism remained the abolition of poverty rather than the abolition of capitalism itself. Socialists, of course, frequently asserted that the abolition of the one was inseparable from the abolition of the other – but rhetoric was no substitute for strategy. And no strategy for the overthrow of capitalism existed. So long as poverty persisted on the scale that it did, and so long as the conventional expectations of the more privileged strata were not frustrated sufficiently to drive them into a revolutionary alliance with the poor, it remained impossible to build a working-class movement with either the power or the ambition to translate the final socialist objective from the language of ultimate goals into the language of practical politics.

The inability of the labour movement to come to grips with the problem of poverty was matched by its failure to recruit among the female half of the working class. In 1901 women made up over 30 per cent of the labour force, but only 7.5 per cent of the total number of trade unionists. About one in six working men were organised in unions. The equivalent figure for wage-earning women was less than one in thirty. The main reason for this difference was not that women were intrinsically less clubbable, but that they were concentrated in those occupations most difficult to organise whatever the sex of the workforce. Despite some valiant efforts trade unionism could make little headway in such a personalised employment situation as domestic service – and in 1911 39 per cent of all employed women were domestic servants. The large numbers of women employed in outwork or in small workshops in dressmaking, millinery, tailoring, shoemaking or the light metal trades, women who often worked on a part-time or seasonal basis, were almost equally difficult to organise. Where employment was secure, regular and concentrated in large workplaces women did organise, most notably in the Lancashire cotton mills which in 1914 accounted for nearly half the total number of women trade unionists. Outside cotton much of the growth of women's trade unionism occurred in the expanding semi-skilled factory trades; among shop assistants, telephonists, postal sorters and – a major growth area – elementary school teachers.

Trade union attitudes to the organisation of women were compli-cated by the widespread hostility of working-class men to women working at all. Since women's wages were generally much lower than men's they were seen as a potential threat to the maintenance of the male wage. Most skilled unions excluded women and bitterly resisted employer attempts to introduce them into the workforce. The fact that such exclusiveness was one reason for women being low paid in the first place did nothing to allay the men's fears. Feminists and craft unionists could agree, in the 1880s, on a TUC resolution in favour of equal pay, but for the men the point of insisting on equal pay was to make it uneconomic for employers to take on women workers. Over the issue of 'protective' legislation designed to exclude women from certain occupations – women in the chain and nail trades of the Black Country and the pit brow lasses became *cause célèbres* in the 1880s – advocates of women's rights fought extended battles against the TUC. As late as 1911 cotton spinners in Wigan were demanding an amendment of the Factory Acts to ban women from the mule room, though the TUC took a more enlightened attitude when the brassworkers proposed a similar measure in 1908.

Fear of cheap labour was only one aspect of the problem. Central to the emergence of a more settled and respectable working-class way of life which underpinned the growth of trade unionism in this period was the construction of the home as an arena of physical comfort and emotional support. Given large numbers of children and the labour intensive character of housework the fulfilment of the domestic ideal required the full-time labour of housewives. Better-off workers in most parts of the country preferred their wives to stay at home. The notion of the 'family wage' – that a man's earnings should be sufficient to keep his wife and young children out of the labour market – was an important element in late nineteenth-century working-class respectability, and it militated against any serious consideration of the case for equal work opportunities for women.

Where women workers did organise successfully male concern to protect job monopolies kept them in a subordinate position. Although most cotton trade unionists were women, there were very few women officials, and the men took care to keep women out of the most specialised and highly paid jobs. Efforts to organise women were further bedevilled by conflict between the middle-class women who took the lead in the Women's Trade Union League (founded in 1874 as the Women's Provident and Protection Society), and male class consciousness. The WTUL operated as an entrepreneur of organisation, helping to set up women's unions and persuading existing unions to recruit women. At the same time it worked as a parliamentary lobby, at first opposing protective legislation, later playing a leading role in the agitation for Trade Boards to establish a minimum rate in sweated industries. The finance for these activities was provided by wealthy philanthropists. In the 1880s the hostility of these women to strikes and militancy and their attempts to organise low-paid women along craft union lines limited their effectiveness. While their approach improved from the 1890s, the WTUL and its offshoot the National Federation of Women Workers (1906) continued to be disparaged as organs of middle-class charity rather than proper trade unions. The rapid growth of women's organisation from the mid-1900s made some impact on male attitudes, but in 1914 the predominant view was still that stated by Will Thorne, the socialist leader of the Gasworkers: 'Women do not make good trade unionists and for this reason we believe that our energies are better used towards the organisation of male workers.'[2]

The structural character of the working class itself made the development of any unambiguously socialist mass working-class movement unlikely. Equally important in explaining the limited impact of socialism were the conscious efforts made to counter its influence. The political articulation of the emergent working-class movement took place in the context of a succession of liberal strategies to contain and subordinate working-class politics.

During the twenty years which followed the passage of the Second Reform Act, the Conservative Party succeeded in broadening its base. In 1885, aided by a revision of constituency boundaries which increased the electoral weight of the 'villa Toryism' of the suburbs, the Conservatives won a majority of the English boroughs. Satisfied by the administrative reforms of Gladstone's first ministry (1868–74); alarmed by the spectre of socialism, by industrial depression, by the rise of competing imperialisms; aware that they now had more to lose than to gain by continuing the campaign against aristocratic privilege, large numbers of middle-class voters turned to the Conservatives as the party of order, stability and national greatness. At the same time the collapse of agricultural rents, as cheap grain flooded in from America and Russia, encouraged the landed aristocracy to pursue new sources of income in industry, hastening the fusion of landed and industrial wealth which underpinned the viability of the new Conservative Party. Finally, the Home Rule crisis of 1885–6, which split the Liberal Party and brought Whigs and Liberal Unionists into the Conservative camp, completed the process – ushering a twenty-year period of Conservative political hegemony.

In face of 'villa Toryism' the most enduring bases of middle-class liberalism from the 1870s were the great sectional causes of the non-conformist conscience. Members of the National Education League (non-denominational education), The United Kingdom Alliance (temperance reform), the Liberation Society (disestablishment of the Church of England), found the essential meaning of Liberalism in the pursuit of their own particular panacea. But beyond these circles of militant righteousness, hatred of the publican and the parson had insufficient appeal to win elections. Something more was needed to appeal to the working-class vote. If the class alliance at the base of popular Liberalism was allowed to break down, Liberal politics, including the demands of the non conformist fads, would have no future at all. The major question confronting the Liberal leadership was whether the maintenance of class alliance would be better served by directing attention towards, or away from, the material needs of the working class. Before the Home Rule crisis of 1885–6, Joseph Chamberlain, leader of Birmingham radicalism, proposed the former course. He was instrumental in the formation of the National Liberal Federation in 1877, intended to provide a democratic basis for Liberalism in the constituencies, to unite non-conformist sectionalism and Lib–Labism around an agreed programme of social reform, and to impose this programme on the Liberal Party in Parliament. This strategy failed. The social demands of the radical programme proved too vague and too modest to mobilise the enthusiasm of working-class voters. Meanwhile, far from persuading middle-class voters of the need to pay 'ransom' to protect the basis of property against socialism, Chamberlain's alarmist talk only succeeded in frightening middle-class voters into the Conservative camp. In most areas the local caucuses of the National Liberal Federation failed to incorporate organised labour, and developed not as popular democratic bodies, but under the firm control of wealthy middle-class Liberals.

Gladstone provided the alternative solution to the problem of developing a coherent Liberal appeal capable of attracting both middle-class and working-class votes. Adamant in his opposition to 'construction', to state-interventionist social reform – which, he believed would sap the foundations of self-help and manly independence – Gladstone sought to direct politics away from socially divisive domestic questions, appealing instead to traditions of democratic internationalism common to both middle-class and working-class liberalism. Working men responded enthusiastically to the Gladstonian appeal. In 1881, for example, a Lib–Lab Miners' MP, Thomas Burt, rejected the view that support among English workers for Irish aspirations reflected any of 'sordid material interest'. It was not appeals to class prejudice, he argued, that would mobilise working-class support for Liberalism, but the moral appeal of a 'great chivalrous idea'.[3] Gladstone's campaign against Disraelian imperialism in the later 1870s united the Liberal Party in a way that Chamberlain's attempt to develop a programmatic radical party could not do. Gladstone and Bulgarian atrocities were, from the outset, closer to the hearts even of the radicals in the National Liberal Federation, than Chamberlain and social reform. The problem of this type of politics became apparent after the 1880 election, when the new Liberal Government, returned on a purely negative basis of opposition to Conservative imperialism, found itself embroiled in the repression of national liberation movements in Egypt and Ireland, and unable to agree on any programme of domestic reform. Eventually the government tackled electoral reform, but, unwilling to risk a confrontation with the House of Lords (or with the Whigs in their own party), settled for a Third Reform Bill that fell far short of manhood suffrage. Following the election of 1885, Parnell's Irish Party held the balance in the House of Commons. This set the scene for the crisis of 1886, in which the Whigs and Chamberlainite opponents of Home Rule allied themselves with the Conservatives, and Gladstone established his undisputed leadership of a purged Liberal Party. From 1886, when Home Rule was soundly defeated in a new election, until his retirement in 1894, Gladstone's lost cause provided a unifying force for Liberal politics which enabled the Party to evade any resolution of the problems of domestic policy. The price of this evasion, however, was impotence. In 1892 the Liberals returned to office, again dependent on the Irish Party. Faced with the inevitable rejection of Home Rule by the Lords, there was nothing they could do. Home Rule by itself could not win an election. They had no agreed domestic programme on which to appeal to the electorate against the Lords. The Grand Old Man retired, defeated, in 1894. The Liberal Government fell a year later.

This decay of Liberalism from the 1880s forms a crucial context for understanding the development of working-class politics in the period. The growth of socialism and of the idea of an independent Labour Party evidently owed a good deal to the inadequacies of Chamberlainite radicalism, to the Home Rule obsession, and to the continuing resistance of business interests in the Liberal Party to any substantial concessions to working-class demands. Nevertheless, Liberalism was far from played out by 1894. Between 1900 and the landslide Liberal victory of 1906, democratic internationalism, provoked by the excesses of Conservative imperialism in South Africa and by the frontal assault of Chamberlain's Tariff Reform campaign, again demonstrated its force as a rallying point for the politics of class alliance. More crucially, in domestic policy, Gladstonian self-help had not gone unchallenged in the Liberal Party after Chamberlain's defeat in 1886.

Consciously and deliberately the New Liberals set out to produce a positive alternative to socialism, a strategy for the elimination of poverty acceptable to the growing numbers of working-class activists who could see no future in Gladstonian self-help. Most of the central figures of New Liberalism were professional men, journalists, writers and civil servants. If the old Liberal nexus of paternalist employer, responsible trade unionist and the nonconformist conscience was breaking down, the professional middle class, rapidly expanding in this period, could offer an alternative, collectivist, route to social harmony. Many of the New Liberals, as young men had been involved in the 'settlement' movement of the 1880s – middle-class colonisers of the East End of London or the poorer districts of provincial cities, who could study poverty on the spot and search out its remedy. As befitted their intermediate social status, the New Liberals grounded their solutions to the problems of poverty in exhaustive attempts to establish the 'facts' independently of the demands or assertions of organised workers and employers. In and around the great social surveys of Booth in London and Rowntree in York, New Liberals wove an ideology of 'social science'. They believed that they had discovered a scientific diagnosis of poverty and scientific remedies for it. The confidence this belief gave them, as advocates of policy and, eventually, as the administrative architects of new state agencies, was no less important historically for being ill-founded.

The sheer extent of poverty was revealed indisputably by Booth's enquiry into the condition of the London working class. It was clear to the New Liberals that working-class efforts at self-help, successful for the few, could never succeed for the many until the state intervened to ameliorate the worst areas of poverty. And where trade unionism failed, the moral incentives of 'less eligibility' – a strictly enforced Poor Law – could not succeed either. Booth and his successors made it clear that it was not individual fecklessness and immorality that lay at the root of poverty, but objective economic circumstances – unemployment, underemployment, low wages. At this point, however, the New Liberals' grasp on reality failed them. There was, before 1914, little attempt to discover an *economic* solution to unemployment. Instead they advocated a number of limited interventions by the state into the worst areas of poverty, reforms intended to place a floor beneath the downward pressure of competition and thereby to create the conditions for the full realisation of self-help and competitive capitalism in society as a whole. Booth described this as a programme of 'limited socialism', calling on the organised workers to turn aside from revolutionary ideas in favour of 'a socialism which shall leave untouched the forces of individualism and the sources of wealth'.[4]

New Liberalism, originating in the context of the middle-class fear of an eruption of the 'dangerous classes' in London's East End in the

1880s, had a special fascination with the peculiar problems of the London labour market, above all the problem of casual labour. While insisting on the economic causes of casuality, they nevertheless viewed its remedy through the moralistic prism inseparable from their endorsement of capitalist competition. They posited the existence of a special class of the very poor, of 'unemployables', at the bottom of the social hierarchy. This class, estimated by Booth as 11.25 per cent of the population, was assumed to be beyond recall: a demoralised residuum of mental, moral and physical inadequates. But for the competition of this stratum on the labour market, the great bulk of the working class might be capable of climbing out of poverty through self-help and trade unionism. The solution, therefore, was 'the entire removal of this very poor class out of the daily struggle for existence'.[5] The problem of poverty would be solved by the establishment of labour colonies which would take the poorest and most degenerate out of the labour market. Their proposals were often ruthless. In 1906 William Beveridge, father of the Welfare State, proposed to offer the very poor the choice between starvation, emigration, or 'complete and permanent loss of all citizen rights, including not only the franchise, but civil freedom and fatherhood'.[6]

The existence of a demoralised residuum was a myth – and a myth a good deal less plausible in the industrial provinces than in London. In reality there was no substantial class of 'unemployables' – as the absorption of the surplus adult labour force into war industry was to demonstrate after 1914. Moreover, the compulsory segregation of the very poor by the state held little attraction for the organised workers to whom New Liberalism was attempting to appeal. Even the most secure of labour aristocrats, though happy to rail against the fecklessness of the poor, would shrink from endorsing the punitive regimentation of a group to which, experience taught, ill luck might reduce himself. Who could be trusted to sort out the merely unfortunate from the unreclaimable?

After the Liberal victory of 1906, little was heard about labour colonies. Instead 'limited socialism' was directed in a much more piecemeal way at particular ills affecting a much wider range of workers than Booth's 'very poor'. Thus school meals for children, medical inspection in schools and non-contributory old age pensions were introduced. The Trades Boards Act made it possible to fix legal minimum wages in sweated trades, putting a floor under the competitive driving down of wages. Labour Exchanges, not very successful in ending the 'anarchy of the labour market', did provide a test, more acceptable than the workhouse test, of the willingness of the unemployed to work – a test used by Lloyd George in establishing sickness and accident insurance schemes. All this legislation had, before 1914, made relatively little impact on the problem of poverty. The importance of New Liberalism for working-class politics lay not in its ability to eliminate poverty, but in its ability to generate social reforms which held out the promise of state action against poverty. From the 1890s onwards, New Liberalism had a profound impact on working-class politics, helping to persuade working-class activists, even while they agitated for an independent Party and, many of them, looked to socialism as an ultimate goal, that their interests lay in co-operation with the new breed of Liberal in a drive to abolish poverty via the legislative intervention of the state. Underpinning the politics of welfare reform was a convergence between a labour aristocratic disdain for the moral incompetents in the slums, and a middle-class view of the poor as something less than responsible citizens, appropriate objects of pity and of social engineering.

Only in the last years before 1914, when a new surge of trade union organisation and unrest opened the way to a more genuinely independent working-class politics, did the Liberal class alliance come under serious threat. The growth of a mass labour movement from the 1870s was facilitated by the emergence of a more homogenous industrial proletariat. At the same time it was held back by certain central features of late-Victorian society and politics. The persistence of extreme differentiations of status within the working class tended to restrict both the size and the political horizons of the labour movement. Simultaneously, the adaptability shown by Liberalism in face of the working-class challenge, played a crucial role in limiting the appeal of socialist ideas.

One further complication should be noted. The shape and pace of economic and social change differed markedly from one part of the country to another, and many of the cross-currents of working-class politics can only be understood in terms of variations in local conditions. As the narrative of the next two chapters unfolds we shall have occasion to emphasise the peculiarities of class relations in London, the special features of the coalfields were Lib–Labism found its most enduring base, and to draw out the contrasting pattern of development in the factory towns of the North which led in the development of independent labour politics.

Notes

1 E.J. Hobsbawm, *Labour's Turning Point*, London 1948, p. 4.
2 T. Olcott, 'Dead Centre: the women's trade union movement in London, 1874–1914', *London Journal*, 2, 1976, p. 43.
3 D.A. Hamer, *Liberal Politics in the Age of Gladstone and Rosebery*, Oxford 1972, p. 307.
4 C. Booth, *Life and Labour of the People of London*, vol. 1, London 1902, p. 177.
5 *Ibid*, p. 154.
6 G.S. Jones, *Outcast London: A Study in the Relationship between Classes in Victorian Society*, Oxford 1971, p. 335.

3

Socialism and the New Unionism, 1884–95

I

The emergence of socialist organisation and ideas in Britain during the 1880s presents a confusing history of sectarian wrangling and utopian hopes. In June 1881 H.M. Hyndman – company promoter, journalist, ex-Tory Radical and author of a popular exposition of Marxism – took the initiative in establishing a Democratic Federation among some of the London Radical Clubs. The original purpose of the Federation was to campaign against government repression in Ireland, for land nationalisation, democratic reforms along Chartist lines, and increased working-class representation in Parliament. Many of the original supporters left when it became clear that Hyndman intended to oppose the Liberals at elections. Subsequently the Federation adopted a socialist programme and, early in 1884, renamed itself the Social Democratic Federation (SDF).

Ireland and the land question did much to promote socialist ideas in the early 1880s. Michael Davitt, leader of the Irish Land League and a firm believer that social revolution in England was the precondition of Irish freedom, worked to promote the land nationalisation cause among British workers. Simultaneously, the agricultural depression and the unparalleled urban unemployment of 1879 encouraged the revival of many of the themes of the Land and Labour League. By the time Henry George, the eloquent American advocate of the 'Single Tax' on land, arrived in England in 1882, a Land Nationalisation Society was conducting a vigorous propaganda. Henry George's popular lecture tours in 1882 and 1883 led many of his listeners to socialism. George himself was not a socialist, but his passionate challenge to the 'invisible hand' of orthodox political economy opened the way for the socialist affirmation that economic life could be regulated to meet human needs.

Hyndman dominated the SDF from the outset. Around him gathered other middle-class recruits, notably William Morris, who had seen Lib–Lab politics at close quarters in the Eastern Question agitation of the later 1870s, and learned to hate it. But the intellectuals did not conjure a socialist movement out of thin air. Though the SDF was hardly a mass organisation in 1884, most of its 400 or so London members were probably working men, drawn from the same small but vigorous clubs of revolutionary artisans, some of them Chartist survivors, who had worked in the left wing of the Reform League, the Land and Labour League and the English branches of the First International. Political exiles – French communards, anarchists, refugees from Bismark's anti-socialist laws – also played a significant role.

Outside London the SDF had little influence, though it made a start in Lancashire – later to be an SDF stronghold – during a strike of the Blackburn weavers in 1884. Propaganda was also undertaken among striking miners and iron workers in the West Midlands, where John Sketchley, an old Chartist, had founded a Social-Democratic Association in 1878. More important were developments in Scotland, where the Highland crofters' struggle against evictions in the early 1880s heightened the reception given to Henry George and Michael Davitt. In 1884 J.L. Mahon, an apprentice engineer, and Andreus Scheu, an ex-patriot Austrian Marxist, set up the Scottish Land and Labour League in Edinburgh. This body, which affiliated to the SDF, gained some influence among the Lanarkshire miners. In Glasgow a separate SDF branch was formed.

At the end of 1884 the new party split. A majority of the executive committee resigned, choosing to establish a new organisation – the Socialist League – rather than attempting to break Hyndman's dictatorship over the SDF which he largely financed, or its paper *Justice* which he personally owned. Most of the leading workers, and the majority of the membership, stayed with Hyndman. The East London anarchists, the Scottish Land and Labour League and a small group of socialist intellectuals who were in close contact with Engels – notably Marx's daughter Eleanor and her lover Eduard Aveling – went into the new organisation. From the outset the Socialist Leaguers were an ill-assorted bunch, held together only by the force of William Morris' personality. Hyndman and Morris, the two men primarily responsible for the introduction of Marxism into Britain, approached socialism in such radically different ways that a split was virtually inevitable. Hyndman's Marxism was doctrinaire and deterministic: it had little place for the liberation of human creative energy from the tyranny of impersonal economic laws. Morris,

designer and poet, came to socialism through the romantic critique
of bourgeois industrialism developed by Thomas Carlyle and John
Ruskin. 'Was it all to end', he demanded, 'in a counting-house on the
top of a cinder-heap, with Podsnap's drawing-room in the offing,
and a Whig committee dealing out champagne to the rich and
margarine to the poor in such convenient proportions as would
make all men content together?'[1] For Morris the essence of socialism
was its promise of a qualitatively different way of life, a vision he
communicated to British socialism in his most influential work,
News from Nowhere.

The immediate cause of the split in 1884 was a dispute over
whether or not the party should contest parliamentary elections.
Morris insisted that until a body of socialist opinion had been
created in the country, it was premature to attempt to get socialists
elected to Parliament. Acutely aware of the dangers of parliamentarianism, he advocated a party of irreconcilables, a 'pure' socialist
party untainted by parliamentary intrigue, or indeed by any intervention beyond making propaganda for socialism. Hyndman had no
such inhibitions. In 1885 his search for cash to finance SDF candidates in the General Election exposed the party to the accusation that
he was being used by the Conservatives to split the progressive vote.
Thereafter Hyndman never quite shook off the odour of 'Tory Gold'.
Nevertheless, the SDF had a future, while the Socialist League,
caught in a purist trap, made little progress. After 1890, when
Morris left, the League fell into the hands of those who preferred the
bomb to the working class as the agency of human liberation, and
disappeared into the underworld of London anarchism.

Socialism originated on the margins of the labour movement. In
the mid-1880s Liberalism held sway among the great bulk of organised working men. The initial response of most trade unions to the
impact of the economic depression was to draw in their horns and
wait for better times. The exceptional depredations of the trade cycle
in the export trades – coal, cotton, shipbuilding – might provoke
trade union leaders to complain of the inequity of a system that could
throw huge numbers of skilled and respectable workmen onto the
streets. Nevertheless, in the slumps of 1879 and the mid-1880s, they
rejected militant policies of resistance to wage cuts and they had no
time for the still more alarming proposals of the socialists. Only by
the fullest acceptance of the logic of the capitalist market, they
thought, could they persuade employers to tolerate the continued
existence of trade unions.

Moderation in industry was matched by moderation in politics. The Third Reform Act of 1884 enfranchised working-class voters outside the boroughs for the first time. While the largely unorganised agricultural labourers could do little but provide voting fodder for middle-class radicalism, the miners (aided by constituency boundaries redrawn to isolate rural society from their disruptive influence) were well-placed to insist on labour men being selected as Liberal candidates. In 1885 six miners were returned to Parliament. But it was not until after 1900 that the Lib–Lab miners' leadership made any serious effort to exploit their electoral advantages to the full. The TUC responded to the Reform Act by establishing a Labour Electoral Association to support Lib–Lab canditatures. The Association encouraged Trades Councils to nominate Labour men, and, where disagreements arose, to demand a ballot of Liberal supporters to choose between their nominee and that of the local party caucus. Lacking funds, and unwilling to promote independent labour candidatures, the Labour Electoral Association had little practical influence. As late as 1900 there were still only eleven Lib–Lab MPS (including the miners) – an increase of only two over the numbers elected in 1885. By and large the trade union leaders accepted the self-help ideology of Gladstonian Liberalism, though the early 1880s saw a mounting demand for state intervention to alleviate the housing crisis, and to promote the emigration of unemployed workers to the colonies. The principle of Employers' Liability for accidents at work, the leading item of the TUC's modest programme of social reform, was partially conceded by the Liberal Government in 1880. But a further sixteen years elapsed before an effective Act was passed – by a Conservative Government. This record of industrial and political pacifism was to provide fertile soil for the emergence of a socialist challenge within the labour movement.

Initially the socialists made headway in the politics of unemployment. From its foundation the SDF agitated amongst unemployed labourers in the East End of London, leading protest marches and deputations to the Boards of Guardians. As unemployment rose in the winter of 1885–6, unrest grew. The crisis was precipitated by Conservative agitation for protective tariffs. On 8 February 1886, when the so-called Fair Traders organised a demonstration in Trafalgar Square, the SDF called a counter-demonstration demanding public works for the unemployed. In the riot which followed windows were smashed and shops looted. Affluent London, which since exposures of slum housing conditions in the early 1880s had been increasingly aware of the East End poor, reacted with a mixture of guilt and terror. Overnight thousands of pounds poured into the Mansion House Fund for the unemployed, while the press demanded prosecution of the socialists. An SDF trade unionist, John Burns – 'the man with the Red Flag' – became the bogey of the hour. Respectable London was so frightened that two days after the riot in Pall Mall it did its best to conjure insurrection out of nowhere. In dense fog rumours flew hither and thither. All over South London 'the shops closed and people stood at their doors straining their eyes through the fog for the sound of the 10,000 . . .', an imaginary army of avenging paupers from Deptford.[2] In many parts of London, including Deptford itself, groups of the unemployed were assembled by the sheer force of middle-class panic. Meanwhile the supposed revolutionaries of the SDF were nowhere to be found. 'We have been overtaken unprepared by a revolutionary incident,' wrote Morris: 'What is the meaning of it? At bottom misery, illuminated by a faint glimmer of hope, raised by the magic word SOCIALISM, the only hope in these days of confusion.'[3] But how to turn that glimmer of hope into an organised movement among the London poor remained a mystery to the socialists.

During the next two years the London streets remained a primary arena of socialist activity, as the League and the SDF fought for the right of public assembly. Already in 1885 the socialists, backed by the radical clubs and massive demonstrations in defiance of the police, had established their right to hold meetings in the East End streets. Following the riots of February 1886, and the return of a Tory Government, the authorities took a tougher line. A new metropolitan police commissioner, Sir Charles Warren, decided to clean up Trafalgar Square, which, during the hot summer of 1887 had been invaded by homeless unemployed, who slept there. While charitable agencies drove cart-loads of food into the Square, the SDF held meetings demanding 'not charity, but work'. Warren tried to clear the Square, egged on by West End shopkeepers who threatened to raise a private army unless the police moved. But everytime the police drove them out, the vagrants and the socialists returned again. When, early in November, Warren banned all further meetings in the Square, the radical clubs and the London Irish joined with the socialists to defy the ban. On 13 November 1887 – 'Bloody Sunday' – police and troops, with great brutality, prevented many thousands of demonstrators from reaching the Square. Three men, one of them a prominent secularist, received fatal injuries. A week later mounted police guarding the Square rode down and killed a bystander, Alfred Linnell. While official Liberalism remained silent, tens of thousands of Radicals, Irish and socialists attended Linnell's funeral. But Warren had won and the Square remained closed to public meetings for the next five years. Meanwhile, it was not unemployment but a new trade union explosion which provided the key to the socialist breakthrough.

II

During the 1880s organised workers experienced the highest and most prolonged unemployment for forty years. In 1886 even the aristocratic Boilermakers were forced to admit that their policy of wage restraint in times of good trade was not being matched by the anticipated willingness of employers to limit wage reductions during the depression. Grievances built up over wage cuts and the stagnation of real wages, the challenge of technological change to the security of the craft in some trades and, more generally, speed-up and the intensification of work. A similar build up of grievances occurred in the rapidly expanding, but largely unorganised, transport industries, where the influx of rural labour needed time, and a favourable economic conjuncture, to find its feet in the industrial world. Throughout industry the growth of larger companies was tending to break personal bonds between workers and their employers.

It was the revival of business activity that allowed this pent up discontent to translate itself into action. Unemployment fell from its peak in 1886, reaching very low levels in 1889 and 1890. Between 1888 and 1892 trade union membership roughly doubled, reaching one and a half million. In 1890, at the peak of the boom, it must have been a good deal higher. Public attention focused on the dramatic upsurge of organisation among the unskilled. Most of the expansion, however, was due to the spread of trade union membership among groups of workers where it was already established.

Since the early 1880s the District Unions of the central coalfields had worked towards a co-ordinated wages policy. Rising coal prices from ths summer of 1888 laid the basis for large wage increases and the replacement of the defunct Miners National Union by a new federation. The Miners Federation of Great Britain (MFGB), established in the winter of 1888–9, opposed any return to sliding scale agreements, made provision for co-ordinated strike action in support of any federated district, and demanded a legal eight-hour day for miners. The exporting districts of South Wales and the North

East remained outside. In the former the sliding scale persisted, in the latter the hewers, already working seven hours, opposed the demand for an eight-hour day which would benefit less-skilled underground workers at the expense of their own privileges. Over the country as a whole membership of coal miners' unions increased by three or four times in the five years following 1887.

Reviving militancy among iron and steel workers underlay the foundation, in 1886, of a new union, the British Steel Smelters' Amalgamated Association. The new union, based on day-wage workers in the rapidly expanding steel industry, opposed the sub-contract system and the sliding scale agreements favoured by the established Ironworkers. In cotton, where trade unionism had survived the depression years remarkably well, there was a rash of strike activity over speed-up, bad materials and disciplinary issues during 1889–91. From 1888 the Amalgamated Society of Railway Servants, which had not authorised a single strike since its foundation under middle-class patronage in 1871, rapidly transformed itself into a militant union. The executive was given power to call strikes without first holding a national ballot and a national campaign for the ten-hour day was launched. During 1889 the membership tripled. During 1890 a major strike won recognition and a sixty-hour week in South Wales. Similar action by Scottish railwaymen failed, but it did bring them into the national union two years later.

Among the craft unions prosperity brought rapid growth and wage advances, won usually without industrial action. There was, however, a wave of local strikes in the building industry after 1889, the largest of which, a six-month lockout of London carpenters and joiners in 1891 over the demand for the eight-hour day, achieved partial success. Among the Engineers militancy, especially pronounced in the strike-prone North East, was focused around the campaign of Tom Mann, a socialist, for the presidency in 1891. Though he narrowly missed election, his campaign served to popularise socialist arguments against the traditional exclusiveness of the society in face of technological change, for the opening up of membership to the semi-skilled and for the eight-hour day. Similar offensives against entrenched conservative leaderships took place in the print unions and in the boot and shoe industry – again with socialists playing a significant part.

At the centre of the New Unionist upsurge was the dramatic five-week London dock strike of 1889. Trade unionism on the London waterfront had survived from the 1870s only amongst the skilled and highly exclusive lightermen, the stevedores who won recognition from the small contractors who employed them, and a few specialised groups of dockers on the south bank of the Thames. The great mass of dockers, casually employed and subjected to the hideous indignities of the 'call-on', had no union, and – despite their successes in 1872 – were generally thought to be beyond recall. When this helpless residuum rose, not in riot but in disciplined trade unionism, they set a powerful example for unorganised workers throughout the country.

The unprecedentedly tight labour market gave the dockers the courage to fight and the ability to win. But it was the leadership and organising ability of the socialists that ensured victory. Though the strike began spontaneously among unorganised dockers a tiny union already existed, founded two years earlier by Ben Tillett. Tillett drew up a list of demands and set about organising the strike. The problems he faced – 30,000 strikers with little tradition of solidarity, or union discipline and no funds – could not have been solved without aid from external sources. The London socialist movement supplied a body of able and experienced agitators, many of whom had already been involved in a successful eight hours' movement among the London gas workers during the first half of 1889. Notable among them were the engineers, Tom Mann and John Burns, who, alongside Tillett, led the strike. The stevedores, themselves well organised, threw in their lot with the strikers, thus ensuring that the docks could not be reopened with blackleg labour. One of the leaders, Tom MacCarthy, had worked closely with Tillett since 1887 and now became Organiser of the new Dockers Union. Partly in response to the massive and orderly demonstrations led by John Burns through the City of London, middle-class money flowed in to support the strike.

By the end of August the strike had reached a point of crisis. Funds were running out and the companies showed no sign of weakening. In desperation the strike committee called for a general strike of all London workers – though the skilled trade unionist of the London Trades Council had in fact shown little solidarity with the dockers and there was no real chance of support from this quarter. The 'No-Work Manifesto' caused an outcry from the press and the middle-class public, whose sympathy to this point had rested as much on their relief at discovering that the avenging barbarians they had feared in 1886 were in reality only respectable and orderly trade unionists, as on humanitarian responses to the misery of the slums.

The threat to extend the strike intensified efforts to end it. A Mansion House Committee was established by the Lord Mayor to bring pressure on both sides to settle. Meanwhile the strikers were enabled to continue, and to withdraw the general strike call, by a new influx of funds from Australia where the struggle of the London dockers had become a *cause célèbre*. Pressured by the shipowners and deserted by the smaller wharf owners, the companies gave way. Headed by Cardinal Manning, the Mansion House Committee secured a settlement giving the strikers 'the full round orb of the dockers' tanner' and, more important, recognition and a virtual closed shop.

The London dock strike did not initiate the New Unionism. It served rather to dramatise and encourage a current of organisation that was already well underway. Outside London dockers were already organising under the stimulus of the sailors. In January and July 1889 the seamen, organised in a national union first established by Havelock Wilson on Tyneside two years earlier, struck for wage advances in most ports outside London and the South Coast. Freights were rising and the strikers were successful, except in Liverpool where the big Atlantic shipowners combined to organise blacklegging. Already in February 1889 a National Union of Dock Labourers had been organised in Glasgow by Edward McHugh, a printer with experience of dockers' unionism in the United States, and Richard McGhee, an Irish engineer and militant Home Ruler. By May the Glasgow union had spread to the Liverpool docks. On Tyneside Havelock Wilson helped, along with other Lib–Lab trade unionists and sympathetic middle-class Liberals, to establish a National Amalgamated Union of Labour (NAUL) in February 1889. Following its victory in London, Tillett's Dockers Union rapidly spread along the East and South Coast, and to Bristol and South Wales.

The victory of the London Gasworkers in June 1889 had played an important part in sparking off the dock strike. Will Thorne, a gasworker and a member of the SDF, had launched the union only three months earlier, with the help of socialist outsiders. The companies, under-mechanised and working on a very narrow margin, had little alternative to meeting the men's demands for a reduction of their excessive hours from twelve to eight. Following their success in London the Gasworkers, aided by local socialist groups, established branches in many provincial towns, especially in the North, gaining the eight-hour day and substantially raising wages. Meanwhile, in

Birmingham, local Lib-Lab craft unionists had already organised a union of gasworkers which spread through the Midlands and parts of Yorkshire.

As in the trade union upsurge of the early 1870s, several of the new organisations expanded to take in workers beyond the industries in which they originated. Both the London and Birmingham Gasworkers, following seasonally employed workers into brickmaking and other industries, organised as general labour unions from the start. Subsequently Thorne's union took in among others rubber workers, dyers in the Yorkshire woollen industry, local authority workers, workers in the Birmingham metal trades, in chemicals, clay-pits and quarries. Part of the reason for this expansion was the desire of the socialist leaders in some new unions to unite workers on a class, rather than a sectional, basis. More important, however, was the fact that successful unions found themselves besieged by other workers demanding to be admitted. Thus the NAUL founded to organise semi-skilled platers' helpers in the Tyneside shipyards, was soon catering for dockers, gas and chemical workers, builders' labourers, and less skilled workers in engineering, iron and steel, and the glass industry in many parts of the North.

In most of the new unions the leaders, often themselves drawn from outside the industry, wielded considerable power over the membership. For one thing there were a great many of them. The Seamen, for example, spent a quarter of their income on salaries in 1890. Nothing better illustrates the authority of the officials than the story of Tom Mann organising a crowd of several thousand hungry dockers anxious to collect food tickets from strike headquarters:

> . . . planting himself in the doorway, his back jammed against one side of the frame, his foot up against the other, he allowed the men to creep in, one at a time, under his leg. Hour after hour went by, while Tom Mann, stripped to the waist, stuck to his post, forcing the men down as they came up to him, chaffing, persuading, remonstrating, whenever the swaying mass of dockers got out of control until at last the street was cleared.[4]

Behind Mann's authority lay, not only his personal charisma, but also the lack of any tradition of collective organisation among the London dockers. The docker creeping under Mann's leg is an extreme case, but the dramatic circumstances in which they emerged, the impossibility of any slow build-up of strength and self-reliance, tended to foster authoritarian leadership in all the new unions.

A further consequence of the relatively weak bonds of spontaneous solidarity among the membership was the unions' need to gain formal recognition from employers if they were to survive at all. Gasworkers, who frequently worked for municipal undertakings, gained recognition more easily than most – local councillors had to reflect on the electoral consequences of a confrontation with their employees. Even in Leeds, where the Liberal council counterattacked in the summer of 1890, the vigorous and often violent opposition of the gasworkers to blacklegs was successful, possibly because it was more difficult for a public authority to break strikes than it was for a determined private employer. In London George Livsey had already routed the union at his privately owned South Metropolitan Gas Company in the winter of 1889–90. Although they could seldom gain a closed shop the gasworkers generally had sufficient bargaining strength to maintain recognition and organisation without it. But for the weakest groups, especially the casually employed dockers and the Seamen who lost control over their members once they put to sea, only the establishment of a closed shop could prevent the organisation being swamped by non-union labour. Unionism on the waterfront was an all-or-nothing affair. Following the Mansion House Agreement in London the contemporary historians of the dock strike wrote: 'The fact that the trade union card has been recognised by men and dock officials as the only passport to work is really the foundation of the Union, and its principal guarantee of permanence.'[5] Union membership was enforced by card inspections at the call-on stands where, twice daily, the men competed for work. Behind these protective barriers the dockers rapidly developed the job-controls that previously they had been unable to construct, imposing larger gangs and reducing the pace of work. During 1889–90 productivity fell significantly in the London docks as a result of such efforts. The union officials, though afraid of provoking the companies into a counter-attack, were unable to prevent the men from pushing their new found strengths to the limit.

The success of New Unionsim during 1889–90 rested on full employment, on the readiness of the police to tolerate vigorous picketing, and on the absence of concerted opposition from employers. None of these conditions lasted long. In 1890, at their peak, the seven largest new unions claimed 320,000 members, though this was probably an inflated figure. On more reliable figures this total had fallen to 130,000 in 1892, and 80,000 in 1896. If the origin of New Unionism had been a relatively peaceful affair, its destruction took place in an atmosphere of violence and class bitterness. Employers had little difficulty in converting middle-class sympathy for New Unionism into hostility, by presenting their counter-attack as a battle for 'free labour' against the 'tyranny' of the closed shop. As public opinion turned against the unions, the police abandoned their neutrality. Vigorous policing during the South Metropolitan Gas strike of December 1889 – which ended in the first major defeat for New Unionism – persuaded even *The Times* that the Home Office was no longer entirely a creature of the unions.

The New Unionist tide on the waterfront turned well before the boom broke in 1891. Already in the spring of 1890 a strike of the Liverpool dockers had been defeated at the hands of blacklegs and troops. Other defeats followed for Tillet's union on the South Coast, and in November the major London dock companies refused to renew the Mansion House agreement. In winter the surplus of labour around the docks was large, and the union offered no resistance. Activists were victimised at the call-on and the membership began to melt away. It was the shipowners' response to the Seamen's union that clinched the fate of both sailors and dockers. In September 1890, incensed by the efforts of the sailors to reinforce their strength by recruiting the ships' officers who controlled hiring, the owners organised to 'resist the new union methods of coercion'. The Shipping Federation established 'Free Labour' offices at which men might pledge themselves to work with union and non-union labour alike, and offered preferential employment to men so registered. The Shipping Federation put the organisation of blacklegging on a scientific basis and were able to dispatch large numbers of men to break strikes wherever they might occur. The counter-attack smashed trade unionism in the docks in a series of confrontations, culminating early in 1893 in a seven-week strike in Hull marked by violence, rioting and even incendiarism with gun boats standing by on the Humber.

III

The trade union explosion of 1889–90 provided the opportunity for socialists to move away from merely propagandist work, or from the quasi-insurrectionary fantasies of unemployed riots, into the potentially much more fruitful area of strike leadership and trade union activity. The existing socialist organisations were, however, ill-equipped to exploit these possibilities. Based in London, where trade unionism was peculiarly weak, and established at a time when the unions were both markedly collaborationist and largely restricted to a narrow aristocratic stratum, the SDF took an extremely narrow view of the potentialities of trade union agitation. An inflexible interpretation of Marx's economics helped to provide a theoretical justification for this attitude. Trade unionism could never do more than separate out privileged groups from the mass of the working class and thus obstruct working-class unity. Strikes could do nothing to raise working-class living standards above the subsistence basis. The persistence of such attitudes resulted in a divorce between Marxist socialism and militant trade unionism that was to have debilitating consequences for the future of socialism in Britain. The sectarianism of the official Marxists was extreme. The SDF officially characterised the trade union work of Thorne, Burns and Mann in 1889–90 as 'a lowering of the flag, a departure from active propaganda, a waste of energy'.[6] Consequently those socialists who saw active intervention in the trade union upsurge as essential to the growth of socialist politics were forced to act independently of the main established party.

The independent socialists made their mark on the trade union explosion of 1889–91 not only by their organising activities but equally by their capacity to translate the ideological challenge to Lib–Labism into immediate agitational demands. In 1886, frustrated by the unwillingness of the SDF to agitate seriously for a mere 'palliative', Tom Mann launched an independent Eight Hours League. Although, in line with SDF policy, the League promised no more than a temporary relief from unemployment when shorter hours were achieved, this qualification tended to disappear as the demand caught the imagination of trade unionists.* To those, both skilled and unskilled, who had experienced the unprecedented unemployment levels of 1879 and the mid-1880s the demand for the legal eight-hour day appealed with all-embracing simplicity as *the* solution to unemployment. State intervention to limit the hours of 'defenceless' women and children had long since been generally accepted, but the proposal to limit the hours of adult males appeared to confront the ideology of self-help head on. For a few years the

---

* 'Inspite of the superior wisdom of party hacks and Socialist sucklings, we adhere to our remedy which is, in truth, not a palliative but a panacea' (*Aberdeen Labour Elector*, 1893).[7] The 'hacks and sucklings' of the SDF continued to insist, with much justification, that unemployment could not be abolished so long as capitalism existed, and with considerable optimism that the chief value of shorter hours was to give workers greater leisure in which to acquire the education they needed to overthrow the capitalist system.

legal eight-hour day demand drew the line between the old-style radical and the new-fangled socialist.

The panacea made rapid headway within the citadel of Lib–Labism, the TUC. Already, at the Congress of 1883, the Railway Servants had allied with an old German Marxist, Adam Weiler, to carry the eight-hour day demand for public sector workers – among whom, by a piece of devious reasoning, they included the railwaymen. In 1887 and again in 1888 the Parliamentary Committee, on the instructions of Congress, conducted plebiscites on the issue of statutory regulation which revealed that the rank and file of many craft unions were moving well in advance of their leaders. The formation of the MFGB in 1889, partly around the demand for a statutory eight-hour day in the pits, and of New Unions, some of which had developed directly out of the Eight Hours League, and all of which favoured statutory regulation, increased the momentum. The climax was reached in 1890 when, in response to the call from the founding Congress of the Second International, demonstrations were organised in London and other cities to celebrate May Day and demand the legal eight-hour day. A few months later the TUC resolved to promote an eight hours Bill, and elected the first socialist, John Burns, onto the Parliamentary Committee.

The campaign for the statutory eight-hour day was, from the outset, closely linked with attempts to establish labour representation in Parliament on an independent basis. Scornful of the sectarianism of the socialist parties, Engels urged his associates within them to devote their energies to the promotion of independent labour politics:

> It is now an immediate question of organising an English Labour Party with an independent class programme. If it is successful, it will relegate to a back seat both the SDF and the SL, and that would be the most satisfactory end to the present squabbles. . . .[8]

That such a party could not yet be organised on the basis of a full and theoretically coherent socialist programme was, he argued, no valid objection. The need of the moment was not theoretical refinement, but practical activity – in the political, as much as the industrial, field. During the late 1880s dissident socialists in both parties came to share Engels' perspectives, and in some cases to act together on them regardless of party.

Independent labour politics took root in areas where industrial conflict created a fertile soil for socialist propaganda. Following the Northumberland miners' strike of 1887, which had attracted a good deal of support from the socialists, J.L. Mahon, a Socialist Leaguer, established a North of England Socialist Federation uniting members of the SDF and the League and hundreds of miners around a programme which included the promotion of socialist parliamentary candidates. The Federation did not long survive the evaporation of the militant spirit. A similar fate befell Tom Mann's efforts to establish a movement for independent labour politics in Bolton following a defeated engineers' strike.

But the most significant pioneering effort of the later 1880s occurred in Lanarkshire, stimulated by a bitterly fought miners' strike early in 1887. Socialists, already at work in the coalfield before 1887, played a significant role in the strike, and were able to point the lesson of its defeat at the hands of Government troops. At least one liberal miners' leader – James Keir Hardie – was forced by the indifference of the local Liberal establishment to question the possibility of achieving social justice through the Liberal Party. Consequently it came as no surprise to Hardie when, a year later, the Liberal caucus rejected his canditature, supported by the miners, for the forthcoming Mid-Lanark bye-election. Refusing Liberal offers to find him a seat elsewhere, Hardie determined to fight the election as an independent miners' candidate. Champion, once secretary of the SDF and now a leading promoter of independent labour politics, put up the money, and arranged for Mann, Mahon and other socialists to assist in the campaign. The result was disappointing, largely because the local Irish voters remained loyal to the party of Home Rule, but the campaign did lead to the establishment of a Scottish Labour Party in August 1888. Without decisively repudiating the Liberals, the new party succeeded in uniting most Scottish socialists with Irish nationalists, land reformers and advanced radicals in an effort to secure the election of MPs pledged to the statutory eight-hour day and other socialist demands.

London remained stony ground for the advocates of independent labour politics. Even after the dock strike of 1889 there was little working-class support for a break from the Liberals. Behind this lay the archaic, almost pre-industrial, character of the London economy. In the absence of large-scale manufacturing industry the tone of middle-class liberalism was dictated more by professional men than by employers. The capitalist character of the Liberal Party, whose dramatic exposure in strikes was so important to the growth of independent labour politics elsewhere, was much less apparent in London. Moreover the rapidity of the middle-class drift towards the Conservatives in the metropolis, together with the predominantly working-class composition of many of the constituencies, prevented the development of a powerful middle-class caucus hostile to working-class canditatures. After the coalfields, London was the chief source of Lib–Lab MPs. Liberal organisation in London was dominated, not by the caucus, but by the Metropolitan Radical Federation based in the working-class radical clubs. Well-established inside the Liberal Party, working-class politics in London were unlikely to develop in an independent direction. The class-consciousness which underpinned political developments in the North was further inhibited by the extreme polarisation between artisans in the luxury trades and the casual poor of the East End, a polarisation only temporarily and superficially disturbed by the triumphs of new unionism. In some of the outer, more industrialised suburbs – Woolwich, West Ham, Poplar, Battersea – the growth of a more homogenous working class did provide a basis for the emergence of independent labour politics from the 1890s. Elsewhere the weakness of trade unionism and the political volatility of the casual poor – who sung Rule Britannia when they rioted over unemployment in 1886 and turned to xenophobic Conservatism as New Unionism declined in the 1890s – ruled out any class conscious alternative to the Radicalism of the artisans.

During the 1880s London Radicalism grew rapidly, mobilised by Bradlaugh's secularist campaign to be admitted to the House of Commons without taking the oath, by the agitation for electoral reform in 1884, and, especially after 1886, by the Irish cause. Nowhere did the prospects of transforming the Liberal Party into a primarily working-class, even socialist, party seem brighter. While the SDF, after its initial failure to win the clubs to socialism, remained indifferent to the possibilities of the radical revival, the other main group of London socialists, the Fabian Society, took a different view. The Fabians urged the Radical clubs not to break with the Liberal Party but to permeate it with socialist policies. Following the establishment of the London County Council in 1888, the Fabians devoted much of their attention to promoting Sidney Webb's 'Municipal Socialism' through the controlling Liberal–Radical Progressive Party. During the 1890s the decline of artisan trades accelerated in the face of competition from factory production in the provinces and sweated workshops in London itself. Encouraged by cheap workmen's trains, an increasing number of artisans migrated to the suburbs. As the artisanate, which had provided the social base for club radicalism, disintegrated, permeation became increasingly irrelevant to working-class politics, even in London. For the next twenty years the gradualist socialism of the Fabians, distinguished by its stress on the role of middle-class intellectuals and administrators in the transition to socialism, played little part in the development of the working-class movement. Meanwhile, in the industrial North, the trade union explosion had created the conditions for the establishment of an independent labour party.

A branch of the Socialist League had been active in Leeds and the West Riding of Yorkshire since 1884, led by a young photographer's assistant from a poverty-striken Irish Catholic family, Tom Maguire. One month before the London Dock Strike, in June 1889, Maguire was helping to organise a successful strike of bricklayers' labourers, and during the next few months League members played a key role in establishing Thorne's Gasworkers Union in a wide range of industries throughout the West Riding. When in the summer of 1890 the Liberals of the Leeds Town Council declared war on the gas stokers and the eight-hour day, the League was well placed to argue the case for independent labour politics. It was, however, the defeat of the Manningham Mills woollen workers in Bradford, not the victory of the Leeds gas stokers, that proved politically decisive.

The militancy of the wool and worsted workers in the West Riding during 1890 owed little to the boom conditions that were so important to New Unionism elsewhere. The industry was in decline. There was a chronic surplus of woollen workers in the labour market, while women and girls, paid extremely low rates, displaced their husbands and brothers. Outside a few of the more skilled sections, trade unionism was chronically weak, and largely confined to a Weavers Union first established in 1883. Five years later the Weavers had only 700 members. In 1889, as an offshoot of a rather conservative Lancashire cotton workers' paper, the *Yorkshire Factory Times* was established. Around this paper the socialist leaders of the weavers sought to build the union, mingling reports of its activity with propaganda for independent labour representation. It was the impact of this propaganda, and above all the victories of the London dockers and the Leeds gas workers that aroused militancy at Manningham Mills. The union leaders, aware of the weakness of their position, initially opposed the strike against cuts in piece prices that broke out in December 1890.

The resulting lockout lasted for five months. Lacking funds and denied assistance for their families by the Poor Law Guardians, the strikers could only survive by mobilising support throughout the West Riding and beyond, thus focusing attention on the outcome of the struggle. Despite considerable sympathy for the strike among local Liberals – Sam Lister, the owner of the Mills, was a Tory protectionist – the Liberal controlled Watch Committee took an extremely repressive line. By the spring the lockout had taken on the character of a general class confrontation throughout the town, and socialists from far and wide descended on Bradford to assert the right of free speech. This did not prevent the collapse of the strike, but it served to dramatise the lessons of defeat at the hands of a Tory employer and a Liberal Watch Committee. Within weeks a Bradford Labour Union had been established, involving the leadership of the weavers and several Socialist Leaguers, to promote labour representation in Parliament and on the town council 'irrespective of the convenience of any political party'.[9] Similar organisations spread rapidly through the West Riding, particularly in the woollen towns, accompanied by a proliferation of labour clubs – twenty-three clubs with about 3,000 members are recorded in Bradford alone by the end of 1892 – which provided entertainment, education and socialist propaganda for many thousands of workers. Equally important was the sudden expansion of Trades Councils in the area under the impetus of socialists and New Unionists intent on directing trade unionists towards independent political action.

While in the West Riding, and many other areas of the country, local organisations pressed ahead with the promotion of independent labour candidates at local elections, it was the General Election of July 1892 that finally precipitated the federation of all this activity into a national Labour Party. Before the election Joseph Burgess, editor both of the *Yorkshire Factory Times* and of a national weekly, *The Workman's Times*, set in motion a campaign for the formation of an Independent Labour Party. Apart from the West Riding, independent organisation already existed in Scotland, where the Scottish Labour Party was now flanked by a Trades Council Labour Party; in Newcastle, under Champion's influence; and in Manchester and Salford where another talented journalist, Robert Blatchford, had brought together SDFers, the local Fabian Societies, Trades Council leaders and others into an ILP constituted on the most rigidly independent basis. Burgess' campaign met with rapid success in other areas, including London and the Midlands. Meanwhile Champion devoted his attention to financing independent candidates at the General Election. In Bradford Ben Tillett, aided by Fabian money, came near to victory in a three-cornered contest, and Champion himself did well in Aberdeen. Havelock Wilson, the seamen's leader and John Burns were returned for Middlesborough and Battersea respectively, but both proved to be more interested in coming to terms with the new Liberal Government than in pressing forward the independent movement. The decisive contest was at West Ham, a constituency of New Unionist dockers and labourers, where Keir Hardie was returned as an independent, though without Liberal opposition, pledged to a vigorous anti-unemployment programme of land nationalisation, municipal workshops and the statutory eight-hour day. At the Trade Union Congress that autumn Hardie chaired a small unofficial meeting which decided to call a national conference to unite the 'Independent Labour Parties in Great Britain'. The foundation conference of the ILP assembled in Bradford during January 1893.

The objective of the ILP's founders was reflected in the programme adopted in 1893. The ultimate goal was socialism, but the conference rejected a Scottish proposal to include the word 'Socialist' in the name of the new party, fearing that this would alienate potential voters. The first priority was to secure the election of independent labour men to Parliament. To this end the party adopted a programme of social reforms designed to avoid antagonising the unions and to appeal to a non-socialist electorate. Both the Fabians and the SDF remained aloof. The Fabians after an unsuccessful attempt to outflank the ILP by appealing to the TUC to establish its own Labour Party, continued to look for socialist openings in the Liberal Party. The SDF, more in sorrow than anger, forecast the subordination of socialism in the ILP to the opportunist pursuit of trade union money and working-class votes.

IV

The expansion of socialist influence in the working-class movement represented by the formation of the ILP, was very largely a result of the activity of socialists in the trade union explosion. The subsequent development of the new socialist party, however, owed as much to the limitations and failures of New Unionism as to its successes. The impact of the 'great Depression' and New Unionism, by challenging the conventional stratification of the working class both in fact and in men's consciousness, momentarily opened the door to a rebirth of revolutionary working-class politics. A few socialists began to develop ideas of revolutionary direct action, anticipating the syndicalist ideas associated with the pre-war industrial unrest twenty years later. But the rhetoric of a united class offensive remained extremely vague and unspecific. There was, indeed, little material basis for any syndicalist strategy of encroaching working-class power in industry. The sectional logic of trade unionism was quick to assert itself against the notion of an all-embracing class unionism. After the first flush of success, for example, the Gasworkers unscrambled their 'general' branches, reorganising on the basis of trade and place of employment. In face of the employers' counter-attack and the return of unemployment, those sections which could not win union recognition dropped out, leaving the general unions as federations of sectional bargaining units rather than organs of a united industrial offensive against capitalism. Even before the counter-attack the New Unionism was clearly something less than a coherent revolt of the poor as a whole. Thus the fight to establish trade unionism in the London docks was also a fight to make dockwork 'respectable' – at the expense of the weakest competitors for jobs. In November 1890, when the Dockers Union decided to close its books, Tom Mann had explained that 'the other men at the Dock gates must clear off; with us there is no room for them'. Trade union action by itself might expand the size of the respectable working class. But it would not eliminate the residuum. There were, explained Mann, 'other social movements to provide for them'.[10]

The 'other social movements', whether they were middle-class charity, the Poor Law, New Liberalism or, indeed, the socialist movement itself were, at best, movements working *on behalf of the poor*, rather than movements *of the poor*. The ILP consisted largely of young skilled workers and their wives, together with sizeable groups of teachers, clerks, shop assistants and other lower middle-class people. ILP organisers soon discovered that the poor had neither the time nor the inclination for political activism. Among the leaders of the ILP the problem of poverty was perceived less as a problem for the poor themselves, more as a problem created by the poor for the organised and respectable working class. Many of their favoured remedies – notably the resettlement of the urban unemployed in rural farm colonies – owed less to any understanding of the economic forces producing poverty, than to a straightforward desire to remove the poor from competition with organised labour in the market place.

It is significant that the ILP emerged out of a defeated strike in Bradford, and that the West Riding of Yorkshire, where trade union-ism was particularly weak, remained for many years its strongest area of support. The growth of socialist politics in the 1890s repres-ents not a political generalisation of industrial militancy, but a reaction to defeat in the industrial struggle, a search for political solutions where industrial ones had failed. Behind this lay the incompleteness and weakness of trade union organisation. During the upsurge of 1889–90, socialist leaders of New Unionism had been anxious to repudiate the allegation made by Gladstonian trade union leaders that their policy would lead workers into craven dependence on the state. 'The keynote', wrote Mann and Tillett, 'is to *organise* first, and take action in the most effective way . . . instead of looking specially to the Government.'[11] Nevertheless their emphasis on the demand for the statutory eight-hour day and on labour representa-tion in Parliament reflected an awareness that the groups of workers they were organising were too weak to win their trade union battles without positive support from the state. The decline of New Union-ism in the early 1890s confirmed socialists in their conviction that it was to legislative intervention, rather than to direct action of the poor themselves, that they must look for the solution to the problem of poverty.

At its peak in 1895 the ILP had perhaps 35,000 members, though no-one really knew. The SDF claimed about 10,500 at the same time, only about a quarter of them dues-paying members. Originating as a loosely co-ordinated federation of local labour clubs and parties, the ILP long retained its decentralised character. The National Adminis-trative Council, as its title suggests, had little executive or policy-making power. The branches often failed to pay their dues to the centre; and, in 1895, national headquarters consisted of a single room housing the Secretary and his assistant. The newspapers, Har-die's *Labour Leader* and Blatchford's *Clarion*, gave the Party a national presence, but the centralising impulse of involvement in parliamentary politics was, for the time-being, weak. The refusal of local Liberal caucuses to run labour candidates continued to bring recruits to the party – notably Ramsay MacDonald, previously a Liberal agent. But despite some good performances in bye-elections in 1893–5, the ILP failed to win a single seat in the General Election of 1895. Hardie, their sole MP, was defeated at West Ham.

Since there was little immediate possibility of pursuing the war on poverty in Parliament, it was primarily in the arena of local govern-

ment that socialist politics took shape in the 1890s. By 1900 the ILP
claimed 106 local councillors, 66 members of School Boards and 51
Poor Law Guardians. Something like one in every thirty paid-up
members of the party held public office. SDF branches were similarly
active in local politics. Well supplied with Fabian Tracts on every
conceivable function of local government, minority groups of socialist councillors concentrated on persuading local authorities to
implement permissive legislation on housing, sanitation, relief works
for the unemployed, and so on. They fought the battle for water
closets – not privy middens – in the new council houses. On the
Bradford School Board Margaret MacMillan pioneered school
meals and medical inspections for children. On the Poplar Board of
Guardians George Lansbury worked for the establishment of Farm
Colonies for the unemployed. In co-ordination with the unions,
socialists campaigned over the pay and conditions of muncipal employees and for 'fair wage' clauses in local authority contracts. Everywhere there were the corrupt practices of the 'builders' ring' on the
Council to be exposed. Though the overall impact of such activities
on the problem of poverty was negligible, the reforms achieved were
real enough to sustain enthusiasm.

The SDF might view municipal politics as 'a phase in the class
struggle against exploiters and not in any sense a petty affair of local
government reform',[12] but this was a difficult perspective to sustain.
It is true that in many localities working alliances between the
socialist parties and the unions and Trades Councils, unattainable at
national level, were formed. The most successful of these was in West
Ham, Keir Hardie's old constituency, where in 1898 the first Labour
Council, led by the SDF, took office. But most such alliances
involved the socialists in compromises with Radicalism. The
advance towards independent labour politics took place in a jungle
of compromises where, at any point, tactical flexibility on the part of
the Liberals would revive Lib–Lab perspectives. At the founding
conference of the ILP the Manchester delegates were defeated in their
attempt to incorporate the Fourth Clause of their own constitution
into that of the new party – a clause binding members to vote only for
Socialists and to abstain when a Socialist candidate was not standing. Only such a policy of rigid independence, argued Blatchford,
could prevent the re-absorption of the ILP into a Lib–Lab alliance in
which the 'independent' labour vote would be used as a bargaining
counter in electoral deals with the Liberals at the expense of the
party's socialist commitments. Blatchford's anxieties were well-

founded as the subsequent history of the Labour Party was to show, and in municipal politics the dangers of 're-absorption' were intensified by the local government committee system which involved a minority group on the Council in everyday power sharing with its political enemies.

The reforming activity of the 1890s did not lead to the abandonment of socialist goals within the ILP. But neither the trade unionism of the 1890s, nor municipal socialism, offered much scope for the development of such aspirations into a realistic strategy for the overthrow of capitalism. Instead ILP politics tended to converge more and more with the non-socialist reformism of the New Liberals. By the late 1890s ILP leaders were to be found working closely with New Liberal intellectuals to formulate an agreed programme of progressive reform. At the same time they resisted firmly proposals for 'socialist unity' with the SDF, despite the strong support for unity among the rank-and-file of both parties.

During the 1890s the disjunction between socialist aspiration and political practice became systematised in the ILP doctrine of 'ethical socialism'. When William Morris offered a moral dimension to the socialism of the 1880s – a vision of the future and an ethic of fellowship in the present – he meant to supplement, not to replace, the dry analytic strength of Hyndman's Marxism. At its best this 'moral dimension' served to reinforce and invigorate a class-conscious socialism without in any way detracting from the clarity of its strategic thinking. But in the hands of those most responsible for popularising socialism during the 1890s ethics became a substitute for strategy, fellowship for class consciousness.

The ex-Socialist Leaguer, Bruce Glasier, believed that questions of strategy mattered little so long as the genius of the cause – fellowship – reigned in the hearts of socialists: a maudlin sentiment quite alien to the spirit of Morris' work.

Ethical socialism also appealed to the Christian sensibility of many of the workers who became socialists. The importance of religion can be exaggerated. Both Blatchford and Glasier were militant atheists; one important source of socialism was the secularist movement; and many other recruits to socialism were, no doubt, like the great majority of the urban working-class, indifferent to organised religion. Nevertheless religion was an important influence in the small manufacturing towns of Yorkshire and Lancashire where both non-conformity and the ILP found their most fertile soil. One of the most curious features of the spread of socialism in the North during the early 1890s was the growth of the Labour Churches. Led by John Trevor, a Manchester Unitarian, who thought he saw God working through the labour movement as once He had worked through the Christian Churches, the Labour Church movement supplied a staging post on the road to secular socialist politics for many people alienated from nonconformity by its bourgeois aura and its identification with the Liberal Party.

Robert Blatchford, whose *Merrie England* was one of the most popular socialist texts of all time, captured the essence of ILP socialism: 'I think that the best way to realise Socialism is – to make Socialists. . . . Give us a Socialistic people, and Socialism will accomplish itself.'[13] Questions of strategy and tactics paled into insignificance beside the propagandist mission – 'to make Socialists'. Propaganda for the socialist ideal was, indeed, of primary importance. But, in practice, no socialist party beyond the merest sect could escape the need to intervene in the everyday struggles of the working class. Within the ILP, ethical socialism served as a substitute for any coherent attempt to relate the practical politics of the party to its socialist goals. This left the leadership of the party with considerable freedom of political manoeuvre – a freedom from any constraints of socialist principle. In this way the ethical socialism of the 1890s paved the way for the subordination of the socialist movement to trade unionism and to the New Liberal revival after 1900.

Notes

1   E.P. Thompson, *William Morris,* London 1977, p. 125.
2   G.S. Jones, *Outcast London. A Study in the Relationship Between Classes in Victorian Society,* Oxford 1971, p. 293.
3   Thompson, *op. cit.,* pp. 409-10.
4   H. Llewllyn Smith and Vaughan Nash, *The Story of the Dockers' Strike,* London 1889, pp. 94-5.
5   *Ibid,* p. 160.
6   H. Collins, 'The Marxism of the SDF', in A. Briggs and J. Saville (eds), *Essays in Labour History,* vol. 2, London 1971, p. 55.
7   K.D. Buckley, *Trade Unionism in Aberdeen, 1878–1900,* Edinburgh 1955, p. 82.
8   Thompson, *op. cit.,* 1955, p. 528.
9   H. Pelling, *The Origins of the Labour Party,* Oxford 1954, p. 95.
10 P. Thompson, *Socialists, Liberals and Labour. The Struggle for London, 1885–1914,* London 1967, p. 51.
11 Tom Mann and Ben Tillett, *The New Trades Unionism,* London 1890.
12 Statement by a leader of the West Ham SDF in 1901, in S. Pierson, *Marxism and the Origins of British Socialism,* London 1973, p. 255.
13 Robert Blatchford, *Merrie England,* London 1908, p. 243.

4

The Labour alliance, 1895–1914

Between 1890 and the labour unrest of 1910–14 there was no major explosion of trade union growth, though union membership rose steadily through most of the intervening years. The vicissitudes of trade unionism during this period underlay political developments in the working-class movement, and went far to determine the ambiguity of these developments. During the 1890s a major employers' counter-attack on the unions opened the way to victory for the advocates of independent labour representation in Parliament, with the establishment of the Labour Representation Committee in 1900. At the same time the limitations of the counter-attack, which resulted not so much in defeat for the unions as in industrial truce and the expansion of collective bargaining, helped to ensure that socialism would have a minor role to play in the emergent Labour Party. While the counter-attack pushed unions towards independent politics, the extent to which they had won a recognised status within capitalist society made the construction of a socialist party on the basis of official trade union machinery an unlikely project from the outset. When the new trade union explosion came after 1910, the political institutions built during the years of industrial peace proved to be entirely inadequate to reflect the new power and aspiration of the working-class movement. By the outbreak of war in 1914 the alliance of socialists with trade union leaders in the Labour Party may have been on the point of collapse.

I

The biggest trade union battles of the early 1890s occurred in mining and cotton. The Miners Federation, established on the principle that wages should reflect the miners' needs rather than fluctuations in the price of coal, faced its decisive test when coal prices fell after 1890. In 1893, in the course of a bitter lockout caused by the union's refusal to accept wage cuts, two miners were shot dead by troops at Featherstone in Yorkshire. The lockout continued for four months, the largest industrial dispute that had occurred in Britain, and the resulting disruption of other industries forced the Government to mediate. The settlement, which miners' leaders claimed as a great victory, maintained wages at their existing level for a further two months (an easy concession since the strike itself had temporarily reversed the price fall), and established a Conciliation Board to settle wage rates thereafter. In reality the miners had been forced to abandon their demand for a 'living wage', and for the next two decades the conciliation machinery regulated wage levels very largely on the basis of price movements. Nevertheless, the very survival of the Federation in 1893 was itself a significant victory, providing a secure framework for the systematic encroachment of union power at pit and local level during the ensuing years of prosperity and expansion in the industry. The revival of coal prices in the late 1890s enabled the MFGB to consolidate its position in Scotland and Wales. Previously weak spots for trade unionism, these areas provided half the Federation's membership by 1900. The miners of Northumberland and Durham were eventually brought into ths Federation in 1907–8, by which time their collective bargaining machinery had recovered from a temporary collapse caused by the very rapid fall in export prices during the mid-1890s.

A federation of Master Spinners, founded in 1891 by the large joint-stock companies of Oldham, launched the counter-attack in cotton. In pursuit of a 5 per cent wage cut the federated firms closed their gates in November 1892. The lockout continued for five months, involving up to 50,000 operatives. Finally in March 1893 Mawdsley, the spinners' leader, settled on the basis of a smaller wage cut and a system of collective bargaining (the so-called Brooklands Agreement) which involved an annual wage round limited to 5 per cent adjustment in either direction; a procedure for referring mill disputes to central negotiation; and the withdrawal of the masters' objection to the closed shop. As in coal, cotton spinners had survived a major employers' attack and established collective bargaining procedures which, though their inadequacies led to recurrent rank-and-file unrest, helped to prevent any major confrontation with the employers for nearly twenty years. Meanwhile the Weavers had achieved their long-standing goal of a uniform price list for the industry, without a strike, in 1892.

Collective bargaining also developed rapidly during the 1890s in many of the craft industries. The Boilermakers' leader, Robert

Knight, had long been concerned to establish sufficiently close relations with the employers to prevent the extreme fluctuations of the
shipbuilding industry from leading to constant industrial conflict.
To this end he developed an autocracy of full-time officials in the
union which operated with minimal control by the membership. As
depression returned from 1890 the Executive took the initiative in
negotiating wage reductions, leading to a six-week unofficial strike
on Clydeside in 1891. Three years later, Knight, overruling the
objections of his members in the area, negotiated a collective bargaining procedure for the North East very similar to the Spinners'
Brooklands Agreement. Comparable agreements followed in other
districts. Meanwhile the threat of technical change to craft controls
was met partly by the vigour of rank-and-file organisation in the
yards.

The most successful response to technical change came from the
print unions, confronted with the rapid introduction of the linotype
machine which set type at four times the speed of hand compositors.
Their militancy in 1889–91 encouraged employers to organise. Both
the London and the provincial unions, aided by the rapid expansion
of the industry which facilitated the redeployment of hand compositors, succeeded in imposing their own terms for the introduction
of new machines. A provincial agreement in 1898 paved the way for
the later development of national collective bargaining in the industry, setting a pattern of high-level negotiations as a supplement to
craft control in the print-shops rather than a substitute for it.

In building, the growth of collective bargaining was both slower
and less complete. During the 1890s a sustained housing boom
facilitated rapid union growth and an upsurge in local strike activity
uncontrolled by union executives. The organised strength of the
unions became more important to building workers as employers
attempted to use an expanded sub-contracting system ('the lump') to
undermine the enforcement of craft controls by the informal solidarity of the trade. But the relative technical conservatism of the industry obviated the need for any concerted employer counter-attack,
while its localistic character inhibited the development of strong
national employers' organisation. In 1899 both sides drew back
from a national confrontation without reaching any settlement of
their future relations. It was only after the turn of the century, when a
slump in building sharply reduced both union membership and local
militancy, that significant advances were made towards national
collective bargaining. From 1904 existing local bargaining agree-

ments were strengthened by the establishment of a national disputes procedure. But some important areas, including London and Scotland, remained outside the national scheme.

It was the large engineering employers, who established the national Engineering Employers' Federation in 1896, who made the most determined assault on trade union power. Feeling themselves squeezed between the pressures of foreign competition and union resistance to the employment of cheap semi-skilled labour made possible by technical advances, these employers became convinced of the inevitability of a showdown with the predominant craft union, the ASE. Asserting the claims of managerial prerogative against shop steward pressure on the frontier of control in the workshops, they argued that the ASE, infiltrated by socialists, was out to gain total control of the internal management of their works. The aggressive president of the Federation, Colonel Dyer, much impressed by Carnegie's ruthless smashing of trade unionism at his Pittsburgh works in the Homestead strike of 1892, declared the employers' determination 'to obtain the freedom to manage their own affairs which proved so beneficial to the American manufacturers as to enable them to compete . . . in what was formerly an English monopoly.'[1]

The actual occasion for the showdown came with the revival of the campaign for the eight-hour day as trade improved. A joint committee of engineering unions in London, where the employers were still unorganised, pressed the issue from May 1897. Some firms conceded, others turned to the national federation for help in resisting. In July the Federation replied to strike action at a handful of London firms with a selective national lockout of ASE members, and the union responded by calling out its members in all Federated firms. Had the issue simply been one of shorter hours, the union's confidence might have been justified. But the employers were determined to force the whole issue of craft control. Though the lockout was never total, the bigger companies used their considerable economic leverage to force sub-contracting firms into line. The ASE, on the other hand, though receiving generous financial support from other British unions and even from overseas, paid the price for its long history of demarcation disputes with other craft unions in the industry. A last minute application to join the Federation of Engineering and Shipbuilding Unions, which Robert Knight had established in 1890, was turned down. The Boilermakers, the Foundrymen, the Patternmakers and a number of other sectional unions remained at work and condemned the ASE for embarking on an adventurist course. Even when the ASE knew it was defeated, the employers prolonged the dispute by demanding an almost complete abandonment of collective bargaining as the condition of a settlement. Finally, after six months, and the loss of seven million working days, a settlement was reached in January 1898.

Collective bargaining on general wage claims was accepted by the Federation, but the union had to abandon both the eight-hour day and, more important, the defence of craft controls. Accepting the employers' 'right to manage', the ASE renounced its own right to negotiate over the proportion of apprentices, the introduction of new machinery or the rate paid to non-unionists. It also abandoned resistance to piecework and the demand for the closed shop. A complex procedure for the avoidance of disputes ensured that most future strikes would be unconstitutional. On paper this represented almost unqualified defeat for one of the strongest sections of the labour aristocracy. In practice, however, the employers, here as in other industries, had failed to smash trade unionism. ASE membership fell little and recovered quickly. Until the outbreak of the First World War craft control in the workshops proved surprisingly resilient. The major effect of the 1898 settlement was to tie up the national leadership of the union in a policy of collaboration with the employers. Meanwhile the more militant districts continued to pursue traditional craft policies, with considerable success.

The defeat of the aristocratic engineers sent a shock wave of insecurity through the whole trade union movement. The crumbling legal position of the unions further intensified this sense of weakness in face of the employers' counter-attack. From the mid-1890s a series of court decisions went against the unions, severely restricting the right to strike and the legality of effective picketing. This legal counter-attack culminated in January 1901 when the Taff Vale Railway Company, following a hard-fought strike in the previous summer, established its right to sue the union for damages. The Taff Vale case was finally settled two years later at a cost of £42,000 to the union. Further cases followed in other industries. The Taff Vale decision, by thus removing the legal immunity of the unions and making them liable at law for the actions of their officials, virtually destroyed the right to strike. Any union taking strike action now placed the whole of its funds in jeopardy.

Despite union fears, the Taff Vale decision was not the prelude to any major new employer offensive. The early years of the new century were years of industrial peace. This was not merely a result of Taff Vale, which was effective as a deterrent to strikes only between 1902–5 (the legal immunity of the unions was restored by the Liberal Government in 1906). Low levels of strike activity characterised the whole period from 1899–1907. Industrial peace was a symptom, not so much of trade union defeat, as of the stalemate reached in many industries during the 1890s. Most of the major confrontations of the 1890s had ended not in outright defeat for the unions, but in the establishment or sophistication of collective bargaining procedures. These procedures survived the test of economic slump after 1902. (Part of the reason for this, however, was that the test itself was not very severe, since the relative buoyancy of prices during this depression restricted the employers' need to cut production costs.) In cotton and in printing wage cuts were generally avoided. In coal, cuts were negotiated without major strain on the existing procedures. In shipbuilding and engineering, cuts provoked strikes in the North East and on the Clyde, but the union leaderships were successful in preventing any general resistance. Here, as elsewhere, employers were concerned to make the new collective bargaining arrangements work, and they were prepared to rely on the national trade union leaderships rather than the tactic of a national lockout, to hold local rebelliousness in check.

II

One effect of the employers' counter-attack in the 1890s was to create opportunities for socialist propaganda in the unions. Socialists naturally predominated in the leadership of the New Unions, and in other sectors where they had taken the lead in building trade union organisation – the Yorkshire woollen industry, Scottish mining. Elsewhere in mining the socialist presence expanded rapidly during the national lockout of 1893 and the South Wales lockout of 1898, but tended to fall away again when peace returned. A more permanent influence was achieved in the North East where the industrial pacifism of the reigning officials and their resistance to unity with the MFGB created a continuing source of support for the socialists among the younger, more militant miners. In those craft sectors, like shipbuilding and printing, where collective bargaining developed on terms most favourable to the unions there was little scope for a socialist-led opposition. In the trades most seriously threatened by technical change in the 1890s, notably tailoring and the boot and shoe industry, socialists put themselves at the head of skilled worker resistance to new production methods – though in neither of these cases were they able to prevent defeat for the unions. In engineering socialist influence played an important part both in the militancy that preceded the lockout of 1897–8, and subsequently in limiting the capacity of the leadership to impose loyalty to the new procedures of national collective bargaining on the more militant districts.

While socialists played an important part in stimulating militancy in particular industries, their efforts to build a general trade union opposition to conciliatory industrial policies met with little success. The idea of an industrial federation of unions for mutual support in strikes had been discussed at the TUC almost annually since the early 1890s. Following the engineers' lockout a socialist campaign for the establishment of a federation won considerable support within the unions both at official level and unofficially through local groups of enthusiasts from different unions. The main effect of this campaign however was to stimulate the Parliamentary Committee into launching its own rival scheme. The General Federation of Trade Unions, established in January 1899, was a more modest project involving the union executives in no substantial financial commitments or loss of autonomy. The Federation subsequently devoted more attention to promoting conciliation than to financing strikes. The failure to establish a militant federation confirmed the emphasis on political, over industrial, struggle in the socialist movement. It would take a new trade union explosion, together with the influx of syndicalist ideas from France and the United States, to jolt socialists towards a political strategy rooted in rank-and-file militancy in industry. Meanwhile the counter-attack of the late 1890s was opening the way for the conversion of the trade union movement, not indeed to socialism, but to independent labour politics.

Lib–Lab resistance to independent labour politics weakened during the 1890s. In 1893 the Parliamentary Committee had blocked the implementation of a socialist-inspired Congress resolution for the establishment of a political fund to promote independent candidatures. In 1894, in a move which reflected the growing centralisation of power in the trade union movement, the TUC abolished Trades Council representation and limited the choice of delegates to trade union officials or those working at the trade. At the same time the card vote was introduced. But none of this did much to stem the pressure for a new political initiative. The engineering lockout, mounting difficulties in the courts, the canvassing of proposals for new anti-trade union legislation, the hostility shown by the Conservative Government after 1895 to trade union deputations, the formation of an Employers Parliamentary Council in 1898 – all pointed towards an intensification of the employers' counter-attack. The case for the establishment of an independent Labour Party was argued in relation to a widespread belief, shared by socialists and non-socialists alike, that the conflicts of the 1890s were only a prelude to an all out offensive against trade union power. In 1893 a National Association had been established to supply 'Free Labour' (blacklegs) to employers, and its services had been used in a number of strikes. Trade unionists had only to look across the Atlantic to see what a full-scale employers' offensive could achieve. The growth of union-smashing trusts in the United States seemed to be mirrored in a wave of amalgamations in British industry in the late 1890s.

The TUC resisted proposals to establish a political levy among affiliated unions in 1897 and 1898. But the next Congress accepted a more modest resolution, moved by the Railway Servants, which called for a special convention of co-operative, socialist and trade union organisations to 'devise ways and means for securing the return of an increased number of labour members to the next Parliament'.[2] This had the advantage of leaving those who preferred to rely on their own political resources, notably the big battalions of coal and cotton, free to do so, while allowing those unions who favoured a pooling of resources to proceed independently of the remainder. The Parliamentary Committee co-operated with the ILP, SDF and the Fabians to convene the conference, which met in the Memorial Hall in London in February 1900. At the conference the ILP steered a careful course between Lib–Lab attempts to restrict the new organisation to the pursuit of limited trade union demands, and the SDF's call for the adoption of a clear socialist objective. The delegates accepted Hardie's compromise resolution, voting to establish 'a distinct labour group in Parliament, who shall have their own whips and agree upon their policy'. Nothing was said about what this policy should be, beyond the anodyne formula that it should consist of 'legislation in the direct interests of labour'.[3] To this end the conference established a Labour Representation Committee (LRC) on which the socialists secured quite disproportionate representation – five out of twelve places. The Committee had, however, little power. No political fund was established, and the financing of parliamentary canditatures remained a matter for the separate organisations proposing them. Ramsay MacDonald was elected

unopposed as secretary, largely because he was prepared to do the
work without payment.

The foundation of the LRC was a triumph for the advocates of
independent labour representation, but it did not overnight transform the character of working-class politics. At first the attempt to
consolidate the LRC was overshadowed by what seemed likely to be
the far more dramatic political consequences of the Boer War. The
Conservative Government's onslaught on the Boer Republics in
October 1899 brought the chronic disarray in the Liberal Party to a
head. Split three ways between the pro-war Liberal Imperialists, an
ineffectively neutral centre, and a pro-Boer left, the final disintegration of the Liberal Party appeared imminent. This circumstance
occasioned many curious new alignments in working-class politics,
as socialists, Lib–Labs and middle-class radicals, united in their
opposition to the war, manoeuvered for leadership in the new party
of social reform that would emerge when Liberalism fell apart.

The LRC was unable to make much headway so long as the
prospect of the break-up of the Liberal Party held the centre of the
stage. In the 1900 'Khaki' election only two LRC candidates were
returned, Hardie and the railwaymen's leader, Richard Bell. Both
had run on a pro-Boer ticket in double harness with Liberals. Meanwhile the Lib–Lab trade union leaders either ignored the new Committee, or, like Richard Bell himself, joined it to counter the influence
of the socialists and steer it away from the pursuit of independence.
Ben Pickard, President of the MFGB, launched a new drive to promote Lib–Lab miners MPs. This was a major blow to the LRC since the
unique political power of the miners – due to geographical concentration they dominated the electorate in a large number of constituencies – would necessarily have to form the backbone of any national
Labour Party.

What saved the LRC from an early death was the impact of the
Taff Vale judgement of 1901. Initial trade union reactions to Taff
Vale were uncertain and divided. Many trade union leaders opposed
demands for the restoration of trade union immunity, believing that
the legal incorporation of the unions would enable them to discipline
militant elements and secure recognition from the employers. Others
pointed out that the Conservative Government, while it might redress some of the uncertainty created by Taff Vale and other judge-
ments, would certainly not restore full trade union immunity from
the law. By 1903, however, the TUC, shocked by the size of the
damages secured by the Taff Vale Company, and convinced by Tory

inaction that nothing could be gained from the existing Government, had come round to the demand for the restoration of immunity. The LRC played Taff Vale for all it was worth as an argument for the need to increase labour representation in Parliament. As a result there was a second wave of trade union affiliations during 1902, and by 1905 the only significant section remaining aloof were the miners. What most unions sought from the LRC, however, was not any long-term alternative to Liberalism, but a sufficiently strong bargaining position to force the next Liberal Government to repeal the effects of the Taff Vale judgement. Ramsay MacDonald and the leadership of the LRC concurred. What they had in mind was bargaining strength *vis-à-vis* the Liberals, rather than strict independence from both established parties.

Paradoxically enough, what enabled the LRC to consolidate itself against Lib–Labism was a major revival of Liberal unity and purpose. The inglorious career of the British Army in South Africa, as the war dragged on in the face of unexpected guerilla resistance, undermined the domestic appeal of imperialism. The ending of the war in 1902 brought no relief to the Government. During the next three years every political issue seemed to add fuel to the Liberal revival. The Education Act of 1902 raised a storm of nonconformist protest. Taff Vale mobilised the labour vote. The import of Chinese labour to work the Rand gold mines appeared to prove the sordid imperialist character of the war, uniting moral protest against 'slave labour' with trade union anxiety at this further evidence of Government-sponsored blacklegging. But it was, above all, Joseph Chamberlain's campaign for Tariff Reform, launched in 1903, which laid the basis for the landslide Liberal victory in the 1906 election. While the Conservative Party plunged into internecine warfare over Chamberlain's dream of imperial self-sufficiency, all progressive forces united in defence of the sacred Liberal principles of cheap bread, free trade and internationalism.

The Liberal revival put paid to ideas of a new progressive party emerging form the ruins of Liberalism. Encouraged by increased trade union affiliations, the LRC toughened up its claims to independence, establishing a Parliamentary Fund which would give the executive material as well as moral power over the candidates it endorsed. Bye-election victories during 1902–3, which increased the Labour group in Parliament from two to five, proved the LRC was a force to be reckoned with. Consequently the Liberal leadership were ready to come to an accommodation with the LRC. Herbert Glads-

tone, the Liberal Whip, and Ramsay MacDonald drew up an agreement allowing, initially, a free run to 30 LRC candidates. Both sides
had an interest in avoiding three-cornered contests which would split
the progressive vote and allow the Tory in. The Liberals, confident
that LRC MPs would act as good Liberals in the House of Commons,
saw 'Labour' candidates as a device for regaining the Tory working-
class vote that had grown alarmingly in the boroughs since the
1880s. The Pact would also save them money. MacDonald, on the
other hand, looked to the Pact as a means of avoiding having to put
the LRCs fragile 'independence' to the test, and of securing the
inestimable advantage over the Lib–Labs of co-operation from Liberal head office in persuading local Liberal caucuses not to oppose
Labour candidates.

The success of the Pact varied markedly between regions. It
worked best in Lancashire where Liberalism was weak, trade union
organisation strong and the working-class vote traditionally split
between the two major parties. It had no effect at all in Scotland
where Liberalism was unchallenged either by Conservatives or by
powerful trade union organisation. Other areas fell between these
two extremes. In the run-up to the 1906 election both sides experienced difficulties from socialist inclined local LRCs and reactionary
Liberal caucuses intent on fighting one another, but the mutual
understanding at the top was sufficient to hold the line. In the event
twenty-four of the twenty-nine LRC MPs elected in 1906 were
returned without Liberal opposition. Apart from its surviving bas-
tion in the coalfields, Lib–Labism could only muster four trade
union MPs. Ironically the Lib–Labs, unsupported by any central deal
with the Liberal leadership, faced much greater resistance from the
local Liberal caucuses than did the 'independents' of the LRC. By
1906 the essence of the LRC's independence lay in the fact that it had
substituted a centralised accommodation with the Liberal Party for
the local arrangements traditionally pursued. The centralisation of
working-class political organisation certainly represented an
advance over the trade and regional sectionalism characteristic of
Lib–Labism. It increased Labour's political muscle sufficiently to
achieve the trade unions' main objective. In 1906 the Liberal Government, under Labour pressure, passed a Trades Disputes Act
restoring the legal immunity of the unions and legalising peaceful
picketing. But the independence of 1906 hardly represented a victory
for the long-term strategy of the ILP. The new Labour Party (for-
mally constituted as such after the election) had arrived on the

political scene not as the grave-digger of Liberalism, but as an integral part of a great Liberal revival.

In their preparations for the 1906 election local LRCs, many of them socialist led, were persuaded and cajoled by MacDonald to prefer Liberal trade unionists to Socialists as their candidates, or to disguise Socialist candidates as pure-and-simple Labour men. Mac-Donald's electoral strategy threatened the ILP tradition of socialist propaganda, of 'making socialists'. Although the majority of the Labour MPs elected in 1906 were in fact members of the ILP, their dependence on trade union finance and on electoral arrangements with the Liberals made it quite impossible for them to behave as a socialist block within the House of Commons. They had no independent electoral base on which to fall back in case of a break with the Liberals. Before 1906 the untested threat of an all-out LRC offensive against the Liberals had helped to persuade Herbert Gladstone of the advantages of coming to terms with Labour. After 1906 the bluff worked the other way: there were twenty-nine Labour hostages in the Commons, most of whom stood to lose their seats if they allowed co-operation with the Liberals to break down. In 1906, amidst the rather synthetic Tory horror at the 'socialist' advance, and the jubilation of the victorious alliance of progressive forces, socialist supporters of the Labour Alliance had ample cause for disquiet. During the next eight years most of their fears were shown to be justified.

III

The ILP had sufficient strength at Labour Party Conferences to pass pious resolutions favouring socialism as an ultimate goal. But this was in no way understood by the delegates to mean that the everyday politics of Labour should be geared to achieving this goal, or that non-socialists would not be welcomed into the party. The compact of 1900 was not to be broken. Thus the 1908 conference, which passed a resolution in favour of socialism by a narrow margin, overwhelmingly rejected a move to write the socialist goal into the party's constitution, as did all Labour Party Conferences before the war. Meanwhile the Labour Party's dependent position in Parliament ruled out any determined effort to promote an independent reform programme, and the party found itself reduced to offering passive support for Government-initiated reforms. Neither the unions, nor their Parliamentary representatives, saw anything to be gained from opposing immediately beneficial social legislation in the name of a distinctively socialist programme of reform. This was shortsighted of them.

Whatever its ameliorative effects early twentieth-century social reform embodied a counter-attack on democratic and working-class institutions at least as formidable as the employers' attack on trade unions in the 1890s. Already in 1902 the directly elected School Boards which facilitated popular control of the education system had been abolished in favour of the more remote authority of the Local Education Authorities. Similarly, the National Insurance Act of 1911 was constructed in such a way as to subordinate the participatory democracy of the most successful of all nineteenth-century working-class institutions – the friendly societies – to the bureaucratic procedures of the commercial insurance industry. What was at issue was whether the growth of state provision for social welfare would represent an extension of democracy and working-class power, or whether it would tend to suppress existing democratic forms in favour of the construction of a bureaucratic welfare machine concerned more with discipline and control than with opening up new opportunities for popular self-government. By the end of the first decade of the century a growing number of socialists were pointing anxiously to the clauses in reform legislation, from Old Age Pensions to Unemployment Insurance, intended to reinforce labour discipline and establish new ways of rewarding the 'deserving' and punishing the 'undeserving' poor.

The Labour Party's acceptance of the Liberal reform programme did not prevent agitation for an alternative approach. The SDF, which had disaffiliated from the LRC in 1901, constituted a standing challenge to the politics of the Labour Alliance, and ILPers, disgruntled by their leadership's alliance with the unions and their policy of electoral compromise with the Liberals, continued to look to 'Socialist Unity' as an alternative strategy.

As in the 1880s and 1890s unemployment stood at the centre of socialist politics. The growth of unemployment after the end of the Boer War led to a series of agitations extending from aggressive mass street collections by demobilised soldiers in London's West End during 1903 to workhouse occupations, sit-ins in fashionable churches, a series of hunger marches from northern towns to London and a major riot in Manchester in the summer of 1905. This activity, largely led by the SDF, forced the LRC and the TUC to pay serious attention to the grievances of the unemployed. From the autumn of

1905 a National Right to Work Council led jointly by the ILP and SDF co-ordinated the agitations, supporting attempts by the unemployed to seize and cultivate Church lands in a number of northern cities. In 1907 the Labour Party, attempting to place itself at the head of this agitation, introduced its own Right to Work Bill which would have placed on local authorities full responsibility for providing either work or maintenance to the unemployed, and established some measure of central Government responsibility for planning and financing public works schemes.

The more militant Labour MPs, led by Keir Hardie, saw in the Right to Work campaign the possibility of co-ordinating the parliamentary and extra-parliamentary politics of labour, strengthening the independence of the Labour Party and developing it in a socialist direction. By the end of the decade, however, Hardie's balancing act between Labour Alliance and Socialist Unity had broken down under the weight of its own internal contradictions. The TUC, while it backed the Right to Work Bill, would have nothing to do with the socialist led agitation in the country, and many of the major Trades Councils were also hostile. The majority of the Parliamentary Labour Party, rallying to the Government as political crises mounted from 1909, showed little inclination to pursue their own distinctive policy in the face of New Liberalism. In any case, economic recovery from 1910 rapidly took the political heat out of the unemployment issue.

The limitations of the labour movement as it emerged before 1914 are perhaps most clearly revealed in its attitude towards the parliamentary franchise. The Reform Acts of 1867 and 1884 had made it possible to contemplate building a Labour Party. But the franchise, hedged around with a complex system of registration, residence qualifications and the exclusion of paupers, remained very restricted. Only about two-thirds of the adult male population qualified for the vote, and all women were excluded. It has been calculated that before 1918 no more than 95 of the 670 Members of Parliament were elected from constituencies predominantly working class in character, despite the overwhelming preponderance of the working class in the population as a whole.

What is revealing, in view of these figures, is that, after 1884, the extension of the franchise never again became a central issue in working-class politics. Indeed Labour and Socialist leaders often spoke as though parliamentary democracy was already an accomplished fact. Certainly among unenfranchised males there was little demand for the vote. They tended to be among the poorer, less organised sections of the working class, and few were excluded permanently. Depending on his particular circumstances a man might fall in and out of the suffrage from one election to the next. This was not, however, the case with the women.

From its foundation in 1893 women had played an exceptionally important role in the ILP. Before she established the Women's Social and Political Union (WSPU) in Manchester in 1903, Mrs Pankhurst had been a local ILP leader. The new militant suffrage movement was rooted in previous campaigning among women cotton workers, and operated initially largely within the network of ILP organisations. But if the suffragette agitation was nurtured in the labour movement, the relationship between them was never an easy one. On the surface, the tension was over tactics, rather than goals. The WSPU demanded the immediate granting of votes to women on the same terms as men. In 1904 the ILP accepted this demand, but the Labour Party rejected it, convinced that the enfranchisement of women under existing electoral law would tend to increase the anti-working-class bias of the electorate. The question of women's suffrage, they asserted, should be tied to a general extension of the franchise – to the demand for Adult Suffrage.

In fact the disagreement was more than merely tactical. Behind the Labour Party's decision lay hostility to feminist assertion and a rooted belief in the innate conservatism of women. The attitudes of male trade unionists towards women followed closely the pattern of their exclusive attitude to the unorganised poor. But there was an important difference. Whereas, in the end, the working-class movement was bound to benefit from trade union growth and political mobilisation among the poor, the solidarities of sex could transcend class boundaries and be turned against the interests of labour. What made this danger seem all too real was the impatient reaction of the WSPU leadership to its rebuff in 1905. Instead of attempting to convert the labour movement, the middle-class women who dominated the WSPU rapidly abandoned their ties with the ILP. As militancy escalated during the next decade, the suffragette agitation isolated itself from working-class politics. Increasingly dominated by Mrs Pankhurst's autocratic daughter Christabelle, the WSPU took on the character of a militant, but socially conservative, crusade of middle-class womanhood intent on bludgeoning the existing political establishment into conceding 'Votes for Ladies'. The Liberal Government responded viciously with jail sentences, forced feeding and the notorious Cat and Mouse Act. Each step in the escalation only served to isolate the suffragettes still further from any possible working-class base.

The flamboyance of the WSPU's militancy has tended to divert the attention of historians from the ultimately more important shift of the non-militant women's suffrage societies towards a working arrangement with the Labour Party. Successive failures for Women's Suffrage Bills in the House of Commons convinced many suffragists that their cause could not be won unless the next general election, due in 1914, returned a clear Liberal and Labour majority. When, in 1912, the Labour Party resolved not to support any extension of the franchise that did not include women, the way was open for an alliance between Labour and the suffragists. In the event the war intervened before this alliance could be put fully to the test. But the enthusiastic support given by suffragists to Labour candidates in several pre-war by-elections anticipated the crucial role that women were to play in building up Labour's constituency organisation after the war.

IV

The dramatic political events which followed the House of Lords' rejection of Lloyd George's budget in 1909 did nothing to enhance the independence of the Labour Party. Two general elections were fought in 1910. The constitutional crisis was eventually resolved by the Parliament Act in 1911, which replaced the Lords' veto by a three-year delaying power. But this merely set the scene for a new crisis over Ireland. As a result of the 1910 elections the Irish Party held the balance in the Commons, forcing the Liberal Government to take up once more the issue of Home Rule. Between 1911 and the outbreak of war in 1914 resistance to Home Rule took an increasingly militant form, as the Conservatives identified themselves with Ulster loyalist preparations for civil war and right-wing mutiny in the British Army. There was little alternative for the Labour Party but to rally to the defence of parliamentary government, Home Rule and the Liberals.

In the two 1910 elections Labour, fearful of provoking Liberal retaliation, had made little effort to expand its parliamentary representation beyond the foothold achieved in 1906. The argument for caution was given added force in 1909 when the courts ruled that the expenditure of trade union funds for political purposes was illegal. The Osborne judgement threatened the financial basis of the Labour

Alliance, and its reversal became a major issue for the party. After three years of procrastination the Government finally legislated, not to restore the status quo but to enable unions to establish a separate political fund from which members should be free to contract out.

After 1906 the Labour Party leadership concentrated on consolidating the party's strength in the country, rather than on attempting to wrest further seats from the Liberals. The one major breakthrough came in 1909 when the Miners Federation at last affiliated, bringing a further sixteen MPs into the Parliamentary Labour Party. This was, however, far from a decisive defeat for Lib–Labism in the mining districts. The attempt to turn Lib–Lab miners' MPs into independent Labour members led to constant friction between the union and the Labour Party; to the loss of six miners' seats in 1910 and three more in subsequent bye-elections; and to the expulsion of a further two miners' MPs for persistently flouting the Labour Whip. In this conflict the Labour Party leaders showed their determination to purge Lib–Lab members and Lib–Lab constituency organisation from the party, even where this meant losing technically Labour seats. Meanwhile, outside the mining areas, there were signs that Labour was gaining strength. Though the party won no bye-elections between 1910–14, its share of the vote tended to increase. Local party organisation expanded around ILP branches, Trades Councils and local LRCs. This steady consolidation of the party's local strength, together with the huge growth of trade union organisation after 1910 that underpinned it, tended to intensify dissatisfaction with the party's dependence on the Liberals. Paradoxically, by 1914 the growing strength of the Labour Party's organisation in the country threatened the party's very survival – dependent as this was on the alliance with the Liberals.

By 1914 there was little sign that the Liberals were in imminent danger from Labour. Any electoral confrontation between the two would have hurt the Liberals by letting in Conservative candidates, but it would have decimated Labour's representation in the Commons. Snowden, who favoured such a course, admitted that at least three-quarters of the Labour MPs would be defeated, most of the socialists among them. On the other hand the maintenance of an electoral pact was becoming increasingly difficult as pressure grew for a much greater number of Labour candidates than the Liberals had been prepared to tolerate in 1910. The national strategists of Liberalism might have been prepared to allow a major new advance of independent labour representation, but it is unlikely that they could have induced sufficient local Liberal caucuses to stand down without putting intolerable stress on the party. On the eve of the First World War, Ramsay MacDonald's entente with the Liberals was coming under increasingly heavy fire from Labour activists. In 1913 there was a major row when MacDonald's own Liberal running mate in the two-member Leicester constituency resigned his seat. The local Labour Party, dominated by one of the largest ILP branches in the country, was determined to contest the bye-election. The National Executive refused their endorsement, convinced that a contest in Leicester would invite widespread Liberal retaliation at the next General Election. Undeterred the local party ran their candidate as an independent socialist, and were soundly defeated. These tensions within the ILP came to a head at its 1914 Conference. Rumours that MacDonald was considering an open alliance with the Liberals, and even discussing the possibility of a Cabinet post for himself in the next Liberal Government, led to an overwhelming vote against any pact with the Liberals, a demonstration of independence fully backed by Snowden, Hardie and other leading ILP parliamentarians.

But it is difficult to see how the Labour Party could have survived the confrontation with the Liberals that now seemed unavoidable. A large minority of trade unionists continued to oppose the party. Nearly 40 per cent of the membership of the nine largest unions voting in ballots for the political levy in 1913 were opposed to union funds being used to support independent Labour candidatures. In some regions, notably among the miners of South Wales and the North East, most working-class voters still rallied to the banner of Gladstonian, rather than the new collectivist, liberalism, let alone to Labour. Many of those who supported the Labour Party did so because they saw it as the working-class element in a broader progressive alliance rather than as the nucleus of an independent, socialist party. If the Labour Party had been forced by its own activists into pursuing real independence, it is doubtful whether the majority of trade unionists would have still been prepared to finance electoral campaigns which let the Tories in. So the most likely development, on the eve of the war, seemed the disintegration of what Keir Hardie had called the Labour Alliance into its constituent parts – a revival of Lib–Labism in the unions and the emergence of a smaller, but genuinely independent, socialist party. The war came just in time to save the Labour Alliance, and to prevent a delayed vindication for the old strategy of socialist unity.

Notes

1   *The Times,* 7 September 1897.
2   H. Pelling, *Origins of the Labour Party,* Oxford 1954, p. 205.
3   *Ibid,* p. 209.

5

The Labour unrest, 1910–14

The labour movement as it had emerged by 1910, socially restricted and politically unambitious, constituted a challenge to capitalist power only in the most qualified and limited sense. A Labour Party struggling for political muscle which nevertheless failed to promote an agitation against the exclusion from the franchise of more than two-thirds of the working class, male and female, was clearly something less than the all-embracing political movement of the class. The exclusive attitudes of organised labour towards women and the poor might derive, in part, from the difficulty of organising those sections of the population. But such attitudes, in turn, powerfully reinforced the inability of the movement to break out of its minority position. Even the more radical activists – the socialists – often based their politics on the assumption that the working class, for the time being at least, was too weak to embark on the independent pursuit of its own emancipation.

I

During the five years before the First World War the whole pattern began to shift. A new upsurge in trade union membership laid the basis for a widening of the movement's social base and its political horizons. The period of relative industrial peace since the turn of the century ended during the depression of 1908–9. A railway strike was narrowly averted in 1907 when, following a dramatic intervention by Lloyd George, the unions were persuaded to accept a conciliation scheme which still denied them effective recognition. The next year saw major disputes in cotton and among engineering and shipbuilding workers on the North-East coast. In the former case wage reductions were enforced in a seven-week lockout that broke fifteen years of peace under the 1893 Brooklands Agreement. In the latter wage reductions were also imposed under threat of national lockouts. These defeats formed the prelude to a new trade union explosion when the depression lifted.

Between 1910–14 trade union membership grew by more than 50 per cent, and strike activity ran at more than four times the level of the previous decade. Behind this lay a low level of unemployment, the failure of wages to keep up with rising prices, and an accumulation of unsolved grievances over conditions, hours and the pace of work which had been building up beneath the facade of industrial truce. In one industry after another strike action, often unofficial, brought previously unorganised workers flocking into the unions. The general unions catering for less skilled workers grew much faster than the movement as a whole. Few industries were untouched by the labour unrest, but its focus was in the two most rapidly expanding sectors of the economy, coalmining and transport.

Since the 1880s, as the search for coal led to the exploitation of deeper and more difficult seams, output per man had been falling in the pits. This, together with a stagnation of coal prices since the Boer War boom and the cumulative effects of safety and hours legislation, led to increasing employer pressure on wage levels. Fear of national action by the MFGB, where membership grew by nearly 50 per cent between 1905–10, prevented the owners from securing a sufficient reduction in costs by attacking general wage levels. Instead they concentrated on cutting down actual earnings at pit level – tightening up on fringe benefits, and on the allowances paid to face workers in particularly difficult positions where they could not produce sufficient to take home average piece-work earnings. In a situation where earnings were already being hit by the decline in output, this issue of 'abnormal places' caused great unrest.

It was the Liberal Government's legislation for an eight-hour day in the mines in 1908 that brought matters to a head. Shorter hours further restricted piece-work earnings, and the disruption of customary shift arrangements caused by the eight-hour system, led to countless local disputes. In the North East an agreement to introduce a three-shift system negotiated without consultation with the rank and file, led to a wave of unofficial strike action in the early months of 1910. In South Wales the fall in piece-work earnings resulting from the Act intensified discontent over the abnormal places issue. In the autumn of 1910 a dispute involving seventy men at one pit belonging to the Cambrian Combine over prices to be paid on a new seam blew up into a strike of all 12,000 miners employed by the Combine. This strike was to continue for almost a year, and the strikers felt that they were spearheading a national struggle on the abnormal places issue. The strike was run by an unofficial joint lodge

committee and crystallised rank-and-file frustration with the conciliatory policy of the leadership throughout the coalfield. In January
1911, following the death of three members of the South Wales
Executive in a rail accident and the resignation of a fourth, militants
were elected to all the vacant places. There was considerable violence
against strike breakers, aggravated by the presence of troops and
imported police. A riot in Ton-y-Pandy in November 1910, following attempts to bring in blacklegs, subsequently became legendary in
the labour movement. A local journalist described what happened:

> The sides of the valley rise rapidly, and clustering at the foot of
> the hills are many irregularly formed rows of houses divided by
> narrow streets. Well acquainted as they were with the topogra-
> phy of the district, the rioters . . . found no difficulty in securing
> comparatively safe and commanding positions. . . . Aided by
> the women, who carried supplies of stones and other missiles in
> their aprons, they stoned the constables in the open streets
> below with terrible fury.[1]

When the police advanced up the side streets some miners retreated
into the houses to continue their barrage from bedroom windows.
Eventually the crowd was dispersed by troops with bayonets fixed.

Refused national support the Cambrian miners eventually went
back, defeated, in October 1911. Meanwhile the strike had served to
concentrate the minds of the national leadership, and in January
1912 the miners voted nearly four to one for a national strike to
establish a minimum level of earnings for all underground workers.
Fearing economic dislocation the Government intervened, supporting the principle of a minimum wage (which was in fact acceptable to
most of the owners), but opposing the MFGB's insistence on an
overall national minimum and on national negotiation of district
minima calculated on the basis of average piece-work earnings.
Unimpressed, the Federation called out nearly a million miners on 1
March 1912. This was the first national miners' strike. Coal prices
rapidly reached famine levels, rail services were cut, factories closed
down, and up to a million other workers were laid off. Within the
month the Government had rushed a Minimum Wage Bill through
Parliament which provided for arbitration to settle the level of
minimum wages, district by district. A second ballot of the miners
showed a small majority for continuing the strike, but the Executive,
afraid that favourable settlements in some districts would break the
unity of the Federation, called off the strike. The district settlements

which followed under the Act were disappointing, far below the levels originally demanded by the Federation. But the strike had strengthened the union. Its membership increased, it had won the principle of a minimum wage, and it had demonstrated its capacity to use national action.

Meanwhile the transport industry had exploded during the summer of 1911. Sparked off by a successful strike of seamen in June, the strikes radiated outwards among dockers, carters, tramwaymen, railway workers, and the miscellaneous factory operatives around the waterfront areas. The poorest workers were drawn into the movement. In London 15,000 women in the sweated workshops of Bermondsey came out, closely followed by cleaners working for the London County Council. This was no ordinary strike movement. The spontaneity and breadth of the strikes posed unprecedented problems both for union leaders, whose ability to gain permanent recognition and bargaining rights for their unions depended on their ability to control the strikers, and for the forces of the state. Union leaders, taken by surprise, rushed to formulate demands and to recruit unorganised bodies of strikers. George Askwith, the ubiquitous Board of Trade conciliator, toured the affected areas, grinding out settlements. In Manchester alone he spent five days in the Town Hall co-ordinating the simultaneous negotiations of eighteen different unions, representing a bewildering variety of workers, all pledged not to go back until the other seventeen were satisfied. And the longer settlements were delayed the more the strikers took on the character of a general social war.

Violence was in any case endemic on the waterfront, provoked by the employers' customary use of blacklegs. Troops were called out in several centres, and Salford was subjected to a virtual military occupation. In Liverpool, with a gun boat standing by on the Mersey, two strikers were shot dead by the Army following three days of guerrilla warfare in the streets around the city centre. Something of the bitterness of the conflict is revealed in the words of Harry Carpener, a Manchester seamen's leader (assiduously noted down by a plain clothes policeman in the crowd):

> This is a fight to the death. I would rather die fighting than standing. We are not going to starve. We are not afraid of our houses being broken into, we are not trembling. The Manchester police are a disgrace to the nation. . . . A police officer who would lock up a man for doing a good job on a blackleg is not

worth his uniform. If you only half do it you deserve locking up. Constables throw aside your uniforms and we won't go in until your grievances are settled. . . . Tomorrow all married men and men with sweethearts bring out your wives and sweethearts into the open. The women won the Liverpool Carters strike. The police won't hurt a woman but she can scratch his eyes out.

Two days later strikers' wives, dressed in rags, marched through the city under the menacing slogan: 'Our Poverty is Your Danger, Stand by Us'.[2] The extent of the strike movement denied the Shipping Federation its usual supplies of experienced blackleg dockers from unaffected ports, and by August most of the provincial strikes had been settled in favour of the men. In London attempts to settle the issue without strike action finally broke down when the dockers rejected a negotiated settlement, struck and forced a substantial improvement of the terms. On the waterfront the strikers were generally victorious, though in London the employers used an ill-judged strike a year later to cancel many of the gains of 1911.

Meanwhile, unofficial action by the Liverpool railwaymen had sparked off a national strike, the first ever on the railways. The executives of the various railway unions were forced to get together and place themselves at the head of the movement. The central demands were for union recognition and an end to the unsatisfactory conciliation procedure established four years earlier. At first both owners and the Government determined to resist. One manager announced: 'The Government at our conference today have under-taken to put at the service of the railway companies every available soldier in the country.'[3] Troops were mobilised, and martial law declared over large areas of the country. Revolvers sold like hot cakes to the alarmed inhabitants of London's West End. In Llanelly, troops protecting a blackleg train fired on the strikers, killing two men. Five more were killed when a goods shed, raided by strikers, went up in flames detonating a van-load of gunpowder. In Liverpool the dockers, who had previously been persuaded with great difficulty by the strike committee to accept a settlement, came out again, and all transport in the city ground to a halt. Mass pickets were mounted and the strike committee, led by Tom Mann, issued permits for the movement of essential supplies of milk and bread – and, when he humbly applied to the committee, to the Liverpool postmaster for the movement of overseas mails. In some areas groups of miners came out in sympathy with the railwaymen, and in Fife and South

Wales there were threats of large-scale strike action by the miners.

Within two days of placing the Army at the disposal of the railway companies, the Government, alarmed at the extent of support for the strikers, and at the probable economic effects of a long drawn out strike, backed down. Lloyd George used the dangerous international situation (the 'Agadir' crisis, over German ambitions in Morocco) to persuade the railway companies to accept conciliation. The union executives called off the strike, ready to grasp at any straw to escape from their embarrassing situation. The eventual settlement went some way towards achieving union recognition, but did little to alleviate the basic complaints of the railwaymen – long hours, low wages and iron discipline. Nevertheless, the strike initiated a period of rapid growth for the railway unions and a new confidence among railwaymen. There were further unofficial strikes over disciplinary matters during 1913.

The transport strikes of 1911 and the miners' strike of 1912 were the most dramatic engagements of the pre-war labour unrest. But militancy continued. In 1913 there were 1,500 recorded strikes, more than ever before, and, outside mining (which was quiescent following the national strike of the previous year), the number of working days lost was greater than in any year since 1892. During the summer of 1913 a 'prairie fire' strike swept through the largely unorganised metal industries of the Midlands, accompanied by the familiar clashes between strikers and the police, and the novel tactic of fund-raising hunger marches dispatched throughout the country. Women workers played a major role in this strike movement. While the craft unions generally viewed the strikers with superior disdain, the general unions registered a spectacular growth in membership and established a permanent foothold in the factories. In Dublin, Jim Larkin led a bitter eight-month strike of transport workers against the employers' determination to destroy his union. The strike, which ended in a draw, was the occasion for much denunciation of the British trade union leaders for their failure to organise sympathetic action. In London the busmen, organised by a union of taxi-drivers, struck in the autumn of 1913, winning union recognition. Guerrilla warfare followed in the garages as busmen used their new strength to challenge managerial autocracy over discipline and scheduling arrangements. Early in the new year the London master builders, provoked by a rash of unofficial strikes over the employment of non-unionists during 1912–13, locked out their workers, demanding that they sign a 'Document' agreeing to work with non-unionists.

After three months the masters agreed to withdraw the 'Document', but the strikers voted against a return to work until further concessions were granted. Weakened by the desertion of the small, aristocratic Stonemasons' union, and under threat of a national lockout, the strikers held out for another four months, until the outbreak of war in August.

In the country as a whole more working days were lost in the building industry during the first six months of 1914 than in the transport workers' revolt of 1911. On the eve of the First World War new upheavals were widely anticipated in mining and on the railways. The militancy which was to create the wartime shop stewards' movement was already apparent among engineering workers whose wages had been held down under long-term agreements negotiated during the depression of 1908–9. Although there were signs that the boom was breaking by 1914, and although many trade union leaders were anxious to avoid new disputes, it seems probable that, but for the outbreak of war, the strike wave would have continued into 1915.

II

In a period when the Labour Party achieved little and was wracked by internal dissension, the trade union explosion provided a base for a renewal of socialist politics. The late 1900s had seen a growing current of hostility to the Labour Party among the ILP rank and file. In 1907, the Colne Valley ILP put up Victor Grayson in a bye-election in defiance of Labour Party instructions not to contest the seat. Narrowly returned as an 'independent socialist', Grayson refused to accept the Labour Whip and embarrassed the Labour Party by his exuberant, unparliamentary advocacy of the claims of the unemployed on the floor of the House of Commons. In 1909 the ILP conference backed Grayson's militancy against the platform, and were only brought to heel by the temporary resignation of the 'big four' ILP leaders, MacDonald, Snowden, Glasier and Hardie. Subsequently most of the ILP rallied to the leadership, but a minority led by Grayson and Robert Blatchford's *Clarion*, defeated in their attempt to recall the party to the politics of unadulterated socialist propaganda, broke away. In 1911–12, in a campaign of great enthusiasm, the ILP dissidents joined with the SDF and various unattached local socialist groups to form a new British Socialist Party (BSP).

The BSP was launched in the immediate aftermath of the strike movement of 1911. For Leonard Hall, an ex-ILP stalwart, the object of the new party was to exploit the socialist potential of the labour unrest:

> Let it be clear, that this is not to be a politicians' party but an agitators' party. . . . The people's real hope and strength lie for the present in the industrial field. When they are strong enough *outside* Parliament to enforce their demands, then will be the time for direct legislation and administrative action.[4]

But Hyndman and the 'old guard' of the SDF retained control of the new party, and insisted on the view that they had held since the 1880s that it was no part of a socialist party's task to interfere with the industrial responsibility of the trade unions. This conflict between pro- and anti-syndicalists was probably the main cause of the decline in BSP membership by nearly two-thirds between 1912 and the outbreak of war. By 1914 there was evidence of widespread demoralisation and inactivity among those members who remained, and the party was suing for affiliation to the Labour Party.

Meanwhile, the ILP fared little better. Between 1909–14 ILP membership fell by a quarter. No less than in the BSP the traditions of the ILP socialism militated against any very close link between the activity of the party and the new currents of direct industrial action, though ILP members were certainly active as individuals in the strike movements. To most of the ILP leaders, intent on sustaining their alliance with trade union leaders in the Labour Party, the unofficial militancy of the labour unrest was an anathema. Snowden condemned not only syndicalism but strikes as well, urging workers to abandon the obsolete weapon of the strike in favour of the ballot box. Hardie, on the other hand, took a forthright position in support of strikers, notably during the Cambrian lockout of 1910–11 and the Dublin strike of 1913. But, despite his great prestige, he was by this time something of an outsider in ILP politics. Similarly his anti-militarist advocacy of the general strike against war found more response among continental socialists than among his fellow British delegates to the Socialist International.

The failure of both major socialist parties to find an adequate response to the labour unrest, led an increasing number of industrial activists to abandon organised socialist politics for syndicalism. In 1910, drawing together a variety of minor groupings inspired by American and French syndicalist ideas, Tom Mann launched the

Industrial Syndicalist Education League. Mann was the perfect per-
sonification of the movement. Enthusiastic, rhetorical and cease-
lessly energetic, an unsectarian, unsystematic, eclectic thinker capable of an extraordinary range of responses; above all an agitator,
always there on the platform, in the strike committee's rooms,
directing, speaking, casting the spell of revolution, bringing 'life and
health and sympathy and hope into the most sordid of human lives'.[5]
In the South Wales coalfield, and in the transport strikes of 1911,
syndicalists played a leading role. Their stress on militancy, rank-
and-file self-activity, solidarity across craft and sectional barriers,
and the tactic of the sympathetic strike enabled them to offer precisely the sort of leadership required by the spontaneous strike
movements of 1911.

The syndicalists rejected state socialism, and directed attention,
with gripping and persuasive simplicity, to the reconstruction of
trade unionism on an industrial basis. These unions were to be both
the chief agency of class struggle in the present, and the embryonic
administrative structure of the Socialist Commonwealth. All syndicalists were agreed that the existing trade unions were too sectional
in their structure, too collaborationist in their policy, and too
oligarchic in their government to act as agencies of revolutionary
transition. But there were fundamental disagreements on what
should be done about this. The Socialist Labour Party (SLP),
founded in 1903 as a breakaway from the SDF, and with little direct
influence outside Scotland, advocated root-and-branch opposition
to the existing unions – bulwarks of capitalism – and the construction of new revolutionary unions. In British conditions 'dual' unionism was a non-starter. A relatively high level of trade union organisation, and the existence of general unions willing and able, when
conditions were ripe, to recruit previously unorganised workers on a
massive scale, left little room for the development of 'dual' unions
outside and antagonistic to the existing movement.

While the SLP strove in vain to establish an alternative leadership
to the existing trade unions, the majority of syndicalists concentrated
on propaganda and education within them. 'The Trade Unions',
wrote Mann, 'are truly representative of the men, and can be
moulded by the men into exactly what the men desire.'[6] The main
thrust of syndicalism in Britain was to canalise rank-and-file militancy into movements for the amalgamation of the existing unions
on industrial lines. The syndicalists could point to considerable
successes in this work – notably the formation of the National Union

of Railwaymen in 1912, which brought all but one of the existing manual workers' unions into a single industrial organisation, and the progress of negotiations during 1913–14 for a Triple Alliance of miners, railwaymen and transport workers. In 1914 the Triple Alliance, which provided for the co-ordination of strike action between its constituent unions, was widely seen as a portent of a revolutionary general strike. In a number of other industries, notably building and engineering, syndicalists established Amalgamation Committee Movements.

There was a paradox at the heart of the apparent victories of syndicalism. Amalgamations and greater unity would certainly be essential if the existing trade union movement was to become capable of mounting a revolutionary general strike and of taking control of the means of production. They were also, however, necessary for quite contrary reasons. The leaders of the railway unions agreed to amalgamate in 1912 because they had learned that unless the Executives could unite they were likely to be surplanted from below. Amalgamation was successful in staving off the threat. To many of the trade union leaders who founded and controlled it, the Triple Alliance was valued, not as a means of promoting and extending sympathetic strike action, still less as a revolutionary weapon, but as a means of preventing spontaneous and unofficial outbreaks, of containing rank-and-file militancy. The subsequent career of the Alliance, as we shall see, fully justified these hopes. No one was more aware than the syndicalists of the dangers of oligarchy, but eloquent exhortation apart, they could find no way of combining rank-and-file control and revolutionary initiative with large-scale and effective trade union organisation.

The central weakness of syndicalism as a revolutionary strategy lay in its failure to confront the necessarily ambiguous role of trade unions within capitalist society – at one and the same time agencies of working-class struggle and of truce with the power of capital. 1910–14 saw an unprecedented strike wave. It also saw the rapid extension of collective bargaining machinery frequently promoted during strikes by the Board of Trade conciliators as the best way of avoiding future conflicts. The settlement of the major disputes in transport and the mines involved the establishment of new collective bargaining machinery. In many other industries – cotton, engineering, printing, boot and shoe – the re-negotiation of existing bargaining procedures helped to avert the escalation of local strikes into national confrontations. The advance of collective bargaining might represent a victory for militancy, but it also served to limit the revolutionary potential of trade unionism, setting up collaborationist and oligarchic tendencies within the organisation. The Seamen, who had initiated the strike wave of 1911, provide an extreme example. After the strike their autocratic leader, Havelock Wilson, established a system of virtual company unionism which lasted for over fifty years. More typical was the unwillingness of the leaders of the National Union of Railwaymen to jeopardise their newly established collective bargaining agreement by supporting local disputes over disciplinary questions on which the companies did not recognise their right to negotiate, or by yielding to demands for sympathetic strike action in support of the Dublin strikers in 1913.

Syndicalists were not unaware of such problems; indeed one source of their support as unofficial strike leaders was the frustration occasioned by the operation of the emergent system of collective bargaining, which strained the relationship between trade union officials and their more militant members. Syndicalist opposition to conciliation and procedural agreements, which prevented the full and immediate use of industrial power when militancy was at its peak and the employer unprepared, appealed to organised workers across many industries. But, short of a revolutionary general strike, syndicalism had nothing to offer in place of the collaborationist logic of collective bargaining once the particular strike was over. It was not until, during the First World War, the shop stewards' movement developed the strategy of independent rank-and-file organisation that revolutionaries began to find a way out of this critical dilemma.

III

The trade union explosion of 1910–14 represented a fundamental challenge to the restricted horizons, both sociological and ideological, within which the development of the labour movement had been confined since the 1880s, and, indeed, since the defeat of Chartism. The penetration of trade union organisation into the poorer strata of the working class, deeper than in 1889–90, made it possible to believe that the labour movement could solve its own 'problem of poverty' by methods of direct industrial action, rather than by an exclusive concentration on achieving social reform through Parliament. At the same time the realisation that the most powerfully organised groups, notably the miners, were now capable of national strike action that could bring the whole economy to a halt, reinforced the appeal of direct action as a weapon in the socialist arsenal. The growth of revolutionary syndicalism reflected this novel sense of trade union power most clearly. But it was by no means confined to those who rejected parliamentary action altogether. Even within the syndicalist movement few, apart from the anarchists, were dogmatic in their hostility to parliamentary politics. In practice syndicalism shaded over into a militant parliamentarianism which stressed, not the superiority of industrial over parliamentary action, but the necessity of co-ordinating the two tactics. Many were confirmed in such a view when, in 1912, the Government harried by the Labour Party in Parliament and worried by the strike outside, was forced to intervene and, partially, concede the miners' demands by legislation. Notwithstanding bitter criticism of the settlement by militant miners, these events encouraged belief in the viability of combining parliamentary politics with the strike weapon. After the war 'Direct Action' was to achieve broad support in the labour movement, understood not as the revolutionary general strike, but as the use of concentrated industrial force to wrest reforms from the capitalist state.

But the labour unrest and syndicalism laid the basis for an upsurge not only of militant reformism but also of revolutionary socialist politics. Judged as a revolutionary socialist current, the syndicalist movement was manifestly inadequate to the tasks that faced it. Loosely co-ordinated, fragmented, and lacking a coherent body of theory, syndicalism failed to organise the grass roots leaders of industrial militancy into a disciplined force capable of leading a fight for revolutionary politics within the labour movement. The established socialist movement failed equally. The pre-war labour unrest created a potential for the growth of a party able to occupy the ground between apolitical syndicalism and the merely parliamentarian ILP. That the BSP failed to realise this potential was largely a result of the grip exercised by Hyndman and the SDF 'old guard' over the new party – a prime example of the triumph of dogma over realism in socialist politics. Nevertheless, the record of revolutionary socialism during these years was not entirely one of failure. The unrest itself threw up a new generation of young working-class activists, a stratum of irreconcilables, toughened in the experience of strike leadership and eager to discuss Marxist and syndicalist ideas. The SLP played an important educational role through its Marxist classes and its publishing programme. The Plebs League, originating in 1909 in a revolt at Ruskin, the Oxford working-men's college, established Marxist education classes in many parts of the country. And the *Daily Herald*, which began as a printers' strike sheet in 1911 and achieved sales of between 50,000 and 150,000, opened its columns to a wide and lively discussion of socialist ideas. All this laid the basis for a new kind of industrially orientated socialist politics that was to crystallise after the war in the formation of the Communist Party.

By 1914 the growing strength and ambition of some sections of the working class threatened to burst the institutional form in which working-class politics had taken shape since the 1890s. The imminent collapse of Labour's electoral pact with the Liberals – and the rejection of the Labour Party by some of the less radical trade union leaderships which would probably have followed any such collapse – placed the emergence of a smaller, but more authentically socialist Labour Party on the agenda. At the same time the strike wave had stimulated currents of opinion which challenged the established division between economistic trade unionism and a reformist politics. Because war broke out in 1914 it is impossible to say whether these trends would have led to the reconstruction of the labour movement on an altogether more combatative basis. In the event, the enormous social and political changes wrought by the First World War enabled the labour movement to consolidate its gains of the pre-war period, and make the break from Liberalism, without destroying what in 1914 was still a fragile alliance between socialists and the major trade unions. Paradoxically, it was the major historical discontinuity of the war, that enabled the Labour Party to resolve its crisis of growth in a manner which maintained at least the appearance of continuity with the organisation established at the turn of the century.

Notes

1 D. Evans, *Labour Strife in the South Wales Coalfield, 1910–11*, Cardiff 1911, pp. 90–1.
2 P. Lloyd, 'The Influence of Syndicalism in the Dock Strike of 1911', Warwick MA, 1972, p. 46.
3 P. Bagwell, *The Railwaymen*, London 1963, p. 292.
4 *Report* of the Socialist Unity Conference, 1911, p. 11.
5 Tom Mann, 'The Strong Right Arm of Labour', *Industrial Syndicalist*, September 1910.
6 Tom Mann, speaking at Manchester Conference of ISEL, *Industrial Syndicalist*, December 1910.

6

The impact of war, 1914–21

The First World War disrupted the continuities of British history more profoundly than any other event of the previous sixty years. At the centre of this disruption was the vast and sudden expansion in the role of the state in social and economic affairs. Before the war state intervention had not proceeded far beyond the ring-holding activities of the nineteenth-century liberal state. Only the social welfare legislation of the Liberals after 1906 had made any significant dent in *laissez-faire*, and, whatever it might portend for the future, this intervention was confined to the sphere of distribution, not production. The problem of supplying men and munitions to the trenches demanded intervention on a quite new scale – control of many industries; controls over the imports, distribution and price of food and raw materials; military, and, to a considerable extent, industrial conscription. By 1917–18 *laissez-faire* capitalism was declared on all sides to be a dead duck. The emergence of a new statist political economy presented major opportunities to, and required major adjustments from the labour movement.

The war effectively destroyed the Liberals as a governing party and facilitated their replacement by a reconstructed Labour Party committed, on paper at least, to the common ownership of the means of production – Clause Four of the 1918 Labour Party constitution. Behind this commitment lay the fact that the rapidity of the transformation of the political economy in wartime had brought the transition to socialism onto the immediate political agenda – or so socialists, of many different schools of thought, believed. This expansion of socialist ambition was accompanied, and reinforced, by a radicalisation of mass working-class opinion. War, of course, had some anti-radical implications – above all in the patriotism it evoked. But patriotism was neither a very stable attitude (moments of patriotic fervour alternated with moments of war weariness and militant protest among the same groups of workers), nor did it necessarily rule out radical social demands. There was no necessary association between support for the war and support for the war profiteer – a popular stereotype of incalculable value to egalitarian and socialist propaganda. The growth of trade unionism during the war involved the breakdown of servile and deferential attitudes among large numbers of previously unorganised workers. This process was closely linked with the liberating consequences of the movement of women from domestic service and sweated workshops into factories and offices. One effect of the war was to greatly accelerate the trend towards a more homogenous working class. Full employment eliminated a good deal of casual poverty; inflation and cost-of-living bargaining eroded customary wage differentials; dilution and the substitution of women for men in many types of work undermined the mystery of craft and the privileges of craftsmen. The impact of these changes on working-class consciousness was complex and often, in the short term, divisive. Nevertheless, it seems clear that the overall impact of the war on working-class attitudes was a radicalising one.

No less important, in its effect on the labour movement, than the construction of the war economy, was its equally sudden dismantling at the end of the war. In 1918 there was an almost universal tendency to exaggerate the probable staying power of wartime statism. Yet by 1920–1 Lazarus had arisen. Amidst the echoes of its funeral orations, *laissez-faire* capitalism came gasping back to life. And if its career thereafter was neither splendid nor very long, this temporary restoration posed for the labour movement the cruelest of tests for those new institutions and strategies developed during the war on the assumption that a large measure of war collectivism was irreversible. Restoration did not occur without major social conflict. During 1919–21 the Lloyd George Government found itself cast as mediator between business pressure for decontrol and the threat by organised labour to use direct action (with possible revolutionary consequences) to maintain and extend the more egalitarian aspects of war collectivism. The resolution of these conflicting pressures during the post-war crisis is one of the most exciting and complex periods of modern British history. By 1922, when Lloyd George fell from power, wartime controls had been largely dismantled. Cheated of 'reconstruction', the organised working class had nevertheless been diverted from a direct assault on state power. Despite its failure to defend war collectivism, the Labour Party had emerged as a major competitor for office. To explain all this is to explain much about the origins of the rules of the game that were to govern British politics during the subsequent forty years.

I

When war broke out in August 1914 the great majority of the Labour Party pledged themselves to support the war effort – some with jingoistic enthusiasm, most with the simple patriotic conviction that whatever had precipitated the conflict it was their duty to support their country until the issue was resolved. The Labour Party concluded a political truce, and subsequently participated in the two coalition Governments formed in May 1915 and December 1916. The TUC declared an industrial truce, and accepted the Munitions Act, outlawing strikes on war work, in 1915. Despite considerable tensions, especially over the introduction of military conscription in 1916, collaboration remained the predominant stance of the labour movement throughout the war.

Trade union membership, which had been growing rapidly since 1910, continued its upward climb, almost doubling between 1914 and 1920. The proportion of women workers, organised in trade unions, grew from 9 to 24 per cent. The very low levels of unemployment experienced during the war and the post-war boom, was the chief cause of this phenomenal growth. Full employment gave workers the capacity to organise. Simultaneously inflation supplied the most pressing motive for workers to take advantage of their scarcity. The cost-of-living index was rising by about 27 per cent each year between 1914 and 1920. As trade union membership grew by leaps and bounds, employers and the Government (which in any case needed trade union co-operation in the prosecution of the war) were forced to grant recognition to the unions far more extensively than ever before. The Munitions Act required employers to recognise trade unions and to tolerate organisation at workshop level. The most striking example of official encouragement to union growth was the short-lived Trade Card Scheme of 1916–17, by which the craft unions in the munitions industries were permitted to administer exemptions for their members from military conscription – a wonderful incentive for reluctant workers to join the union!

These gains in the potential power of the trade union movement were not matched by the capacity of the leadership to use this power to full advantage. On the crudest measure of trade union effectiveness the leadership failed – for most of the war wage rates lagged behind the rise in prices. It is true that earnings figures, were they available, would modify this picture. But the rise in earnings, as distinct from rates, owed little to the activities of the trade union leaders, stemming in the main from increased effort (overtime and payment by results), from changes in the structure of the labour force (e.g. promotion to better paid jobs), and from militant shopfloor activity often undertaken in direct opposition to official union policies. Whether a tougher posture by the leadership could have gained larger wage increases, and gained them sooner, is a matter for speculation. It is clear, however, that in their dealings with the Government the trade union leaders did not maximise their advantages.

During the first two-and-a-half years of the war the labour leadership had shown a readiness to oblige which went far beyond the minimal requirements of patriotism. In 1915, confronted with a Munitions Bill intended to bring about 'the greater subordination of labour to the direction and control of the state',[1] and to redress the industrial balance of power in favour of the employers, the trade union leaders made no attempt to demand concessions on prices or rents in return for their sacrifices in the industrial field. Similarly in December 1916, when Asquith's coalition Government was finally ousted by Lloyd George and his Conservative allies, the Labour leaders voted to enter the new coalition without exacting anything but the vaguest and most minimal concessions from the Prime Minister. Few trade union leaders, outside the Miners Federation, appeared to understand that support for the war effort was quite compatible with the adoption of a tough bargaining posture. So pusillanimous was the record of Labour's representatives that a writer in the New Statesman was moved to interpret the decision to join Lloyd George's coalition as a sad end to the effort to create an independent, let alone a socialist, working-class party in the House of Commons.

Nevertheless, during the last eighteen months of the war the tone of the leadership became more assertive. Within a year of entering the Lloyd George coalition, the Labour Party was undertaking the two major internal transformations that were to place the prospect of a Labour Government on the immediate political agenda. The federal constitution of the party was reformed to permit individual membership (in addition to membership via an affiliated organisation) laying the basis for the construction of Constituency Labour Parties. This established the framework necessary for the massive growth of the party's electoral machine during the inter-war years. More immediately important was the elaboration of overall policy statements on foreign affairs and for post-war reconstruction. The seal was set on this new ideological independence by the addition of Clause Four to the party constitution – establishing 'the common ownership of the means of production' as its long-term goal.

By what alchemy was the party, which to all appearances had committed suicide in December 1916, so swiftly transformed? Objective changes in the situation of the Labour Party were important. In the first place the Liberal Party disintegrated in the aftermath of the Lloyd George–Asquith split, virtually forcing the Labour leaders, despite their support of the coalition, to take steps to fill the resulting political vacuum. Secondly, the enormous growth of trade union strength – and during the war trade union affiliations to the Labour Party grew even faster than the unions themselves – presented the leaders both with an increased demand for labour representation in the House of Commons and with the financial resources to secure it. The Franchise Act of 1918, which enfranchised almost all men, and women over 30, greatly increased the chances of success for Labour candidates. These underlying factors persuaded the Labour Party during the last eighteen months of the war to set its sights on power. But precisely what they meant by 'power', and to what ends they intended to use it can only be understood by closer attention to the immediate context.

The first need, if the Labour Party was to fill the vacuum left by the disintegration of the Liberal Party, was to heal the breach over the war. In August 1914 the great majority of ILP members, and five of the seven ILP-sponsored MPs, had disassociated themselves from Labour's support of the war. Ramsay MacDonald resigned the leadership of the Labour Party to Arthur Henderson, in order to be free to oppose the war. The ILP issued a statement expressing solidarity – 'across the roar of the guns' – with their anti-war comrades in Germany. Most ILP opposition to the war rested on a pacifist basis, and found its characteristic expression in resistance to the right of the state to conscript men for military service, organised in the No Conscription Fellowship. MacDonald adopted a rather different position – accepting that 'whatever our views may be of the origins of the war, we must go through with it'.[2] MacDonald saw his task as maintaining 'the mind of peace' in time of war – mobilising those forces, Liberal as well as Socialist, who blamed secret diplomacy for the catastrophy and who believed that only democratic control of foreign policy could ensure a just and lasting peace settlement. To this end he helped to establish the Union of Democratic Control

(UDC) which provided him with a platform independent of the pacifist ILP.

The February Revolution in Russia gave a boost to the British anti-war movement. It also served to persuade Henderson and the majority of the Labour Party of the need to present their pro-War stance in a more positive and attractive form than the uncritical support for Allied victory with which they had contented themselves since 1914. Following an official visit to Russia in the summer of 1917, Henderson was convinced that British Labour should respond to the call of the Petrograd Soviet for an international socialist conference – including 'enemy' socialists – to discuss peace terms. The Government disagreed, and Henderson resigned from the War Cabinet – though he did not suggest that the party as a whole should break with the Coalition. Subsequently Henderson, Webb and Ramsay MacDonald got together to produce a statement of Labour's War Aims. The primary intention of these initiatives was to convince the Russians, and particularly the Petrograd Soviet, of the non-imperialist nature of the Allied war effort, and thus to prevent a separate Russian peace. In this they failed: but the rhetoric of a 'democratic diplomacy' and a 'people's peace' were sufficient to bring the ILP dissidents back into the fold, re-uniting the party and helping to split up the gathering momentum of the extra-parliamentary anti-war movement.

Agreement on war aims could be reached in 1917–18 because the split in the Labour Party had never been so profound as to prevent a continuing dialogue between pro- and anti-war socialists. Some of the more violently jingoistic elements did their best to get the ILP excluded from the Labour Party, and they succeeded in 1917 in changing the basis of elections to the National Executive, strengthening trade union control of the party. Nevertheless, in the end it was the jingoes who found themselves excluded. Unity was maintained, above all, by joint activity over domestic issues. The social consequences of war created tasks and opportunities for the labour movement to which many of its leaders turned with some relief, leaving on one side the contentious issue of the war itself. 'Let us do our own work like the French peasant cultivates his fields close to the firing lines,'[3] said Sidney Webb, and he spoke for an uncommonly wide range of opinion on both sides of the pro-war/anti-war divide. The institution which most perfectly expressed this spirit was the War Emergency Workers National Committee. Established within a week of the outbreak of war, the WEWNC represented both the political and industrial sides of the labour movement, and involved most of its leading figures. While the Labour Party and the TUC were heavily compromised by their collaboration with coalition Governments, the WEWNC did much to maintain Labour's independence, both in its agitations over immediate issue, and in the forum it provided for the formulation of long-term goals.

The domestic impact of the war generated a spirit of class assertion in the labour movement which informed the reorientation of the Labour Party at the end of the war. Particularly important was the sense of having achieved significant footholds for working-class power within the wartime operations of the state. Rent control was established in December 1915 following rent strikes in Glasgow and other areas. During the winter of 1917–18 many working-class grievances over food distribution were met by the implementation of policies first proposed by the WEWNC and the Co-operative movement, and forced on the Government by fear of working-class unrest. Local Trades Councils played a key role in articulating working-class grievances, in mobilising pressure on the authorities, and in establishing a measure of democratic participation in the administration of some of the controls. In the major industry scheduled by the Labour Party's reconstruction programme for immediate national-isation, the mines, wartime control had been experienced as a concession that the union had wrested from the state and imposed upon the employers. The impact of such experiences on the labour movement was reflected not only in demands for the permanent national ownership of this or that industry or service, but, more generally, in the emergence of socialism as an operative goal. The WEWNC played a central role in channelling this new class assertion into the Labour Party, developing the slogan 'Conscription of Riches', from a merely propagandist and rhetorical counter to military conscription, into a demand for the common ownership of the means of production. Soaring prices, closely associated with the profiteering of ship owners and others, served to dramatise the evils of capitalism. When Arthur Hunderson pledged the party to strenuously resist any attempt at decontrol after the war, and to campaign to strengthen the popular grip upon the economy, many Labour Party members must have interpreted this as a commitment by the Labour leadership to place itself at the head of a working-class offensive to consolidate and extend the footholds already established for the political economy of labour within the state system.

This was not exactly how Henderson saw it. Ramsay Mac-Donald's pre-war stricture – 'class consciousness leads nowhere'[4] – remained fundamental to the belief of most Labour leaders. Perhaps the most significant fact about the adoption of Clause Four is that it took place at a time when the Labour Party remained firmly committed both to the war effort and to participation in the coalition Government. Labour politics in the last eighteen months of the war were about the balance between working-class ambition aroused by the struggle for participation in the war economy and fuelled by growing war weariness, on the one hand, and on the other, the commitment to class collaboration both for its own sake, and in the interests of national victory. The reconstruction programme – *Labour and the New Social Order* – was in fact extremely modest in its aims. Only the nationalisation of basic fuel and transport industries was proposed. The implementation of this programme would have meant not state socialism, but state-aided capitalism. Party spokesmen stressed the need for class collaboration in the restoration of private industry after the war, rebuking those who insisted that the workers could no longer be persuaded to work for private profit. Clause Four, studiously vague on the critical issue of workers' control, was intended as much to contain as to express the ambitions of the Labour Party's rank and file. The political and trade union leaders were ready to adopt socialist aims in 1918, partly as a manoeuvre to contain their own left wing, and partly because they believed that major advances could be made along the road they had mapped out without provoking a capitalist counter-offensive.

The Labour Party's reconstruction programme was adopted in the belief that the collectivism of wartime was most unlikely to be dismantled, whatever the Government in power after the war. The enthusiastic statism characteristic of the central governing group did much to foster this illusion – the nationalisation of the railways, at least, seemed inevitable. 'The Labour Party', wrote Henderson, 'has proceeded upon the assumption that reconstruction is inevitable,' and the force that made it so was, he continued, not the assertion of any particular class interest, but 'the new democratic consciousness and the new social consciousness which have come to birth in the long agony of the present struggle'. In the event the reconstruction ethos proved a flimsy basis on which to rest Labour's commitment to socialism. There can be little doubt that had they foreseen the scale of conflict that would be necessary to achieve even the modest advances demanded, the leadership would not, in 1918, have made its rash pledge to 'strenuously resist' any attempt to dismantle the more desirable features of the war economy.[5]

II

While the wartime experiences tended to reinforce class-collaborationist perspectives, important sections of the workers experienced wartime state intervention not as liberating, but as repressive. They saw in the wartime state not an actual or potential ally, but an agency used by the employers to reinforce their class power. This tended to confirm syndicalist fears of the state, not least because it was precisely the politicians most directly responsible for the New Liberal social reforms – Lloyd George and Winston Churchill – who took the leading role in the construction of the wartime 'Servile State': and it was the same corps of eager young bureaucrats in the civil service who supported them in this.

Within the ILP pressure built up for a fundamental revision of the traditional attitude to the state and to political action. Conscientious objection, resting more often than not in the religious sensibilities of ILP members, implied a limitation on the right of the state to enforce its will against individual conscience in matters of life and death. At the same time the growing involvement of the party's rank and file, in some areas, with wartime industrial unrest reinforced pressure for a departure from a merely electoral stance. In Glasgow, where membership leapt forwards while nationally it stagnated, the branches were said to be 'sick of politics' and eagerly embracing the Guild Socialist heresy.*

In South Wales, by 1918, the Divisional Committee of the ILP was calling for an extension of party activities into the industrial field – where 'the real issue with the capitalist class is met'.[6] By the end of the war conscientious objectors and industrial militants were co-operating in attempts to commit the party to Guild Socialist ideas of workers' control. However, the wartime influx of ex-Liberals, coming into the party via the UDC and primarily concerned with foreign affairs, reinforced the middle-class character of the party, militating

---

* Guild Socialism originated before the war as an attempt to find a middle way between syndicalist and Fabian ideas. It laid particular stress on schemes for workers' control in industry. It's appeal was initially to middle-class intellectuals. During and after the war Guild Socialist ideas made headway among working-class activists in a number of important industries. As a coherent political position Guild Socialism did not long survive the Russian Revolution which divided Guildsmen – and women – between those who approved of a revolutionary strategy and those who did not.

against any turn towards a more industrially orientated political perspective.

Industrial militancy was in the forefront of the wartime battle against the 'Servile State', and a convergence of anti-war politics with the industrial unrest was the key to the development of an effective alternative to the politics of the Labour Party. It was among the Marxist parties to the left of the ILP, and the broader stratum of trade union activists influenced by syndicalist ideas, that such an alternative began to develop during the war. After an initial period of industrial peace, militancy revived as workers struggled to keep up with the rising cost of living. During 1917 and 1918 strike activity reached roughly half the level characteristic of the pre-war labour unrest. In wartime conditions, when trade union leaders were pledged to industrial peace and, in many industries, strike action was illegal, this level of strike activity involved the growth of organised rank-and-file movements. The leadership of industrial miltancy devolved onto those politically conscious activists who were prepared to defy both the trade union bureaucracy and the state. All this presented an unprecedented opportunity for the development of revolutionary politics.

In 1915 the South Wales miners struck successfully for a wage advance in defiance of the Munitions Act. The threat of further strike action, particularly from South Wales, secured major gains for the miners during subsequent years. Strikes against the conscription of miners were only narrowly averted in 1917 and 1918. By the end of the war unofficial movements had a powerful presence both in South Wales and in Scotland. On the railways a rank-and-file movement of Vigilance Committees played a major part in pushing the NUR executive into forward wage movements. But it was the workers in the metal-working industries who occupied the forefront of industrial militancy, accounting for nearly a third of all wartime strike activity.

This militancy was centred among skilled engineering workers in the munitions works. The influx of women and semi-skilled men into munitions factories and on to jobs previously performed only by the craftsmen – dilution – appeared to undermine and render worthless the means by which skilled engineers had habitually sought to defend their interests in the labour market. The wartime shop stewards' movement recognised that any struggle to restore undiluted craft privilege would be both undesirable politically and hopeless. It attempted, with some success, to break down divisions between craftsmen and less skilled workers, to develop an industrial policy which united the interests of the two groups, and to construct all-grades organisation in the workshops. The leaders of the movement were, by and large, revolutionaries drawn from the Socialist Labour Party and the syndicalist movement. These men saw in the craftsmen's militant revolt against bureaucratic trade unionism the germs of a revolutionary spirit on which they could build. But the movement contained, as well, the germs of a merely sectional struggle for the restoration of lost status. Its development hung between these possibilities.

While shop stewards' organisation within the workshops spread widely during the war, the shop stewards' *movement* – local Workers' Committees based directly in the workshops and capable of leading the mass of the workers independently of the existing trade union authorities, became fully established in only a handful of the larger munitions centres. The shop stewards' movement originated in 1915–16, during the struggle over dilution on the Clyde. Defeated by the Government the Clyde Workers' Committee nevertheless laid the basis for the spread of the movement, spelling out the basic principle of independent rank-and-file organisation:

> We will support the officials just so long as they rightly represent the workers, but we will act independently immediately they misrepresent them. Being composed of delegates from every shop and untrammelled by obselete law or rule, we claim to represent the true feeling of the workers. We can immediately according to the merits of the case and the desire of the rank and file.[7]

In May 1917 supporters of the Workers' Committees led a national strike – the largest of the war – against the removal of the craftsmen's exemption from conscription and the extension of dilution from munitions to ordinary commercial work. Because of the issues at stake in this strike the movement veered very much in the direction of a struggle to regain lost status, to the dismay of its leadership.

The development of the political potential of the movement hung on its relationship with anti-war politics. In June 1917, following the February Revolution in Russia, anti-war socialists in the ILP, BSP and other organisations mounted a national rank-and-file convention in Leeds to call for an early 'people's peace', and the establishment of what they chose to call 'soviets' in Britain. Very little came of the conference, partly because the Government sternly repressed any attempt to establish the Workers' and Soldiers' Councils projected at Leeds, and partly because the majority of those involved (which included MacDonald and Snowden) were concerned to demonstrate to the Labour Party the need to adopt a more independent foreign policy, rather than to advance the revolutionary movement. The shop stewards' movement was, for the time being, more concerned with sectional wage claims than with lending force to the elbow of the anti-war movement.

It was during the winter of 1917–18, while the Labour Party was reuniting around its War Aims Memorandum and Clause IV, that Britain came nearest to producing a mass revolutionary anti-war movement – defined by Theodore Rothestein of the BSP as 'definite resistance to the war on the basis of a general strike in munitions factories and kindred industries.'[8] During the Autumn of 1917 a series of wages battles in which skilled and unskilled fought side by side served to reduce the craft sectionalism of the shop stewards' movement. At the same time peace propaganda intensified and war weariness grew among a working class faced by the bloody stalemate on the Western Front and acute food shortages caused by German submarine warfare. During the last weeks of January 1918 it was touch and go whether or nor the munitions workers would erupt into a political strike, demanding immediate peace negotiations on the Bolshevik terms of no annexations, no indemnities. At the last moment, however, the engineering craftsmen drew back from their political challenge to the state, into the militant, but extremely sectional, demand for continued exemption of skilled workers from military conscription – and the drafting of more dilutees in their place. Nothing came of this sectional militancy, partly because the revolutionary leaders of the movement refused to have anything to do with it.

The war had wrought dramatic changes in the British socialist movement. While ILP opposition to the war initially destroyed much of its influence in the Labour Party, by 1917–18 the convergence of ILP and Labour Party foreign policy had begun to heal the breach. Meanwhile the Labour Party, directed by Sidney Webb and Arthur Henderson, had written socialist objectives into its constitution and adopted a relatively comprehensive and ambitious programme for reconstruction after the war. Confronting this confident and united reformism, was a revolutionary left strengthened by its association with wartime industrial unrest. But the revolutionaries remained disunited, and faced an extended period of negotiations and of theoretical clarifications before they could regroup after the war within a united Communist Party. In the meantime their power in industry was to be decisively weakened by the post-war collapse of the shop stewards' movement. When, in 1919, the rapid dismantling of the war economy rendered Labour's new perspectives largely irrelevant, it was not the revolutionary movement that filled the breech, nor the ILP, but the revival of a quasi-syndicalist direct activism rooted in the left wing of the trade union bureaucracy.

III

During 1919 the fate of war collectivism was decided, and the commitment of the Labour leadership to the maintenance and extension of state control over the economy was put to the test. The Labour Party, deprived of its expected representation in the House of Commons by the 'hang the Kaiser' election of 1918, could do little to resist the rapid dismantling of the war economy. Simultaneously the wartime rhetoric of a 'democratic diplomacy' was rudely shattered by the Versailles Treaty, the militarism of the Coalition Government in Ireland, and the spectre of a new war raised by British intervention in Soviet Russia. Faced with the impotence of the parliamentary Labour Party many trade union leaders began to talk the language of Direct Action, of the political general strike. The phenomenal growth of the unions during the post-war boom, and their militancy, lent plausibility to this threat. Outside mining, as many working days were lost during 1919 in strike action as during the four pre-war years of the labour unrest put together. Strike activity remained at unprecedented levels for the next three years. If Labour had been cheated out of its proper influence in the political system, it was up to the unions to restore the political balance. Direct Action called into question, on a wider scale than ever before or since, the division between political and industrial action around which the labour movement was constructed. The miners' leader Frank Hodges declared to the 1919 TUC:

> I am astonished that, in view of the impotence of the Labour Party, caused by circumstances over which it has no control, it does not more frequently come to the industrial movement and say, 'We are overweighted and crushed by a great political despotism. Come to our assistance in order that we may have power at our elbow to shatter the institution and remould one on better lines.'[9]

Britain remained on the fringes of the international revolutionary crisis of 1917–21. If revolution failed in the defeated continental states, it was never likely to succeed in victorious Britain. Nevertheless, for a time, working-class assertiveness and the context of international revolutionary chaos, created a profound anxiety in the minds of Britain's rulers. Mutinies in the army and navy at the end of the war, though hardly revolutionary in intention, served to undermine Government confidence in their ability, in a crisis, to use armed force against strikers. The spread of trade unionism in the police force, following a strike in London in the summer of 1918, constituted a further threat to the maintenance of order. A report of a Cabinet meeting on industrial unrest held in January 1920 illustrates the state of panic created by the threat of a Triple Alliance strike. Lloyd George (who was probably pulling his colleagues' legs, for devious reasons of his own) solemnly informed the Cabinet that the air force could attack with bombs and machine guns, if, as Churchill feared, ground troops could not be relied upon to put down an insurrection. Walter Long had spent the weekend checking over the firearms in his house, only to report, disconcertedly, that none of them was less than 200 years old. Bonar Law so often referred to the need to arm the stockbrokers that the Cabinet secretary had visions of militant stockbrokers manning the barricades. Panic, however, was not the characteristic response of the Government. Led by Lloyd George, the Cabinet showed considerable understanding and tactical skill in handling, and eventually breaking, the working-class offensive of 1919–20.

One result of the wartime expansion of the role of the state in the economy was the politicisation of economic conflict. Already before 1914 the economic disruption caused by strikes of miners or of transport workers had forced the Liberal Government to take a more active role in the resolution of industrial conflict. During the war, the state had in many cases virtually replaced the employers as the major authority with which unions negotiated, and, consequently, the prime target of union militancy. Lloyd George's post-war Government faced a difficult choice. Every wage claim threatened to become a political issue, every strike a direct confrontation between trade unionism and the state. To overrule employer resistance to hours and wage claims, to concede to labour demands for the maintenance of controls, nationalisation, housing programmes, etc., might avoid an immediate confrontation: but only by storing up trouble for the future through a progressive politicisation of industrial conflict. On the other hand a policy of resistance to Labour's demands, of reneging on reconstruction pledges, of dismantling war collectivism, seemed likely to result in an immediate explosion of working-class anger, a general strike, even, conceivably, a revolutionary bid for power. By 1921 the Government had succeeded in resolving this dilemma. While avoiding a general strike, they managed to abandon most of the reconstruction programme, dismantle most of the apparatus of control, and go far towards depoliticising the sectional strikes and lockouts that accompanied the employer counter-attack on inflated wartime wage rates. This operation was possibly the most significant defeat ever suffered by the British labour movement.

1919 opened with a Government victory. In the case of the engineers, whose wartime power was now suddenly undermined by the run down of munitions production, the Government was prepared to back employer resistance. In January, when the Clydeside engineers struck for a forty-hour week in defiance of a nationally negotiated settlement of forty-eight hours, the Government sent in troops and tanks to break the strike. Defeated on the Clyde, and exposed to large-scale unemployment throughout the country, the power of the shop stewards' movement was effectively crushed by systematic victimisation during the early months of 1919. Other sections, however, could not be so easily dealt with. In February, faced with simultaneous demands from railwaymen and miners – the latter demanding nationalisation as well as wage and hours concessions – the Cabinet decided to play for time. Drastic deflation, demanded by the Treasury and the City of London, was rejected in favour of a continued programme of Government borrowing and social expenditure. A National Industrial Council was convened to allow labour leaders and employers an official platform on which to formulate joint demands on the Government – the main result of which was a Government pledge (later broken) to introduce a statutory forty-eight hour week and minimum wage legislation. Meanwhile the miners, who with their Triple Alliance partners remained unimpressed by the National Industrial Council, were persuaded to suspend strike action and accept a Royal Commission, on which they were heavily represented, to report on their claims. Unsure of the likely response of the miners to the interim report of the Sankey Commission, the Government insured against a Triple Alliance strike by meeting most of the railwaymen's demands.

It was only by the deployment of all his persuasive powers that Robert Smillie, the left-wing leader of the Miners Federation, was able to persuade the miners to accept the establishment of the Sankey Commission in February and its interim report in March. The latter went some way to meet their wage and hours demands and appeared to open the door for nationalisation. Through the early summer of 1919 socialists rejoiced at the spectacle of Bob Smillie tearing apart the owners' witnesses. Capitalism, it appeared, was on trial, and it was manifestly losing the argument. Sidney Webb, a labour nominee on the Commission, believed that the Commission had both averted the disaster of a revolutionary general strike and that it established a precedent for similar 'state trials of the organisation of each industry', wherever trade unionism was powerful enough to force serious consideration of the nationalisation demand.[10] But social transformation by Royal Commission was an illusion. While in the robing room of the House of Lords the mock trial of capitalism proceeded, outside the decisive moment for action by the labour movement to secure its wartime gains passed unexploited. In the event those revolutionary miners, like Will Lawther, delegate from the Red village of Chopwell, who opposed the Sankey Commission from the outset as a delaying manoeuvre by the Government, showed better political judgement than either Smillie or Webb.

Whatever Lloyd George's intentions in the spring of 1919, and they are obscure, by the summer neither he nor the great majority of his Cabinet had any intention of nationalising the mines. For one thing back-bench opinion in the House of Commons had moved sharply against nationalisation under the impact of a business campaign against a Government bill which seemed to portend creeping nationalisation of the railways. When a majority of the Sankey Commission reported in favour of nationalisation in June there was an outcry not only from the mine owners but also from other businessmen reacting as much against the implicit threat to capitalist property in general, as to the specific issue of mines' nationalisation. Nationalisation of mines, in itself – as Sankey and others pointed out – was perfectly compatible with the maintenance of capitalism: but, unfortunately for the miners, the nationalisation of their industry had become a symbolic issue in the wider political struggle. At the same time the Cabinet was now confident that rejection of mines' nationalisation would not precipitate revolution. Police trade unionism had been crushed by early August, Home Office reports suggested that the militant temper of the rank and file had subsided, and the Triple Alliance had shown its reluctance to initiate direct action. Confident that the immediate danger had receded, the Government began to reverse the conciliatory policies adopted earlier in the year. Lloyd George's announcement, in August, rejecting mines' nationalisation was accompanied by a refusal to introduce effective legislation on hours' limitation or minimum wages, and moves towards a more orthodox, deflationary economic policy which involved scaling down the housing programme and other social expenditure. The miners responded to the rejection of Sankey, not by strike action but by launching, rather late in the day, a national propaganda campaign. Meanwhile the Government's confidence that it had regained control of the industrial situation led it into a new confrontation with the railwaymen that brought the country once again to the brink of a general strike.

Hit by rapidly rising prices, the NUR had put in a new wage claim. In September 1919 the Government replied with a scheme withdrawing temporary bonuses paid during the war and standardising wages at a level which, far from raising them, involved a substantial cut. Even Jimmy Thomas, the right-wing NUR leader, could not avoid strike action over this – though, anxious to avoid a political confrontation, he did obstruct attempts by the NUR Executive to involve the Triple Alliance. Once the railwaymen came out the leaders of the Transport Workers Federation (TWF) came under great pressure from their members to authorise sympathetic strike action. A hurriedly convened 'Mediation Committee' of leaders of unions affected by the strike persuaded the Government that if they persisted with their attack on railway wages, widely seen as the beginning of a general counter-offensive against wartime wage gains, widespread sympathetic action could not be avoided. Sobered, the Government backed down, agreed to maintain existing wage levels for a year, to establish national collective bargaining in the industry on a permanent basis and to negotiate a guaranteed minimum wage indexed to the cost of living. Once again confrontation had been avoided, though only at the price of conceding a major victory to the railwaymen.

The next major upheaval arose not over an industrial question, but over intervention in Russia. In March 1920 London dockers prevented the loading of the *Jolly George* with arms for Poland. In August 1920, when the victories of the Red Army seemed likely to precipitate a new Allied intervention against Soviet Russia, the TUC and Labour Party established a joint Council of Action, threatening to use 'the whole industrial power of the organised workers' in the event of British involvement. Lenin, misinformed and rather carried away, saw in this response by 'the British Mensheviks' the establishment of a revolutionary situation of dual power. In reality, as the British revolutionary John McLean suggested at the time, the labour leaders probably knew they were kicking at an open door, that the Government had, in fact, little intention of sending troops to Poland. The mobilisation of widespread anti-war sentiment around the Council of Action produced an easy political triumph for Labour, without running any serious risk that the Direct Action bluff would be called. There was, it seems, in the establishment of the Council of Action, a sizeable measure of Jimmy Thomas's reputed technique: 'When the buggers are giving you trouble, give 'em a mass meeting. That gets it out of their system.'[11] In many localities the Councils of Action, established on the basis of existing Trades Council and Labour Party organisation, showed some inclination to push matters further. There were calls for strike action to end the economic blockade against Russia, and to force the withdrawal of troops from Ireland. But nothing came of efforts to promote a national delegate convention of local Councils – a necessary preliminary for the establishment of a leadership willing to put the Direct Action threat into practice. The importance of the Russian issue to British labour had more to do with war-weariness and fear of conscription, than with any more explicitly revolutionary solidarity or intention. After 1920 the normalisation of trade relations with Russia remained a major issue in Labour politics. Ironically it was an issue which helped to provide socialist credentials for the pursuit by the first Labour Government in 1924 of a strictly orthodox solution to the problem of unemployment.

By the Autumn of 1920 the question of miners' wages, intimately linked with the question of state control of the industry, was back at the centre of relations between organised labour and the Government. War control had involved the creation of a national profits pool, a system which made it possible for the Miners Federation to negotiate wages nationally. Any return to district settlements, which enabled the owners to play off one district against another, would be fiercely resisted by the Federation, both as a threat to miners' living standards and to the survival of the Federation itself. Since the owners insisted that decontrol must mean a return to district settlements, the miners had no choice but to fight on the 'political' issue of control, even after they had accepted in the spring of 1920 that the nationalisation of the mines was no longer an immediately attainable objective. In October 1920 the miners struck for a wage advance, having abandoned an earlier claim, designed to win public support, for simultaneous price reductions, and in spite of attempts by both Smillie and the other Triple Alliance unions to get them to accept arbitration. As in the case of the railway strike a year earlier, it was the threat of sympathetic action (this time from the NUR, in defiance of Thomas) which forced the Government to compromise, offering an immediate wage rise, a bonus dependent on future output, and negotiations with the owners for the establishment of a national wages board to be completed by the end of March 1921. The leadership accepted this package, despite a narrow majority against it, and despite the prophetic warning of a Derbyshire militant: 'We can starve the Government into subjection now, just the same as they will do to us next March. . . . Everytime we go to Downing Street we get weaker.'[12]

Shortly after this settlement coal export prices began to fall, turning Government control of the industry from a profitable enterprise into a substantial drain on public funds. In February the Government announced its intention to bring forward the date of decontrol to the end of March. There was now no possibility that the owners would agree to establish a national wages board. Decontrol meant the ending of the profits pool, a return to district settlements, and given the price fall, major wage cuts. On 1 April the miners struck, having earlier asked the Triple Alliance for support. After considerable hesitation, and by narrow majorities, the NUR and TWF agreed to strike from Friday 15 April. The Government showed no sign of backing down on the central issue of the profits pool and national collective bargaining. On the day the strike was due to begin Thomas seized on some incautious remarks by the miners' leader Frank Hodges the previous night about the possibility of accepting temporary wage reductions and created sufficient confusion to persuade the NUR and TWF to call off the strike. The bitterness caused by this betrayal – Black Friday – was intense. In London, busmen seized their union headquarters to protest. But behind Thomas's ability to get the strike called off, behind the determination of the Government not to compromise, lay the fact that already since the summer of 1920 unemployment had been growing rapidly, weakening the will and capacity of the rank and file to fight. The miners went back after three months on strike at rates that, in many cases, left them worse off than before the war. Black Friday marked the end of the Triple Alliance as an effective weapon, and the beginning of a major counter-attack on wage levels. Key sections of the trade union movement went down to defeat in a series of confrontations. Others accepted reductions without striking. In the aftermath of Black Friday none of the major unions were prepared to contemplate a co-ordinated resistance to the counter-attack. Outside mining the largest confrontation was the two-and-a-half month lockout of engineering workers in 1922 which finally crushed the power of the shop stewards (already drastically weakened by unemployment) and forced the unions to accept the reassertion of managerial authority in the factories. By 1924 money wages had been cut by up to a third, and trade union membership had fallen from 8 million to 5.5 million.

IV

The key to the Government's success in its handling of the post-war industrial crisis is to be found in the grasp shown by leading politicians of the ambivalent nature of trade unionism and of the threat it posed to the established order. Right at the beginning of the crisis, Bonar Law had put his finger on the essential point: 'Trade union organisation was the only thing between us and anarchy, and if trade union organisation was against us the position would be hopeless.'[13] So long as there was any danger of a revolutionary outcome to a confrontation between trade unionism and the state, the Cabinet showed considerable skill in avoiding confrontations and in finding allies among the trade union leadership. Jimmy Thomas is an obvious example, a man the authorities knew they could rely on in successive crises. Other union leaders were no less anxious to avoid confrontation whether because they believed that it could only harm the electoral prospects of the Labour Party, or because they believed that a general strike would of necessity end in civil war.

Even among the left-wing advocates of Direct Action, it was not impossible for the Government to find allies, albeit reluctant ones, at moments of crisis. In March 1919, for example, Lloyd George warned his colleagues against proposals to arrest the miners leaders:

> Smillie is an extreme man, but the fight he put up against the extremists induced them to accept the [Sankey] Commission and proves that he has some measure of statesmanship in his equipment. If the leaders are under lock and key, the movement will pass into the hands of hot-heads and feather-brains of the Noah Ablett type.[14]

This assessment of Smillie seems a fair one. The nationalisation of the mines might well have been achieved had it been demanded more forcibly in the critical early months of 1919, when working-class militancy was at its height, the forces of order weak, and the Government's fear of revolution most acute. Yet it was the persistent efforts of Smillie and Hodges, the two leading advocates of Direct Action, which prevented the miners striking at that moment. The unleashing of a revolutionary struggle for power, which, in their own view, could only result in the destruction of disciplined trade union organisation, was no part of the Direct Actionists' strategy. Rather than risk that, they declined to use the power of the strike precisely at the moment when – because the Government feared revolution – it stood the greatest chance of success. 'If you carry out your threat and strike', Lloyd George is reported to have told the leaders of the Triple Alliance, 'then you will defeat us. But if you do so have you weighed the consequences?' Faced with the prospect of a revolutionary seizure of power, the Triple Alliance leaders had no hesitation: 'From that moment on', Smillie remarked many years later, 'we were beaten and we knew we were.'[15] The Direct Actionism of the left-wing trade union leaders represented a policy of brinkmanship which they were bound to lose because, unlike their opponents, they were not prepared to go over the brink.

During 1919–20 the talk of Direct Action created fertile soil for the revival of syndicalist illusions in the revolutionary potential of trade unionism. A wide spectrum of socialist opinion looked to the Triple Alliance to initiate decisive action against the Government. It is a virtue of the 'hot-heads and feather-brains of the Noah Ablett type' – the revolutionaries who formed the Communist Party – that they resisted such illusions and developed a clear-headed critique of the inadequacy of the left-wing trade union officials as leaders of a potentially revolutionary confrontation. Drawing on the experience both of Russia in 1917 and of the wartime shop stewards' movement in Britain, they attempted to build a rank-and-file movement independent of the officials, warning that demands for a more powerful lead from the established trade union officials might prove counterproductive:

> The General Staff of officialdom is to be a dam to the surging tide of independent working-class aspirations and not a directing agency towards the overthrow of capitalism. . . . The unity we have appealed for becomes a unity to stop action by the mass rather than unity which shall lead them to victory.[16]

In the aftermath of the railway strike of October 1919 the communists came to believe that any large strike would take on the character of a confrontation which would only be resolved either by the complete defeat of the unions, or by the establishment of soviet power.

Little came of this strategy, if only because the Government and the trade union leaders took pains not to present the revolutionaries with the general strike on which they had pinned their hopes. Black Friday and mounting unemployment undermined the plausibility of Direct Action. Meanwhile the substantial electoral advances achieved by the Labour Party in municipal elections in the Autumn of 1919, in parliamentary bye-elections and in the General Election of 1922 did much to restore faith in parliamentary action. In 1922, with 142 MPs, Labour became the second largest party in the House of Commons. A Labour Government was now in sight. When the militant Clydeside ILPers triumphed in the 1922 election they came down to London believing they represented the spearhead of a final assault on capitalist power. Ironically, their opening shot in the battle was to elect Ramsay MacDonald as leader of the Labour Party. The next few years were to deal as cruelly with parliamentarian illusions as the last few years had dealt with syndicalist ones. Nevertheless, the defeat of Labour's post-war offensive fell a long way short of cancelling out the gains of wartime. As the next chapter will argue, the war had initiated long-term changes in the structure of British society, the effect of which was greatly to enhance the capacity of organised labour to resist the disasters of the inter-war years.

Notes

1   Lloyd George, quoted in *The Times,* 4 June 1915.
2   Lord Elton, *The Life of James Ramsay MacDonald,* London 1939, pp. 252, 276.
3   R. Harrison, 'The War Emergency Workers' National Committee', in A. Briggs and J. Saville (eds), *Essays in Labour History,* vol. 2, London 1971, p. 222.
4   J.R. MacDonald, *Socialism and Society,* London 1905, p. 128.
5   A. Henderson, *The Aims of Labour,* London 1917, pp. 20, 24.
6   M. Woodhouse, 'Marxism and Stalinism in Britain, 1920-26', *Fourth International,* July 1967, p. 68.
7   J. Hinton, *The First Shop Stewards' Movement,* London 1973, p. 119.
8   *The Call,* 3 August 1916.
9   TUC Congress *Report,* 1919, p. 296.

10   M. Cole (ed.), *B. Webb's Diaries, 1912-1924,* London 1952, entry for
     12 March 1919, p. 153.
11   M. Foot, *Aneurin Bevan,* vol. 1, London 1966, p. 33.
12   J.E. Williams, *The Derbyshire Miners,* London 1962, p. 638.
13   P. Bagwell, 'The Triple Industrial Alliance, 1913–1921', Briggs and
     Saville, *op. cit.,* p. 106.
14   C.J. Wrigley, 'Lloyd George and the Labour Movement', London PhD,
     1973, p. 414. Ablett was a leading militant and revolutionary in the
     South Wales coalfield.
15   A. Bevan, *In Place of Fear,* London 1952, pp. 21-2.
16   Hinton, *op. cit.,* p. 311.

7

Working-class organisation between the wars

I

Between 1920 and 1939 unemployment never fell below 10 per cent. At the depth of the world slump, in January 1933, three million workers, or nearly a quarter of the insured workforce, were unemployed. Behind these figures lay the breakdown of the nineteenth-century world economy, precipitated by the disruptions of war. Falling prices for food and raw materials on the world market hurt Britain's export industries only less than it hurt the primary producing countries themselves. The growth of the staple export industries – coal, textiles, shipbuilding, iron and steel, heavy engineering – was halted and reversed. Increasingly, before 1914, these industries had relied on supplying the underdeveloped world. As the prices realised by primary producers for their exports declined, so also did their ability to import manufactured goods. Other factors also contributed. Increasingly other countries became self-sufficient in goods they had previously imported from Britain – most dramatically in cotton where exports fell from over 7,000 million yards in 1913 to under 1,500 million in 1939. Meanwhile the British staple industries, burdened with surplus capacity and unable to earn the profits necessary to modernise, lost out to more efficient foreign rivals. The attempts of British governments in the 1920s to restore and maintain the gold standard, the symbol of Britain's nineteenth-century economic predominance, involved an overvaluation of sterling which further weakened the export industries. The trend of the inter-war years was away from the free movement of goods, capital and labour over which Britain had ruled for a century before 1914, and towards economic nationalism. This trend was powerfully reinforced in 1931 when Britain finally abandoned the attempt to reconstruct the liberal world economy, went off the gold standard, and adopted protection herself.

The decline of the staple export industries, in which trade union strength had been concentrated before 1914, struck at the heart of the established labour movement. The number of coal miners fell by over a third from 1.25 million in 1920 to under 800,000 in 1939, and membership of the miners' union fell in proportion. Iron and steel, shipbuilding and cotton were similarly affected. In the worst years (1931–2), 35 per cent of coal miners, 43 per cent of cotton operatives, 48 per cent of steelworkers and 62 per cent of shipbuilding workers were out of work. In parts of Wales, Scotland, Lancashire, the North East and the West Riding, the heartlands of nineteenth-century industrialisation and now the 'depressed areas', mass unemployment of this order persisted throughout the 1930s.

This picture of decay should not be overdrawn. Despite the decline of the old industries, industrial output, productivity and, for large sections of the working class, standards of living rose. Alongside the traditional economy a new basis of economic growth was emerging, albeit unplanned, incomplete and too slowly to take up the slack created by the decline of older industries. By 1935 15 per cent of the labour force was employed in the new science-based industries which had employed only 5 per cent in 1907. The rapid growth of new industries – cars, aircraft, electrical engineering, chemicals, synthetic textiles – provided one basis for the partial recovery of the British economy during the 1930s. Equally important was a boom in the building industry which employed more than one worker in fifteen during the 1930s. The growth of new industries and the building boom were linked in two ways. Firstly, both were dependent on a growth of domestic demand: only a small proportion of the products of the new industries were exported. The precipitate fall of world food prices released income in Britain to spend on housing, transport and consumer durables. Secondly, the new industries, not tied to the areas of traditional industry by the need for bulky raw materials or fuel – the growing use of electricity was a prime symbol of industrial modernisation – were established predominantly in the South East of England and the Midlands, near to their potential markets. The consequent shift of population from the old depressed areas into the new expanding ones created a demand for new houses, while the growing use of motor cars and buses made possible the suburban sprawl that characterised new building in the 1930s.

By the 1930s it was commonplace to speak of the 'two Englands', contrasting the half-empty satanic mills of the depressed North with the 'glittering white structures of concrete, glass and steel, surrounded by green lawns and beds of tulips' which passed for factories on the Great West Road.[1] Behind the facade, industrialism, as George Orwell suspected, was as ugly as ever. Employer hostility to trade unionism was generally more acute in the new factories than in older industrial centres where the masters had learned to live with organised working men. The unions were slow to adapt themselves to the problems of organising in the new industries, large areas of which remained unorganised until the Second World War. The multiplicity of unions, the lack of any central recruiting drive, fear of victimisation and the growing distances separating home from workplace compounded the difficulty of establishing stable centres of organisation among the diverse immigrant populations of the new areas.

Apart from the new industries, manual employment was growing in three main areas between the wars: building and its ancillary trades, road transport and the food manufacturing and distributive trades. Building was never a well-organised industry, and only about a quarter of building workers were union members in the late 1930s. In road transport the busmen formed a militant section of the Transport and General Workers, but road haulage, dominated by small individualistic firms, remained a problem. In distribution, whose rapid growth was closely associated with the turn of British industry towards the home market, trade union membership, in any case a very small proportion of the workforce, did not keep pace with rising employment.

The depression did nothing to increase female participation in the trade union movement. After the war most women returned to traditional roles as domestic servants or housewives. The expanding female workforce in distribution, clerical work and the new industries remained low paid and poorly organised. Employment of married women grew slightly, reaching 10 per cent by 1931, but trade union opposition to competition for jobs from this source remained strong. The 'marriage bar' was common in white-collar occupations, and was even introduced in the Lancashire cotton mills which had previously employed a high proportion of married women. Unemployment of the male breadwinner forced some wives to go out to work, though managing on a reduced income increased their domestic labour at the same time. In more prosperous working-class families, participating in the consumer boom of the 1930s, a renewed emphasis on domestic comfort kept women firmly in their place.

The largest occupational shift of all, from manual to white-collar work, represented a further set-back to the labour movement. In 1911 about one-fifth of the occupied population were white-collar workers; by 1938 the proportion had risen to around a quarter. Some groups of clerical workers, on the railways and in the civil service for example, were well organised, though the latter were forced to break their affiliation to the TUC by the Trades Disputes Act of 1927. But it took no Act of Parliament to dissuade other groups of middle-class unionists – technicians, scientists, profes- sional workers, local government workers or even school teachers – from identifying with the manual workers. White-collar trade union- ism as a major force in its own right and within the broader trade union movement was to be a post-1945 phenomenon. The middle class reacted to adversity more by intensifying their efforts to mark themselves off from the workers than by identifying with the labour movement. Middle-class unease brought comfort to the political right – an alignment cemented by Conservative reductions in income tax on middle incomes during the 1930s. There was no appreciable narrowing of the social distance between the middle class and the workers: their separation being reaffirmed in many areas by the construction of the new council estates. Even where middle-class support for the labour movement did grow during the 1930s, the now well-remembered leftism of (some) intellectuals was balanced by those lower middle-class people who, for example, helped to sustain Herbert Morrison's right-wing machine in the London Labour Party.

II

Despite the failure of 'reconstruction' after the war and the lack of any major social reforms by the two Labour Governments of the period, a gradual expansion of state welfare provisions did some- thing to counteract the debilitating effect on the labour movement of economic depression and shifts in the occupational structure. Ini- tially this expansion owed much to the fear of revolution, a crucial consideration behind the post-war expansion of the state's commit- ment in two of the major areas of expenditure, unemployment relief and housing. The provisions were not generous, and desperate efforts were made to prevent the growth of the welfare budget. Nevertheless between 1913 and 1924 the proportion of the national income spent by central and local government on social services almost doubled, from 5.5 per cent to 10.3 per cent. By 1938 the proportion had risen again to 13 per cent. The major changes in unemployment insurance occurred immediately after the war. Lloyd George's unemployment insurance scheme of 1911 covered only a small number of industries. It was extended during the war, and made universal (with the exception of agricultural workers and domestic servants) in 1920. In 1921 dependents' allowances were added to the benefit scales, and the 'dole' – originally paid to unemployed ex-servicemen who had no insurance stamps – was built into the scheme, allowing so-called 'uncovenanted' benefit to those who had exhausted their insurance entitlement. These measures laid the basis of unemployment relief for the inter-war years. Lloyd George's non-contributory old age pension was extended in 1919, but the major expansion of pensions during ths period was Neville Chamberlain's 1925 Act introducing the contributory pension.

Rent controls, first introduced in 1915, were maintained to some degree throughout the period. This discouraged private provision of rented accommodation and was a major factor, together with the intensified housing shortage caused by the cecession of building in wartime, behind the introduction of Government subsidies. Of the four million houses built between the wars over a quarter were council houses. During the 1920s most private housing was constructed with Government subsidies, though in the 1930s, when the great bulk of private houses were built, subsidies were insignificant. Despite Government intervention and the housing boom, the shortage, particularly of cheap accommodation, was still acute in 1939. In the fields of education and public health no major innovations were made, although provisions were improved in a number of ways. A few more working-class children, helped by scholarships, stayed on at school beyond the age of fourteen. The growth of secondary modern schools did little to ameliorate the rigid stratification of the education system, especially since they remained starved of finance. Secondary school fees were not abolished until 1945. Medical services for the manual worker remained a confused mixture of voluntary and compulsory insurance, free and paid doctors, means tested public benefits and charity – all of which could be involved in the treatment of a single illness. After 1929 the old Poor Law hospitals were turned over to County Councils, and during the 1930s their standards improved. Maternity and infant welfare services expanded rapidly. Subsidised school milk, from 1934, did something to combat malnutrition among children.

The overall impact of these and other extensions of state welfare expenditure was to reverse the pre-1914 pattern in which the working-class paid more in taxes than it received in social services. By 1937 5–6 per cent of the national income was being redistributed by the state to lower income groups, though a good deal of this went to the better-off workers and the lower middle class who benefited disproportionately from housing and educational expenditure. The redistribution would have been greater, had not debt payments on wartime Government borrowings – a means of redistributing income towards the rentier – accounted for such a large proportion of Government income: over 40 per cent during the 1920s.

State intervention in industry soon resumed its growth, largely at the behest of the very business class which had demanded decontrol at the end of the war. Far from the restoration of a free market economy, the inter-war years saw a rapid growth of collectivism within industry itself, as amalgamations and take-overs concentrated ownership and the revival of trade associations, after a temporary post-war collapse, increasingly restricted competition between separate firms. By 1935 nearly 45 per cent of gross industrial output in the industries surveyed by the Census of Production was produced by 135 industrial conglomerations employing 5,000 or more workers; and there were thirty-three trades in which the largest units accounted for 70 per cent or more of the total workforce. In 1937 one survey concluded that: 'As a feature of industrial and commercial organisation free competition has nearly disappeared from the British scene.'[2]

Governments promoted this development. The urgent needs of big business overcame lingering commitments to the ideal of free competition. Most dramatically the introduction of a general protective tariff in 1931, already foreshadowed by protection for 'key' strategic industries and for many of the new industries in the 1920s, helped to shore up agreements to restrict output and maintain prices among domestic producers. On the railways, in agriculture, mining and cotton, amalgamations and agreements to restrict competition were underwritten by Act of Parliament. In some service industries the state intervened more directly, establishing public corporations to run broadcasting, electricity supply, passenger transport in London, and overseas airways. Advocates of 'rationalisation' in the 1920s and of 'planning' in the 1930s justified these developments as replacing wasteful competition by efficient large-scale production controlled by an enlightened managerial élite. In this fertile soil, class collaborationist perspectives flourished among the labour leadership, notably in the Mond-Turner talks after the General Strike, but also in the Labour Party's attempts during the 1930s to equip itself ideologically as the agent of a statist renewal of capitalism.

It would take a Second World War to make such a transformation possible. Meanwhile, the collectivism of the 1930s was more a symptom of capitalist decay than of its renewal. In some cases, particularly in the new industries, concentration did serve to increase efficiency, but in the main both amalgamations and trade associations were more concerned with restricting competition, maintaining prices, and keeping inefficient producers in business. Consequently the interventions of the state did little to reconstruct and modernise the economy. That would have required not statutory backup for restrictive agreements, but nationalisation of substantial sections of basic industry and a measure of centralised planning of the economy as a whole. No government in the inter-war years was prepared to contemplate intervention on this scale.

III

The early 1920s saw a consolidation of trade union structure in a spate of amalgamations involving all sections of the movement. Industrial unionism, the hallmark of progressive trade unionism before the war, made little headway. While the miners had something approaching an industrial union, its federal structure remained a source of weakness. The NUR, the prime achievement of industrial unionism before the war, remained locked in conflict with the drivers' union, ASLEF, with the AEU (itself an amalgamation of engineering craftsmen) in the railway workshops, and with a section of its own membership who broke away in 1924 to form a separate signalmen's union. As road transport challenged the railways, the NUR's ambitious plans for a single transport workers' union were frustrated by the refusal of the T&GWU to consider handing over its busmen and lorry drivers. It was above all the consolidation of the two great general unions, the T&GWU (1921) and the NUGMW (1924), that determined the future pattern of trade union structure, to the detriment of the tidy-minded plans of industrial unionists. The T&GWU originated as an amalgamation of dockers and road transport workers, but the Workers Union, which merged with it in 1929, brought in a wide range of semi-skilled workers in engineering, building and other industries. As trade union membership revived in the 1930s these other sectors soon outnumbered the original core of the union. The NUGMW had a more miscellaneous membership from the outset. In 1937 its major strengths were in local authority employment, gas, electricity supply, engineering and building. Both general unions were well placed to survive the depression by holding onto their membership in 'sheltered' jobs and subsequently using this strength as a base from which to expand elsewhere as economic conditions improved.

Despite favourable TUC resolutions and earnest enquiries, the General Council, during the 1920s, quickly abandoned plans for industrial unionist reorganisation, preferring the role of mediating between the existing competing unions. Its policy, eventually formalised in the Bridlington Agreement of 1939, was to freeze existing trade union structures, discouraging breakaways and new unions, while encouraging co-operation, federation and amalgamation wherever this could be done without offending powerful sectional bureaucracies. The General Council, which appointed its first full-time secretary in 1923, extended its authority in other ways too. Although the General Strike put paid to its attempts either to lead or to mediate in industrial disputes, its activity as a policy-making body and pressure group on behalf of the movement as a whole continued to grow after 1926 under the guiding hand of the General Secretary, Walter Citrine.

The wartime advance of national collective bargaining was not, except in mining, reversed after the war. The delays involved in national collective bargaining procedures often operated to the advantage of the unions in a period when wage cuts, not advances, were the main subject of negotiations. National collective bargaining concentrated the unions' strength on maintaining the minimum rate, which tended to be a larger component of actual earnings in depressed than in prosperous times. Nevertheless, in some industries, like engineering, the maintenance of national collective bargaining may have harmed the membership, holding stronger areas and sectors down to the levels attainable by the weaker. By the 1930s militants in the booming aircraft factories were pressing for a separate national agreement, and the General and Municipal Workers had successfully returned to local negotiations in electricity supply. Generally, however, union officials joined employers' organisations in the defence òf national collective bargaining procedures from which much of their authority flowed, though few went so far as the Boot and Shoe Operatives who, in 1921, used employers federation money to finance a strike to enforce the national agreement on a maverick employer. More commonly, where the intensity of competition made industry-wide bargaining difficult or impossible, the state stepped in with Trade Boards, Whitley Councils and special Acts of Parliament as for the railways in 1921 and cotton in 1934. Despite declining membership, trade unionism, after the First World War, had become an accepted institution and its professional leaders were acquiring a status which, especially after the General Strike, opened up the prospect of a more extensive and profound development of class collaboration than had been possible before 1914.

Shortly after the engineering lockout in 1922, the AEU executive had accepted further wage reductions despite their rejection by a ballot vote of the membership. This was symptomatic of a general shift in the internal balance of power in the trade unions, away from the rank-and-file initiative of the previous decade, to the consolidation of bureaucratic power that characterised trade unionism between the wars. Mass unemployment sharply reduced the ability of rank-and-file trade unionists to resist collaborationist policies. Simultaneously the advance of national collective bargaining put a premium on the development of professional trade union bureaucracies, expert in negotiation rather than militant leadership. And the sheer size of unions, after the amalgamations of the early 1920s, tended to increase the gulf between executive committees and the membership. While trade union membership fell, the number of full-time officers actually increased. Nowhere was the trend more clearly revealed than in the general unions, where size, the heterogeneity of the membership and the relative lack of traditions of rank-and-file militancy all tended to enhance oligarchic rule by the full-time officials. The well-paid right-wing oligarchy of the NUGMW was protected against challenges from the left by the scrapping of biennial elections for officials. From 1926 full-time officers were first appointed by the Executive and, after two years, confirmed in office for life by an election. Promotion within the bureaucracy was made possible without any election at all. In such a system union officialdom was peculiarly remote from membership control, and even tended to become an hereditary caste. Several of the national officers of the NUGMW after the Second World War had started their careers as clerks in union offices, appointed by fathers or uncles. In the T&GWU full-time officials had never been elected, except for the General Secretary, Ernest Bevin, who wielded immense personal power as the one force holding together the semi-autonomous trade groups into which the union was divided. Bevin's dictatorship was, however, limited by the militant traditions of the union's original trade groups, the dockers and busmen.

IV

Powerless to impose its own economic solutions, weakened by industrial and political defeats, by mass unemployment and by adverse shifts in the occupational structure, the most remarkable thing about the labour movement between the wars was its resilience. The buoyant, inventive class assertion of the previous decade rapidly gave way to bitter and largely unsuccessful defensive strikes in the declining sectors during the 1920s (and the early 1930s in cotton). Nevertheless, in the worst years of the slump, trade union membership, though only half the peak figure of 1920, was still well above the level of 1911. In 1938, after some recovery, 30 per cent of the total labour force was unionised compared with less than 20 per cent in 1911. The great betrayals of the General Strike in 1926 and of the Second Labour Government in 1931 penetrated deep into the memory of the labour movement, but in face of the inexorable decline of the industries from which organised labour had traditionally drawn its muscle, there seemed little enough to be done about them at the time. The grim years of mass unemployment alienated millions of workers from the system. It was an alienation characterised not by revolt, but by a stubborn hanging on for better times. Explosions of rank-and-file anger occurred, but they petered out quickly: no new militant leadership emerged to turn the movement in more effective directions. Perhaps there were none. For a generation after the post-war crisis working-class political initiatives were frozen into the long wait for the return of a majority Labour Government. Despite its collapse in 1931, the Labour Party's vote rose from 4.2 million in 1922 to 8.3 million in 1935.

In part this stubborn resilience reflected the new institutional stability in the movement derived from its decade of advance before 1920; in part it reflected a sea-change in working-class political consciousness brought about by the depression itself. Underpinning both of these was a greater cohesion within the working class. Between the wars the two great landmarks of nineteenth-century working-class stratification – the aristocracy of labour and the casual poor – tended to dissolve, leaving an altogether more homogenous bloc at the base of the social pyramid. It was the divisions between North and South, between employed and unemployed, that struck contemporaries. But these were in fact less far reaching than the division between the respectable working class and the poor in nineteenth-century England which, to some degree, they had replaced.

The decline of those industries where traditional skills had been at a premium was itself a heavy blow to the old labour aristocracy. Beyond this, technological change tended to reduce the relative size of the skilled workforce, most dramatically in engineering workshops where the proportion of skilled workers fell from 60 per cent in 1914 to 32 per cent in 1933. More important than any decline in the number of skilled jobs, however, was the erosion of differentials. During the inflationary years of the First World War, when cost-of-living bargaining became the norm, the incomes of the lower paid had risen much faster than those of skilled workers. During the next twenty years differentials were not restored to any significant extent. And while declining differentials undermined the material basis of the old labour aristocracy, its psychological basis never recovered from the shock of dilution – when the mysteries of the craft had been exposed to vulgar eyes and quickly mastered by plebeian workers or even women. After dilution it would no longer be possible for the nineteenth-century notion that there were two distinct classes of humanity, the skilled and the unskilled, to gain easy acceptance in the working-class mind.

Even more important than the decline of the labour aristocracy was the transformation of poverty at the other end of the scale. Again the impact of war had been crucial. The unprecedented labour shortage eliminated overnight much of the abject poverty that had driven pre-war social reformers to talk of racial degeneration and propose the segregation of the 'unemployable'. There was, of course, no lack of poverty between the wars. Rowntree's 1936 survey of York showed 18 per cent of the working class living in poverty: but this compared favourably with the 28 per cent of 1901. The degree of poverty was limited by the greatly extended provision of state unemployment benefit, including dependents' allowances, that had been wrung out of the post-war Coalition Government as a bulwark against revolution, and which no inter-war Government succeeded in withdrawing. For the poorest the dole may well have meant better food than casual employment, and it brought the maintenance of an adequately furnished home nearer their reach. For all workers the underwriting of life's most critical situations by state benefits may well have helped to strengthen those ties of kinship and neighbourly community which underpinned working-class solidarity and which, before the war, were constantly disrupted by the sheer magnitude of the disasters of unemployment, sickness or too many children. The expansion of new industries in old centres of casual and sweated labour, statutory wage-fixing in the worst organised industries, and the growth of secure employment in government services like the post office and in local government further contributed to the shrinking of the reservoir of casual labour.

Increased homogeneity in the working class helped the labour movement to survive. But there was little possibility in these years that it could transcend its traditional limitations. Especially after the General Strike of 1926 the narrowly electoral politics of the Labour Party grew at the expense of extra-parliamentary forms. Whole areas of potential mobilisation – the street, the housing estate, the workplace – were systematically fenced off by the nervous and conciliatory leadership of an increasingly bureaucratised movement. While their control was never absolute, it was certainly debilitating. The inability of the movement to develop trade union strategies and political demands appropriate to the needs of the female half of the working class continued to limit its potential base. In some ways the syndicalist current, with its stress on the primacy of class struggle at the point of production, had tended to reinforce the traditional male-centredness of the movement. After the First World War, as before, the labour movement turned an excluding face towards sections of the working class which it had failed to organise. It resisted forms of activism which appeared to threaten the authority of its leaders and the viability of their various accommodations with capitalism. Consequently it remained an accomplice in its own impotence.

Notes

1 G. Orwell, *The Road to Wigan Pier*, London 1937, p. 140.
2 A.F. Lucas, *Industrial Reconstruction and the Control of Competition*, London 1937, p. 64.

8

Labour Government and General Strike, 1924–31

In 1924 the Labour Party formed its first Government. This, and the subsequent experience of office in 1929–31, was to prove more threatening to the unity and coherence of the labour movement than any of the upheavals or defeats of the previous decade. The enthusiasm with which Labour politicians in the 1920s accepted the offer of probationary membership of the political elite prefigured the even more disastrous experiences of the 1960s and 1970s. The established partnership between a reformist Labour Party and an economistic trade unionism entered a state of acute crisis as soon as Labour's access to state power put that partnership to the test. It took the ousting of Ramsay MacDonald, Labour's first Prime Minister, and the virtual take-over of the Party by the General Council of the TUC in the early 1930s to repair the resulting damage to the unity of the movement. As subsequent experience was to confirm all too clearly, the entry into government spelt doom for the labour movement.

I

In 1923 Stanley Baldwin, who had played a decisive role in the break-up of Lloyd George's coalition in the previous year, led the Conservatives into a general election on the issue of Tariff Reform. The Conservatives lost their overall majority in the Commons and Labour emerged as the second largest party. It was the well-founded confidence of most of the established political leaders in the political moderation of Labour under MacDonald that allowed Labour to form its first Government early in 1924 – only a minority of Conservatives felt that the socialist menace justified the re-establishment of a Liberal–Conservative coalition to keep Labour out.

The Labour leadership saw their first experience of office as an opportunity, not to polarise politics by courting defeat on major issues of principle, but to demonstrate their capacity to govern 'responsibly'. The Cabinet, well-padded with experienced politicians recruited from Liberal and Tory ranks, was punctilious in its observation of established rituals – provoking one Clydeside shipyard worker to shout at an ILP meeting: 'A worker's government, ye ca' it! It's a bloody lum [top] hat government like a' the rest.'[1] Certainly the Government's attitude to strikes confirmed this judgement. The TUC was alarmed when 'their' Government invoked the Emergency Powers Act against Bevin's threat to bring out the London underground workers in sympathy with the tramwaymen. John Wheatley, the only left-winger in the Cabinet, was responsible for its main domestic achievement. Wheatley's Housing Act owed a good deal to his ability to negotiate dilution with the unions, but little to any previous socialist thinking on the subject. Although the chief issue in the election, apart from free trade, had been unemployment, Snowden's policy at the Exchequer was entirely orthodox.

The Government saw foreign policy, rather than direct economic intervention, as the key to combating unemployment. This reflected the retreat from collectivism into Liberal internationalism which had marked Labour Party thinking after the dismantling of the war economy. MacDonald's enthusiasm for a compromise settlement on German reparations payments starkly contradicted party policy of opposition to reparations in principle and provoked a bitter resolution at the 1924 TUC. The other main plank of the Government's foreign policy, negotiation of a trade agreement with the Soviet Union, was welcomed by the unions, but opposed by the opposition parties who accused the Government of betraying the interests of the British bondholders whose property had been expropriated by the Bolsheviks. It was over the Russian issue that the Government fell in October 1924. During the election campaign which followed, anti-communist hysteria was whipped up by the publication by the Foreign Office of the 'Zinoviev Letter' – allegedly a missive from the President of the Communist International explaining that the Russian Treaties would open the way to revolution in Britain. Ramsay MacDonald's failure to prevent the Foreign Office from taking this letter seriously – it was in fact a forgery – contributed to the Conservatives' overwhelming victory at the polls. Anti-communism probably made little headway among Labour's working-class supporters, and the party's vote actually rose quite substantially. The Tory victory rested on the decimation of the Liberals, as the middle class, alarmed by enemies more imaginary than real, rallied to the party of property.

Within the Labour Party, opposition to MacDonald's leadership and policies remained fragmented and ineffective. The construction of constituency Labour Parties, envisaged in the 1918 constitution, proceeded slowly. Until the later 1920s the party's local presence continued to rest essentially on the Trades Councils and, especially in Scotland and the North, the ILP, whose membership had grown rapidly since the war. The evident lack of socialist purpose displayed by the Labour Government, persuaded the ILP of the need to rally the movement, as events had rallied it in 1918, behind a programme of 'Socialism in Our Time'. The core of the new programme was the demand for a 'living wage', to be determined by a public inquiry and to be achieved by legislative coercion of employers and direct state benefits, including family allowances. The capitalist crisis antici- pated when a future Labour Government implemented this policy, was to be met by nationalisation of the banks and certain basic industries, and by a battery of controls over prices, credit, investment and foreign trade. The programme was intended to combine a simple and powerful mobilising demand – the 'living wage' – with a detailed and practical programme of action for the next Labour Government.

As a focus of opposition to MacDonald, 'Socialism in Our Time' gained little support. The idea of a public inquiry to establish a living wage created little enthusiasm and the whole notion fell foul of trade union concern for free collective bargaining. In particular the major- ity of unions opposed family allowances which they thought would be used to hold down wages. The 1927 Labour Party Conference referred the ILP programme to a joint Labour Party–TUC commit- tee, where trade union hostility delayed matters for several years.

A potentially more promising core of active resistance to Mac- Donald's politics was to be found in the grass-roots struggle over unemployment. During 1920–1 unemployed protest movements had come together in the National Unemployed Workers Movement (NUWM). Inventive in its militancy, the movement raided factories where overtime was being worked, occupied council offices and workhouses, organised squatting and resistance to eviction, and was involved in almost daily battles with the police. Women played an important part in this activity. In 1922 the NUWM led the first national hunger march. It also represented individual claimants before insurance and poor law authorities. Politically the movement was dominated by the Communist Party and many of its leaders, like the secretary Wal Hannington, were victimised engineering shop stewards. Panicky authorities, noting the role of ex-servicemen in the movement saw its activities as a portent of revolution: 'It must be remembered', wrote the Director of Intelligence at Scotland Yard, 'that in the event of rioting, for the first time in history, the rioters will be better trained than the troops.'[2] The main object of the Communist Party, however, was not to use the unemployed as insurrectionary shock troops, but to win immediate benefits (which it did) and establish close links with organised labour. In the engineering lockout unemployed workers' committees did much of the picketing. Between 1922 and 1925 – by which time, due to the temporary upturn in trade, the movement was less active – the NUWM gained official TUC backing for some of its work.

The political significance of the NUWM lay less in the basis it provided for the development of militant labour politics under Communist leadership, than in the boost its activities gave to the development of militant labour politics in local government. British socialism, in the mid-1880s, the early 1890s and again in the 1900s, had been reared in the politics of unemployment. Before 1914 social-ist candidates had made substantial inroads into the machinery of local government, and of poor law provision. Already the generosity shown by socialist poor law Guardians to the unemployed had caused bitter conflicts with the central authorities. After the war this process was resumed with renewed urgency and with greater success as Labour control in local government advanced. It was the jailing of George Lansbury and most of the Labour-controlled Poplar Borough Council 1921 that gave its name to the most significant inter-war development in the politics of unemployment – Poplarism. For years Poplar had granted outdoor relief at a high rate to the able-bodied unemployed. When unemployment reached its peak in 1921 they were faced with the necessity of cutting these rates, or defaulting on payments due to certain Metropolitan funds. They chose the latter, arguing that more affluent areas of London could well afford to subsidise the East End unemployed. Jailed for their pains, the councillors organised the other prisoners – and the guards – and held borough council meetings, serenaded from outside the walls by the band of the Poplar Workhouse School. The Government gave way, conceding the substance of Poplar's claim.

For a time Poplarism thrived in local labour politics. In a number of areas the hated poor law was being transformed into an agency of the working class. It was not difficult, however, for the Government, by withdrawing effective power from locally elected authorities, to undermine any policy of encroaching control on the foothills of state power. From 1926, when many Labour-controlled authorities ran up large deficits supporting the locked-out miners, the Government began to reassert its control. Legislation was introduced to bring the Boards of Guardians under tighter control, and Government commissions were sent in to cut down relief scales in Durham, South Wales and the East End of London. In 1929 Neville Chamberlain, the architect of Conservative social policy between the wars, abolished the directly elected Guardians altogether, replacing them by Public Assistance Committees appointed by the County Councils. The Labour Party, itself committed to the abolition of the poor law and the responsibility of the national exchequer, rather than impoverished local authorities, for the relief of unemployment, opposed any attempt to shore up the power of the Guardians. The ILP, from whom a lead might have been expected, was busy with grandiose schemes for 'Socialism in Our Time'. So a fund of working-class resistance to the depression was dissipated in uncoordinated battles with the 'dictator', Chamberlain. During the 1930s unemployed activism and local authority defiance of central government continued, but no effective way was found to direct this militancy into the national politics of the Labour Party.

II

The first experience of office had put considerable strain on the alliance between Labour and the trade unions. Members of the General Council expressed bitterness at the failure of the Government to consult them any more than previous administrations. There were attempts to oust MacDonald and install Henderson, always closer to the unions, as leader of the party. In 1925 Bevin, irritably and unsuccessfully, tried to persuade the Labour Party Conference to oppose minority government in the future. In general, however, the trade union leadership reacted not by attempting to reform the Labour Party, but by withdrawing from joint activities, concentrating on the separate development of their own political platform in the General Council, and pursuing influence through direct industrial pressure on the Tory Government. It was this latter development which provided the key opportunity for the left to resume the class offensive of the previous decade.

Industrial militancy, reviving since 1924, focused around events in the coalfields. Faced with falling markets and profits the mine owners gave notice of an end to national wage agreements and of major

wage cuts to take effect from 31 July 1925. The Miners Federation
was determined to resist. It gained the support of the General Council, the railwaymen and the dockers for an embargo on coal movements in the event of a strike. At the very last moment, worried by the
economic effects of such a stoppage, the Government intervened,
granting a nine-month subsidy to the owners to enable work to
continue at the old wages, in return for which the Miners agreed to
co-operate with a Royal Commission to investigate once again the
efficiency of the industry. This apparent victory was greeted with
euphoria in the unions – 'Red Friday' had exorcised the evil spirit of
'Black Friday'. A minority within the Cabinet resented the Government's climb down. So did the mine owners who wanted to slog it
out and, curiously enough, Ramsay MacDonald – who saw the
Government's action as an open invitation to revive pernicious
notions of Direct Action.

In fact Red Friday represented a truce, not a victory. It gave the
Government nine months in which to perfect its strike-breaking
organisation. More important, by forcing the Miners to accept a
Royal Commission, the Government had driven in the thin edge of a
wedge that was eventually to split the Miners from their trade union
allies. The Samuel Commission, 'impartially' composed of two Liberals, a banker and a cotton boss, reported in March 1926. It
proposed, for the long term, reorganisation of the industry under
private ownership, and, meanwhile, substantial wage cuts. (But it
rejected the owners' demands for district negotiations and longer
hours.) The only link between these two recommendations was a
vague suggestion that the miners should not be expected to accept
wage cuts until some definite agreement had been reached between
owners and union that 'all practicable means for improving' the
organisation of the industry should, at some future date, be adopted.

Little was done by the unions to prepare for the crisis. The General
Council contented itself with setting up an Industrial Committee
which listened with polite indifference to Citrine's plea for detailed
contingency planning for a General Strike. Nothing was done to
clarify the relations between the Council and the MFGB in the event
of a strike. The leadership had little inclination to prepare for a strike
which it had every intention of averting. It was the publication of the
Samuel Report that provided the General Council with the opportunity to make a positive intervention. Neither side welcomed the
Report. The owners showed no enthusiasm for reorganisation. The
Miners stuck to their demand: 'Not a penny off the pay, not a second

on the day.' Even if they could be persuaded in principle to accept temporary wage cuts in return for reorganisation, they had been offered no realistic guarantee that reorganisation would in fact follow. Only the Government could provide such guarantees. The basis of the General Council's policy during April 1926 was to persuade the Government to put its weight behind reorganisation, hoping that in return the miners would accept the cuts.

Unfortunately, apart from a handful of progressive industrialists – who were to turn up again after the Strike in Mond-Turner talks – the General Council were the only people to take the Report seriously. The Government, whose relationship with the owners remained close and friendly, had no intention of forcing through reorganisation by legislation. By the end of April the General Council found itself trapped between Government indifference and the Miners' determination to resist. On the 29th a Special Conference of Trade Union Executives authorised the Council to call a national strike. Next day the Government activated the Emergency Powers Act and the TUC sent out strike notices, to take effect from midnight on Monday 3 May. Despite the sympathy of rank-and-file trade unionists with the miners, it is quite possible that the General Council would have settled for cuts without any firm promise of reorganisation had the Government handled the eleventh-hour negotiations with more tact. In the event the General Council found itself leading a General Strike from which it expected to gain nothing. Not surprisingly it patched up a settlement over the heads of the MFGB as soon as one could be arranged.

The General Strike was the left's major opening in the inter-war years. This was the situation which the revolutionaries of 1919 had eagerly anticipated – the opportunity for rank-and-file workers' councils, led by revolutionary socialists, to seize the leadership of the working-class movement from reformist politicians and trade union bureaucrats, and to transform the strike from an action in defence of the miners' wages into a revolutionary struggle for power. Whatever credibility this cataclysmic vision might have held immediately after the war, by 1926 it was a non-starter.

From its foundation the Communist Party had concerned itself primarily with the politics of industrial struggle. It was, consequently, by far the most important political organisation operating within the unions. While the first Labour Government was in office, in 1924, and industrial militancy showed signs of revival, the CP launched the National Minority Movement. Building on existing rank-and-file movements in mining, engineering and the railways the Movement grew rapidly during the next two years. By the eve of the strike the 883 delegates at a Minority Movement 'Conference of Action' could claim (with a good deal of double counting) to represent nearly a quarter of the total membership of the trade unions.

It is, however, easy to exaggerate the strength of the Minority Movement. The party itself remained small, growing from 3,000 members in 1924, to 6,000 at the time of the General Strike. In conditions of continuing unemployment, the Minority Movement, despite its broad appeal within the unions, remained 'a sentiment rather than an organised force'.[3] 'How can you build factory organisations', asked J.T. Murphy, leader of the wartime shop stewards' movement, 'when you have 1,750,000 walking the streets? You cannot build factory organisations in empty and depleted workshops.'[4] But without a basis in such organisation the Minority Movement could not build a genuinely independent rank-and-file movement, or constitute itself as an alternative leadership to the established trade union officials. Unable to challenge the trade union bureaucracy directly, the Movement was dependent on the open or tacit support of left-wing officials for its advance. The weakness of the Minority Movement became clear when the left-wingers failed to produce any alternative policy to the General Councils' eventual desertion of the miners, in which they were fully implicated. Not surprisingly, there was a good deal of confusion in the CP during the run up to the Strike about what could be expected from the General Council's left wing. The Communists might have achieved more, had they recognised the very limited possibilities of revolutionary politics in the 1920s, rather than acting on the assumption that it was possible for socialists to secure a mass following around a revolutionary programme at a time when the whole working-class movement was in retreat.

During the General Strike the solidarity and enthusiasm of the workers surprised both the Government and the TUC leaders. Despite – or perhaps because of – the General Council's lack of preparation, the vigour and ingenuity shown by local strike committees and Trades Councils in organising the strike was impressive. The General Council sought to limit the Trades Councils' role to that of supporting the strike committees of individual unions and to maintain the vertical, sectional chains of command. In practice, in most areas, the strike committees merged into the Councils, if only to sort out confusions caused by contradictory instructions from the different national executives. Trades Council offices were a ferment of activity, organising picketing, meetings and entertainments, issuing permits for the transport of food, producing lively cyclostyled strike bulletins despite harassment from Bevin who thought they should confine themselves to distributing the General Council's own leaden *British Worker*. In Newcastle, where the Council of Action, prompted by the Communist Page Arnot, was particularly effective, the strikers were able to force the local Government Commissioner to propose joint control of the movement of food supplies from the docks.

The Government stood firm, confident that the trade union leaders would find a way to call off the strike. To encourage them, Winston Churchill, hugely enjoying himself as editor of the official *British Gazette*, characterised them as leaders of a revolutionary conspiracy. Jimmy Thomas, the Railwaymen's leader, mined from within, predicting attacks from Fascist mobs and the wholesale arrest of the leadership. The General Council grasped at the first straw that offered, a memorandum from the Chairman of the Samuel Commission which had no official status, and, after nine days, called off the strike with nothing gained for the miners, and without any guarantees against the victimisation of the strikers. Stunned, and angry, the strikers refused to go back until reinstatement agreements had been negotiated with their employers. But go back they did.

Despite the vigour of the Trades Councils there were strict limitations to their initiative. For the local activists, as for the mass of the strikers themselves, the goal of the strike was always a defensive one. Even the CP's modest attempts to raise the demand for a General Election and the nationalisation of the mines seems to have fallen flat. Above all, the alternative leadership necessary to carry the strike forward simply did not exist. The CP could not have been more active – up to one third of the 3,000 people prosecuted for offences committed during the strike were Communists, about 20 per cent of the party's membership – and it was aware of the need to develop a new rank-and-file leadership from below – 'a more revolutionary leadership . . . than was possible from the ranks of the local or district officials' who actually ran the strike. But, commented Page Arnot sadly, 'this stage was never reached . . .'.[5]

Had the strike occurred as the culmination of a period of trade union advance, a period in which rank-and-file self-activity had thrown up a rank-and-file leadership – in 1919 for example – the outcome might have been very different. But that is precisely why it did not occur in 1919. In 1919 Cabinet ministers had whispered about the danger of revolution behind closed doors, and done what they could to conciliate the trade union leaders. It was an indication of ruling-class confidence in 1926 that the Cabinet was prepared not only to provoke a strike where one might well have been avoided, but also, through the militant personality of Winston Churchill, to invent and publicly proclaim a revolutionary conspiracy that had no basis in fact. The object of the invention, which succeeded, was to frighten the TUC leadership into submission. Such tactics could only be pursued by the Government because, as they well understood, the danger of social revolution was very much more remote in 1926 than it had been seven years earlier.

It is possible that had the Miners accepted defeat in May 1926 they would have been able to negotiate a settlement including reductions for all but the worst paid men, but maintaining national negotiations. The miners, however, were determined to fight on – which they did against the advice of many of their leaders through six months of poverty and often ferocious police repression. In the end starvation, blacklegging and the threat of company unionism drove them back to work on terms which included longer hours (by Act of Parliament), wage cuts, and worst of all, a return to district agreements. By the end of 1930 real income had sunk below the levels of 1914, even for those miners not on short-time or unemployed. Some miners' families were paying off debts incurred during the lockout as late as 1972.

III

In other industries there was no equivalent fall in wages, though the immediate effect of the strike was to prevent unions from striking to push up wages when profit levels recovered during 1927–9. More remarkable was the relative stability of money wages after 1929, during the world slump. Despite unprecedented unemployment, falling prices and falling trade union membership, there was no repeat of the wage-cutting of the early 1920s. Economists complained of 'wages rigidity' preventing the necessary downward adjustment of British costs and export prices. The General Strike, despite its collapse, had nevertheless taught employers that there were limits beyond which it was dangerous to push their workers.

Certainly the existence of the dole placed a floor beneath wage cutting. Outside coal, textiles, exceptionally hard hit by the world depression, was the only major industry to experience large-scale wage reductions. These were bitterly resisted: two-thirds of all working days lost in strikes and lockouts between 1927 and 1934 were in textiles.

The first cuts were imposed in the summer of 1929 following a lockout of nearly 400,000 cotton operatives. Eighteen months later the weavers successfully resisted attempts to speed-up work by doubling the number of looms for which each worker was responsible. At the height of the conflict, in the summer of 1932, a new round of wage reductions and the revival of the 'more looms' question, led to the greatest clash Lancashire had seen since the Plug Riots of 1842. Despite the tenacity of the cotton workers, whose leaders again and again found themselves pushed into battles which they were convinced would be lost, the strike was defeated on both counts. After 1932 a vicious circle of speed-up, competitive wage-cutting and factory closures was only prevented from destroying collective bargaining in the industry altogether by the Government's agreement to give statutory force to agreements between the unions and the master's federation.

The 1932 cotton strike saw the extensive use of the Trades Disputes Act of 1927 against pickets. The passing of this Act had symbolised the Conservatives' victory over the unions in the General Strike. While the Act avoided the most excessive demands of employers – repeal of the 1906 Act or the banning of strikes in 'key' industries – it outlawed sympathetic strikes and strikes designed to 'coerce the Government, either directly or by inflicting hardship on the community', and extended the legal restrictions on picketing. While little use was subsequently made of these clauses, their wording, deliberately vague, was designed to maximise the deterrent effect of the law. In the nature of things it would be very hard to say how far it succeeded in this. Other clauses restricted the right to strike, outlawed the closed shop in public sector employment, and prevented civil service unions affiliating to the TUC or Labour Party. But most important was the substitution of contracting-in for contracting-out of the political levy. This cut the Labour Party's income from affiliation fees by over 25 per cent between 1927 and 1929, and restricted the number of union-sponsored candidates at the 1929 election. The main effect of this evidently partisan attack on the political levy, however, was to draw the unions and the

Labour Party closer together. It also stimulated the development of Labour's constituency organisation, by forcing the party to place more emphasis on recruiting individual members.

While the Trades Disputes Act created a good deal of bitterness, Communist efforts to mobilise pressure for direct action against the Bill came to nothing. The widespread demoralisation which followed the General Strike was accompanied by the rapid dissolution of the amorphous left-wing of 1925–6, leaving the CP isolated and exposed to disciplinary action from the right. Despite the failure of the CP's campaign for affiliation to the Labour Party in the early 1920s, its members were active and, in a number of localities, powerful within the party. A leadership intent on proving itself 'fit to govern' would not long tolerate the existence of such an organised focus of opposition. Already in 1925 the Liverpool Conference of the Labour Party had voted to debar Communists from individual membership and from acting as trade union delegates to party conferences. Resistance to this decision from Communists and other left-wingers was stimulated by a wave of sympathetic protest against the jailing of the CP's Executive Committee in December 1925. In September 1926, by which time seven London Labour Parties had been expelled for refusing to implement the Liverpool decision, a National Left Wing Movement was established to sustain the disaffiliated parties, to oppose further expulsions and to fight for a left-wing policy inside the Labour Party. There was little chance of success for any of these objectives. Too weak to affect Labour Party policy, the very existence of the Left Wing Movement, under obvious CP direction, gave the Labour Party leadership an excellent pretext for purging troublesome parties. By 1929, twenty-six local Labour Parties had been expelled, and the rules against Communist membership of the party had been further strengthened.

The exclusion of the Communists was accompanied by a new attempt to establish the basis for a policy of industrial peace. By the autumn of 1927 the furore over the Trades Disputes Act had died down sufficiently for the TUC to respond favourably to the invitation of a group of employers led by Sir Alfred Mond of ICI to discuss areas of common interest. Despite vocal opposition from some of the more left-wing unions the Mond-Turner talks (Turner was Chairman of the TUC) continued until spring 1929.

The direct and tangible results of the Mond-Turner talks were negligible. But they played an important part in shaping the long-term goals of the more far-sighted trade union leaders. The businessmen and professional managers who associated themselves with Mondism represented large and progressive companies whose interests were best served, not by keeping trade unionism at arm's length, but by incorporating its leadership in an effort to secure stable labour relations and the active co-operation of a disciplined workforce. For Alfred Mond the future lay not with the embattled, individualist mine owners, or their counterparts in engineering, but with the corporate organisation of industry under professional managers who would see themselves as a third force between capital and labour.

As in the First World War, many trade union leaders found themselves drawn towards this corporatist vision of industrial organisation. Even so tough and unsentimental a man as Ernest Bevin confessed to an instinctive feeling of kinship with the professional manager, a feeling which no doubt underpinned the agreement he negotiated with Lord Ashfield, Mondist director of the London Traffic Combine. Ashfield agreed to encourage trade union membership, in return for union co-operation in the rationalisation of the industry. Deals of this sort helped to give practical meaning to the General Council's commitment to approaching 'a new industrial order . . . not by way of a social explosion, but by a planned reconstruction in which the unions will assume a larger share of control in directing industrial changes.'[6] The Bevin–Ashfield relationship was later to contribute to the rise of the unofficial London Busmen's movement, because it threatened job-control in the garages. When they spoke of 'control', of 'improving the status of the worker', the Mondists meant not the encroaching control of workers on the shop floor, but the recognition of trade union officials as managers of a labour force disciplined by an employer-enforced closed shop.

IV

In the 1929 election Labour emerged, for the first time, as the largest party in the House of Commons, though outnumbered by the combined forces of Conservative and Liberal MPs. Few Labour members opposed the formation of a second minority government, though the ILP group led by the Clydesider James Maxton argued that instead of trying to govern as a minority, the Cabinet should devote itself to preparing socialist legislation, court defeat in the

Commons, and welcome a new election on issues defined by itself. Ramsay MacDonald's Cabinet, however, had no intention of living dangerously. It proceeded instead 'on the assumption that once a Labour Government is in office, its primary duty is to find a means of remaining there.'[7] The alienation of the Maxton group, who were frequently to vote against the Government over the next two years and finally to take the ILP out of the Labour Party, was one consequence of this policy. Much more important was the rift that opened up between the goals of the party leadership and those of the General Council of the TUC.

The central problem facing the new government was unemployment, which rose inexorably from 1.2 million in June 1929 to 2.5 million in May 1931. The Government's approach to unemployment was dominated by Philip Snowden, Chancellor of the Exchequer. Snowden believed that 'socialism' – extensive social reform and state purchase of private industry at market value – was a luxury to be financed, in the first instance, out of the revenue produced by a prosperous capitalist economy.

In the absence of prosperity it was, therefore, impossible to advance towards socialism. Snowden rejected Keynesian ideas of deficit financing and public works as a means of stimulating the economy, accepting the orthodox Treasury view that reduced Government expenditure was the proper response to economic depression. Unable to implement a ruthlessly deflationary policy – because of the effects such a policy would have had on the Government's support within the labour movement – the Cabinet simply drifted into financial catastrophe. Snowden's stubborn orthodoxy, and the support it received in the Cabinet, rested partly on mere unimaginativeness, partly on a reluctance to confront the power of the Treasury and the financial establishment in the City of London. In addition there was the belief that the maintenance of economic internationalism, symbolised by the Gold Standard and free trade, and incompatible with the adoption of Keynesian measures, was essential not only to eventual economic recovery, but also to the maintenance of international peace. Any departure from internationalism on the economic front, any move towards protectionism and national (or imperial) autarchy, would sow the seeds of inter-imperialist rivalry leading to a new world war. After the First World War the Labour leadership soon pushed the collectivist commitments they had learned in wartime into the background. But their commitment to economic and diplomatic internationalism remained. In effect, the second Labour Government grafted working-class internationalism onto the older stock of free trade imperialism and thus tied the fortunes of the party to those of the City of London.

The trade union leadership, who shared the Cabinet's view that any immediate advance towards socialism was out of the question, nevertheless could not be content with the policy of drift. The extent of unemployment during the worst years of the world slump – it reached 22.5 per cent at the beginning of 1932 – threatened the very existence of trade unionism. That the unions survived with the loss of no more than 50 per cent of their peak post-war membership can be attributed in no small part to the existence of unemployment benefit. Contributory unemployment insurance, and when that was exhausted the 'dole', constituted a vital limit on the effects of mass unemployment on wage levels and trade union organisation. Understanding this, the least that the trade unions expected from 'their' Government after 1929 was that it would resist Opposition attacks on unemployment benefit. Their disillusionment was rapid.

The reaction of the trade union movement to the second Labour Government was not, however, entirely a defensive one. Within the General Council, under the intellectual leadership of Bevin and Citrine, it is possible to discern elements of an alternative economic strategy. This strategy was no less class-collaborationist than that adopted by the Government, and it was therefore sharply distinct from the 'Socialism in Our Time' policies of the Maxton group. But it did have the considerable virtue of proposing collaboration with the more progressive, rather than the more reactionary, sections of the ruling class. Thus Bevin, developing the themes of Mondism, advocated an alliance of both sides of 'industry' against the City, an alliance which would involve a Keynesian policy of deficit budgeting and public works to stimulate investment, and the insulation of the British economy from the worst effects of the world slump by protective tariffs. If necessary he was even prepared to sacrifice the ultimate sacred cow – the Gold Standard. While the General Council remained dubious about tariffs – the implicit challenge to internationalist traditions was too great to be swallowed all at once – there was a growing readiness to consider proposals for protection on their merits, and considerable appeal in the argument that by granting or witholding tariffs governments would be able to force the pace of 'rationalisation' on reluctant industrialists. Not all employers, of course, were reluctant. Support for a vigorous,

Government-led policy of 'capital-development' and rationalisation was expressed by several of the big businessmen who served on MacDonald's Economic Advisory Council during 1930. The Liberal Party was committed, since its 'Yellow Book' of 1929 which Keynes inspired, to a similar general economic strategy.

Whether an expansionist strategy would have been politically viable, or indeed economically effective, had the Government adopted it must remain a matter of speculation. What is certain, however, is that the Cabinet preferred to govern hand-to-mouth, rather than attempt to construct, from the materials available, a power base for modernising British capitalism. Their chief attempt at 'rationalisation' was the Mines Act of 1930. Even the Liberals attacked it for its failure to bring realistic pressure to bear on the individualistic mine owners. In 1930 one of the junior ministers responsible for unemployment policy, Sir Oswald Mosley, resigned in order to fight for his own expansionist solutions to the problem. Widespread sympathy – most importantly among Trade Union MPs – for Mosley's criticisms made no impact at all on Government policy. Subsequently Mosley, in the face of the united hostility of the leadership, came within an ace of winning the support of the Party Conference for serious consideration of his proposals.

By the winter of 1930–1 the Government was living on borrowed time, only avoiding defeat in the Commons by setting up Inquiries which were bound to report in favour of the Opposition policy. In June 1931, one such inquiry, the Royal Commission on Unemployment Insurance, recommended a 30 per cent cut in standard benefits. Confronted by TUC-organised demonstrations, and protests from all sections of the Parliamentary Party, the Cabinet rejected the cut in favour of a milder attack on 'anomalies'. It pushed this through the Commons with Opposition support against the votes of Maxton's and Mosley's followers. On 31 July, the day after Parliament rose, the report of the May Economy Committee (established in March as a result of a Liberal amendment to a Conservative censure motion) was published, recommending large cuts in public expenditure. The May Report's prediction of a £120 million budget deficit unless cuts were carried through precipitated a run on the pound. When the Government sought foreign credits to defend sterling it was firmly told by the bankers that it would first have to reach agreement with the Opposition Parties on a programme of cuts in public expenditure. The majority of the Cabinet favoured agreement with the Opposition, but the minority, stiffened by the adamantine refusal of the General Council to accept cuts in unemployment benefit, was too large to be disregarded. 'The General Council are pigs', remarked Sidney Webb, who favoured the cuts. Arthur Henderson, on the other hand, concluded that only the fall of the Government could preserve the unity of the labour movement.

On August 23 the Cabinet resigned, expecting a Liberal–Conservative coalition to replace them. To the astonishment of most Labour ministers, Ramsay MacDonald emerged next day as Prime Minister in a National Government, including Conservatives, Liberals and two other leading Labour figures, Philip Snowden and Jimmy Thomas. By implementing the cuts that Labour had rejected, the new Government temporarily stabilised the situation. But in September, the Government was finally forced off the Gold Standard which MacDonald had abandoned his party to preserve. In October, under Tory pressure, the 'emergency' National Government rendered itself permanent by calling a general election in which Labour was reduced to a mere fifty-two seats, less than it had held since before 1914. Its proportion of the vote, however, had only fallen from 37 to 30 per cent. It was the lack of Liberal–Conservative competition that decimated the party's representation in Parliament.

Notes

1 R.K. Middlemass, *The Clydesiders*, London 1965, p. 141.
2 B.B. Gilbert, *British Social Policy, 1914–1939*, London 1970, p. 75.
3 T. Bell, *A Short History of the British Communist Party*, London 1937, p. 100.
4 J.T. Murphy, speech at Communist International 1922. Quoted in J. Hinton and R. Hyman, *Trade Unions and Revolution: The Industrial Politics of the Early British Communist Party*, London 1975, p. 14.
5 J. Klugmann, *History of the Communist Party of Great Britain*, vol. 2, London 1969, p. 162.
6 Walter Citrine, 'The Next Step in Industrial Relations', 1927. Reprinted in W. Milne Bailey, *Trade Union Documents*, London 1929, p. 434.
7 R.H. Tawney, 'The Choice Before the Labour Party', 1934. Quoted in M. Foot, *Aneurin Bevan*, London 1966, p. 88.

9

The thirties

Following the collapse of the Labour Government, it was the TUC General Council which held the party together, insisting, despite the reluctance of the new leader, Arthur Henderson, on the expulsion of MacDonald and the others. In December 1931 the General Council increased its representation on the National Joint Council of Labour, a consultative body representing the Parliamentary Party, the National Executive and the TUC, and used it to impose its will on the Labour Party as a whole. The ability of the General Council to dominate the Labour Party in the 1930s rested not only on the decisive role it had played in August 1931, but also on the overwhelming predominance of trade unionists in the Parliamentary Party following the 1931 election. Half the Labour MPs were sponsored by the Miners Federation alone.

Between 1931, when the Party Conference demanded that any future Labour Government must undertake 'definite socialist legislation', and 1934, when the party settled its domestic policy for the remainder of the decade, a major reassessment of the politics of parliamentary gradualism was undertaken. The early 1930s saw a fundamental debate about what Tawney called 'the radiant ambiguities of the word Socialism'. Party intellectuals organised in the Socialist League (established 1932) and Cole's New Fabian Research Bureau (established 1931) discussed the lessons of the crisis and issued an avalanche of advice. One conclusion was that to avoid destruction by a financial crisis any future socialist Government would have to nationalise both the Bank of England and the joint-stock banks. Beyond this there was talk of taking emergency powers over finance and investment, abolishing the House of Lords and reforming House of Commons procedure. The Socialist League was strident on the need for emergency legislation if a Labour Government was to survive its first few months in office and get down to a long-term programme of nationalisation. But others also appreciated Tawney's 1934 aphorism: 'Onions can be eaten leaf by leaf, but you cannot skin a live tiger paw by paw.'[1] Atlee and Dalton, the effective leaders of the party from 1935, were agreed that 'the next Labour Government must start off with a well-planned rush',[2] and that any attempt at sabotage by financial interests should be met with emergency powers. Serious and detailed consideration was given to the nationalisation of particular industries, and the 1934 programme, *For Socialism and Peace*, included a more extensive nationalisation programme than ever before.

Nevertheless the Labour Party in 1934 was very far from being an unambiguously socialist party. No government could have carried through the advance programme advocated by the Socialist League without a massive mobilisation of extra-parliamentary support. Few recognised this. Discussion of nationalisation and of economic planning was partly a response to the Soviet Five Year Plan, but it also reflected a renewed surge of non-socialist argument about the need for greater state intervention in the economy. As in the First World War, the Labour Party and Trade Union Leadership were far from clear about the distinction between their 'socialist' policies, and those advanced by Liberals and radical Conservatives, and they remained prone to the illusion that a consensus on immediate measures could be reached without jeopardising the long-term socialist goal. Citrine's impatient reaction to a meeting of Socialist League intellectuals which he attended in 1933 – 'We were discussing ultimate Socialist objectives of a theoretical character. I did not propose to waste my time further doing so'[3] – was characteristic of the pragmatism of the trade union leadership. Attempts to evaluate immediate reforms by the yardstick of the ultimate socialist goal, like William Mellor's warning to the 1934 Labour Party Conference that bureaucratic plans for socialising Iron and Steel had more in common with the Corporate State than with socialism, were greeted with incomprehension by the trade union leaders. There was indeed an extensive discussion within the trade union movement over the question of control within nationalised industries, but this focused around the pros and cons of official trade union representation on the controlling Boards – Bevin's idea of 'status' – rather than on any genuine proposals for worker participation. A campaign by Cole and the New Fabian Research Bureau to revive Guild Socialist schemes of control backed, surprisingly, by Charles Dukes of the General and Municipal Workers, did achieve some success at the 1933 Labour Party Conference which agreed to the right of workers to 'an effective share in the control and direction of socialised industries'. But this was passed only after a more specific demand for 50 per cent trade union representation had been dropped. The unreality of these debates is revealed by the fact that Charles Dukes, who led for the left, was simultaneously presiding over the increasing bureaucraticisation of his union, and was shortly to be doing his best to smash the genuine revival of a movement for workers' control in the aircraft shop stewards' movement of the later 1930s.

From the standpoint of the trade union leadership, the leftward shift of party policy in the early 1930s reflected not so much a new seriousness in their formal commitment to socialism, as a temporary reaction to short-term difficulties encountered on the 'Mondist' road to status within the power elite of a reconstructed capitalist society. In the depths of the depression neither Governments nor employers had much incentive to consult powerless trade unions. So the union leadership turned their energies to the Labour Party. But as prosperity returned, trade union interest in planning socialism within the Labour Party receded. From the mid-1930s Citrine's emphasis on the research functions of the General Council and on patient lobbying of the Government began to bear fruit in TUC representation on Government Committees. Some material gains resulted, notably in 1938 when the movement for holidays with pay was greatly strengthened by legislation. By the end of the decade Citrine – who had a good deal more in common with Neville Chamberlain than did most labour leaders – was a regular visitor to the back-door of No 10 Downing Street, preparing the way for TUC collaboration in the construction of a new war economy.

II

While the Labour Party and the TUC discussed the programme for the next Labour Government, sections of the rank and file fought the results of the last one. The 1931 cuts provoked demonstrations by school teachers and civil servants, and, most menacingly, a naval mutiny at Invergordon. The main effect of the mutiny was to provoke a new run on the pound which finally forced Britain off the Gold Standard. While Invergordon never held the insurrectionary implications attributed to it by many at the time, it did succeed in limiting the extent of the cuts in the Navy. Meanwhile there was a storm of protest from the unemployed. The cuts in unemployment benefit were accompanied by the imposition of a family means test on the so-called 'transitional payments' to those who had exhausted their contributory benefits. Some of the new Public Assistance Committees refused to operate the means test, and many others – not all of them Labour controlled – were reluctant to operate it rigorously. Government attempts to impose the cuts led to the suspension of two authorities – Durham and Rotherham – and violent clashes between police and unemployed demonstrators in other areas. In Belfast two men were shot by police. In Birkenhead, following violent clashes with demonstrators, the police themselves rioted, raiding tenement buildings and beating up the occupants. During 1932 over 400 members of the Unemployed Workers Movement were jailed. The established labour leadership, despite their apparent shift to the left, showed no inclination to lead this militancy. The TUC encouraged Trades Councils to set up their own unemployed organisations, but the main purpose of this was to divert support from the communist-led NUWM. Nothing much came of it, except where Trades Councils defied the TUC and co-operated with the Communists.

The drive to restore Treasury control over unemployment relief, initiated by Neville Chamberlain after the General Strike, culminated in 1934 with the replacement of the Public Assistance Committees by an Unemployment Assistance Board (UAB) under centralised control. Under the UAB the wide variations in rates of benefit – partly the result of local working-class pressure – were to be replaced by a single national scale. When it became apparent that this would involve cuts in many areas, the anger of both unemployed and employed workers was intense and demonstrative. Local authorities (including Tory controlled ones), Medical Offices of Health, religious bodies and MPs of all parties responded to this anger and joined the protests. Within a month the Government backed down, suspending the implementation of the new scales for two years. The Standstill Act of 1935 was the greatest victory achieved by the agitation of the unemployed since the immediate post-war years. It is indicative of the strength of that agitation that, through the rest of the decade, the UAB found itself unable to avoid paying out benefits which, in many cases in the depressed areas, exceeded wages paid to employed workers. At the same time it is indicative of the overriding strategic weakness of organised labour, and of the defensive – rather than offensive – character of the victory of 1935, that those wages themselves remained below the officially accepted poverty line.

A myth has grown up around the 1930s as the 'red decade'. In fact, for most of the thirties the socialist left was extremely weak. By 1932 the ILP had come to the end of its road as an organised opposition within the Labour Party. Exaggerating the political possibilities created by the wave of militancy against the cuts, and exasperated by tightening discipline in the Parliamentary Party, the ILP decided to sever its historic connection with the Labour Party. Disaffiliation was encouraged by the Revolutionary Policy Committee, a pro-Communist group within the ILP, which believed that the time was ripe for building a mass revolutionary alternative to the Labour Party. In the event ILP membership declined from 16,700 in 1932 to 4,400 in 1935. A close working alliance with the CP during 1933–4, and commitment to an openly revolutionary policy, only accelerated the decline as older members in Lancashire and South Wales left in defence of their distinctive political traditions. By 1935, when the pro-Communists seceded to join the CP, the ILP was little more than an isolated revolutionary sect. Only in Glasgow, where Maxton and three other ILPers retained their seats in the 1935 election, did the party continue to have a significant local presence.

If disaffiliation was disastrous for the ILP, the alternative course was hardly more encouraging. Those ILPers, led by E.F. Wise, who opposed disaffiliation helped to establish the Socialist League. The League, predominantly middle class and London based, never had more than 3,000 members. Its main effort was directed to the policy debate within the Labour Party. Although the crunch did not come until 1937, it was already clear by 1934 that the League had failed to establish a serious presence with the party – all of its 75 amendments to *For Socialism and Peace* were defeated by overwhelming majorities at the Party Conference.

Despite the lunacies of the Communist Party's 'Third Period' policy, it proved to be the only socialist organisation capable of sustaining and expanding a genuine base in the working-class movement during the 1930s. During the agitation against the cuts in 1931 membership doubled in three months, reaching 6,000. It grew rapidly again from 1936, surpassing the previous peak (after the General Strike) and topping 17,500 by 1939. This renewed growth partly reflected the party's continuing work among the unemployed (as late as 1937 a quarter of the membership were unemployed); partly the influx of intellectuals in the later 1930s; but, most significantly, the party's involvement in militant trade union activity.

Trade union membership recovered strongly after 1933. Although the overall level of strike activity remained low, the number of strikes, mostly small and short, increased very rapidly as some measure of prosperity returned to parts of the economy. A great deal of this strike activity was unofficial and in several important industries Communists found themselves in the leadership of effective rank-and-file movements. The model for Communist industrial work in the thirties was provided by the London Busmen's movement. Significantly this rank-and-file movement had originated, in 1931–2, in opposition to the party's attempt to build an independent 'breakaway' union. The busmen had won a uniquely independent position within the TGWU in the amalgamation of 1921. They had their own Central Bus Committee with direct access to the Executive. Working in an industry sheltered from the worst of the depression, they were one of the few groups of workers who had successfully resisted wage cuts in the 1920s. The rank-and-file movement, established in the face of union acceptance of proposed wage cuts in 1931–2, was elected directly from the garages and provided the busmen, through the lively journal, *Busmen's Punch*, with a platform independent of union control and critical of union policy. Opposing the frittering away of militancy in local strikes, the movement directed the busmen's grievances over speed-up and worsening traffic conditions into a campaign for shorter hours which culminated, on Coronation Day 1937, in an official strike. Bevin's handling of this strike was informed more by his obsessions with Communist subversion than by any commitment to winning shorter hours. He set his face against extending the strike among other London Transport workers or among the provincial busmen. The strike failed, and subsequently, the TGWU crushed the rank-and-file movement. Nowhere did the collaborationist and anti-communist mentality of the trade union leadership in the 1930s have more disastrous results for ordinary trade unionists.

On the railways a Vigilance Movement established in 1933 was the driving force behind the campaign to restore wage levels in the later 1930s. Despite persistent large-scale unemployment and a union leadership traumatised by the defeat of 1926, militancy also revived in the mines. The battle against company unionism took a dramatic turn with the South Wales stay-down strike of 1935 – a novel and desperate tactic, but easily the most effective way of keeping blacklegs from the coal face. Two years later company unionism was ousted from the industry in a somewhat compromised victory following an overwhelming ballot in favour of national strike action. A similar vote for 'the miner's two bob' in 1935 was used by the MFGB leadership to secure rises on a district basis. Despite evidence that the membership was prepared to fight, the Miners' leader, Ebby Edwards, preferred to look – in vain – to Government intervention in the industry to restore national bargaining and to 'rationalisation' to create the conditions for a restoration of the cuts.

It was in engineering that the Communists gained their most significant and lasting successes. During the 1920s trade unionism in the engineering industry had shown little sign of recovery from the hammer blow of the 1922 lockout. Existing factory organisation was largely destroyed, and whole new mass-production sections of the industry were developed by employers intent on retraining non-union shops. In 1931 the AEU Executive accepted further cuts without any attempt to test the willingness of its depleted membership to resist. Between 1933 and 1939 membership of the AEU almost doubled, and the number of its shop stewards trebled, while the General Unions expanded rapidly among less skilled engineering workers. Behind this revival lay, firstly, economic recovery – above all the growing pace of rearmament from 1935 – and, secondly, the activism of Communist and other militants, many of them ex-shop stewards from the First World War who had spent the intervening years organising the unemployed. An apprentices' strike in 1937 played a major part in stimulating organisation. By the outbreak of war union membership in the previously vitually unorganised aircraft factories reached 90 per cent, and the Communists had a leading position in the powerful aircraft shop steward movement. As on the buses and the railways, the Communists' successes reflected their gradual abandonment of the 'third period' attempts to organise alternative unions. Instead, the emphasis was placed on the development of shop steward organisation in close co-operation with the union District Committees. In a number of cities the Trades Councils became organising centres of the trade union revival, despite the indifference shown by the TUC, whose fear of encouraging Communists outweighed their desire to recruit members.

III

The trade union revival occurred too late to influence the electoral politics of the 1930s. By the General Election of 1935 the Labour Party had recovered much of the ground lost in 1931, but though it trebled its representation in the House of Commons this still left the Conservatives with an unassailable majority. Labour remained predominantly a party of the older industrial areas and some of the poorer parts of London. In the South and West of England it made few electoral gains, and it took the industrial mobilisations of the Second World War to achieve the political breakthrough in Birmingham. While Labour made some significant advances in local government, capturing the London County Council in 1934, it was international questions which dominated the politics of the later 1930s. The advance of European fascism posed grim and urgent tasks for socialist and working-class politics in Britain. It was not without some sense of relief that working-class activists of many different shades of political opinion threw themselves as never before into the politics of the world struggle. With stalemate on the home front, there were positive advantages to be gained for the labour movement by switching its offensive from domestic to international issues.

These new possibilities could not be exploited without a sharp internal struggle in the labour movement, the main victims of which were pacifism and left-wing attempts to develop a consistently proletarian internationalism. At the Labour Party Conference in 1935 the right settled accounts with the pacifist tradition, represented in the person of the party's octogenarian Christian Socialist leader, George Lansbury. With Mussolini poised to invade Abyssinia, a General Election in the offing, and the evidence of strong public support for collective security revealed by the Peace Ballot of 1934–1935, Bevin made short work of Lansbury's pacifism. Following the TUC's lead, the Party Conference voted overwhelmingly in favour of League of Nations sanctions, including if necessary military sanctions, against Italian aggression. Lansbury resigned, making way for Clement Atlee. By affirming Labour's identification with collective security and the League, the 1935 conference also put paid to the attempts of the Socialist League to develop a revolutionary socialist foreign policy. The Socialist League refused to make any distinction between aggressive and defensive capitalist states. Consequently it rejected collective security and pinned its hopes on international working-class activity to prevent war. As recently as 1933 the Labour Party had reaffirmed its belief in the pre-1914 idea of an international general strike against the threat of renewed imperialist war. But the trade union leaders, acutely aware of Hitler's destruction of the German labour movement, had little difficulty in discrediting this policy.

In the 1935 election the Tories effectively outmanoeuvered Labour's effort to place itself at the head of public demands for resistance to Mussolini's aggression. Baldwin presented himself as the champion of collective security and the League of Nations. The deception proved short-lived, and over the next four years the Government's pursuit of imperial security through appeasement placed the British labour movement at the forefront of resistance to fascism in the West. Quite how this resistance was to be made effective remained, however, a subject of bitter dispute between left and right until 1939.

The campaign for a United Front against fascism was initiated by the Communist Party in 1933. At first this meant little more than unity with the disaffiliated rump of the ILP, a tactic clearly intended to recruit as many members of the disintegrating party as possible. During 1934, however, the Soviet Union joined the League of Nations, and French and Spanish Communists negotiated electoral alliances with other left-wing parties. Following the Seventh Congress of the Communist International in 1935, the British Communist Party renewed its request for affiliation to the Labour Party. In the summer of 1936 the victory of the Blum Popular Front Government in France and the fascist rebellion against the Spanish Republic added further fuel to United Front demands. The left won a quarter of the votes at the 1936 Labour Party conference in favour of Communist affiliation. A similar vote was cast against the leadership's support of Government policy in denying arms to the Spanish Government. It was widely believed on the left that a fascist victory in Spain would make a new world war inevitable. At the same time an association of Constituency Labour Parties was formed to campaign against the domination of the party by predominantly right-wing union leaders. In an attempt to draw these diverse currents together, Stafford Cripps and the Socialist League patched together a new United Front campaign in January 1937 in association with the Communists, the ILP, the Left Book Club (established in the summer of 1936) and *Tribune* (founded as an organ of the United Front campaign itself). In a series of enthusiastic meetings the left sought unity around a programme of defence of the Spanish Republic, opposition to rearmament by the Tory Government, support for the struggles of the unemployed and the affiliation of both Communist and Independent Labour Parties to the Labour Party.

Far from being persuaded by the rise of facism of the need for unity on the left, the Labour leadership took its stance on the defence of democracy against dictatorship whether of right or left. While, in the later thirties they were willing to accept Stalin as an ally against Hitler – Stalin, after all, did not threaten their control of the labour movement – they remained adamantine in refusing to co-operate with the British Communists or the Socialist League. The United Front campaign of January 1937 was launched by the Socialist League in defiance of a ban on joint work with the Communists. Predictably the Labour Party enforced its discipline, banning the League and forcing its members to choose between disbanding their organisation or expulsion. Encouraged by the Communists, who had more use for sympathisers inside than outside the Labour Party, the League chose wisdom as the better part of valour and dissolved in May 1937. Subsequently the leadership combined repression with conciliation. The Constituency Parties were allowed to elect their own representatives to the National Executive. This enabled Cripps and some other left-wingers to secure election. At the same time the right persuaded the party to abandon its opposition to rearmament, making much play with the contradiction, more apparent than real, between the demand for 'Arms to Spain' and 'no arms for Britain'.*

The Socialist League proved easy game for the Labour establishment. But where the United Front had tougher roots, official bans and prescriptions proved much less effective. All over the country Communists and Labour Party members worked closely together. Hundreds of workers, as well as the more celebrated poets, fought fascism in Spain. In South Wales a Council of Action established in

* Until 1937 the Parliamentary Party voted each year against the arms estimates. Opposition to rearmament as such was not the primary reason for this stance. In part it was a response to the enormous profits being made by defence contractors as the arms budget swelled. In 1938 Dalton remarked: 'We are making millionaires nearly as fast as we are making aeroplanes.'[5] More important, opposition to the estimates was justified on tactical grounds as the only way in which the party could make clear its dissent from Conservative foreign policy which appeared more likely to use British armaments in support of imperialist aims, than in the defence of democracy against fascism.

1936, and representative of all working-class organisations and parties, was a model for the United Front agitation. It drew on traditions of extra-parliamentary protest in the coalfield, and gave expression to a remarkable spirit of class solidarity evoked by events in Spain. The disciplinary action which destroyed the Socialist League in 1937 had no discernible effect on the South Wales Council of Action or on its equivalents in other parts of the country.

The failure of the United Front campaign persuaded the anti-fascist movement to reconsider its strategy. Fascism could only be stopped by a military alliance of Britain, France and the Soviet Union. Since unity on the left in Britain had failed to secure this, increasing emphasis came to be placed on the building of a much broader Popular Front. Already in 1936 there were voices, strongest in the Co-operative Party, calling for a Popular Front, on the model of Blum's socialist-radical coalition Government in France. From the end of 1937 the Communist Party put its growing weight behind such demands. Popular Frontist politics implied acceptance of the idea, previously denied by many supporters of the United Front, that bourgeois democracies could withstand fascism, and that the defence of democracy should take precedence over the struggle for socialism. The central strategic preoccupation of the Popular Front campaign was to engineer a split in the Conservative Party – signs of which were not lacking, especially following the resignation of the Foreign Secretary, Anthony Eden, in February 1938 – which would enable Labour to enter a coalition government with anti-appeasement Conservatives and Liberals.

The Popular Front campaign of 1937–8 met with resistance both from the left and the right of the labour movement. Doubts about the reliability of the Soviet Union as an ally against fascism were fed by the show trials in Moscow, and reports of the less than fraternal behaviour of the Communists in Spain. After a bitter struggle on the *Tribune*, which ended in the sacking of the ex-Socialist League editor William Mellor, the paper of the Labour left threw its support behind the Popular Front and allowed the Communists to censor criticism of the USSR. The apparent readiness of Popular Front supporters to subordinate class struggle to anti-fascist unity evoked a deeper anxiety among some socialists. George Orwell denounced 'the nauseous spectacle of bishops, Communists, cocoa-magnates, publishers, duchesses and Labour MPs marching arm in arm to the tune of *Rule Britannia*.'[6] In a more analytical vein, the ILPer Fenner Brockway condemned imperialist peace and imperialist war with equal venom, arguing that the socialist movement was in no position to determine how long the former would last, or when the latter would begin. The pursuit of peace in a capitalist world was a delusion. The proper task for the working-class movement was relentlessly to fight capitalism, whether in peace or in war, not to seek to make anti-fascist alliances with it. This was a bleak and comfortless doctrine, whose appeal was limited to those more puritanical socialists who could not bring themselves to enter the ambiguous and treacherous territory of Popular Front politics.

The Labour leadership opposed the Popular Front on rather different grounds, mobilising labourist sentiment in defence of 'our traditional independence', and urging members to fight fascism by working for a Labour victory at the next General Election, due in 1940. An alliance with the Communists, they argued, would do nothing to enhance Labour's chance of victory in that election. This cut little ice with Popular Front campaigners, who saw no evidence in bye-election results that Labour could win the election in any case, and felt that the pace of fascist advance demanded a more immediate response. Cold-shouldered by the Labour Party, the Popular Front campaign petered out in frustration by the summer of 1938. However, Labour's rejection of the strategy underlying it was a good deal less absolute than appeared on the surface. The party was clear in its opposition to appeasement and support for a Russian alliance as the cornerstone of an alternative foreign policy. The National Executive declared its readiness to enter a coalition government if the preservation of peace and democracy depended upon it. Privately the leadership was ready to drive wedges into the Conservative Party in the event of a real internal crisis on the Government benches. The rapid swing of public opinion against appeasement that followed the momentary peace-in-our-time euphoria of Munich in the autumn of 1938, created conditions for a new Labour Party offensive, Popular Frontist in all but name – and, of course, in its enduring rejection of Communist overtures.

The success of two Popular Front candidates at bye-elections late in 1938 persuaded Cripps to launch one last quixotic effort – leading to the expulsion of himself, Nye Bevan and a few others from the party. They badly misjudged their moment, for in March 1939 Hitler's invasion of Prague forced Chamberlain, in public at least, to abandon the appeasement policy. This was a victory of sorts for the Popular Front agitation, since fear of an alliance between disgruntled Tory backbenchers and the Labour Party had as much to do with Chamberlain's change of course as any genuine rethinking of his belief in the possibility of reaching an enduring accommodation with Nazism. During the closing months of peace the Labour leaders denounced the absurdity of Chamberlain's offer of guarantees to Eastern European states against further Nazi aggression unaccompanied by any serious effort to secure the military alliance with the Soviet Union that alone could make those guarantees plausible.

It was in the politics of the Popular Front (in all but name) that the labour movement found the lever necessary to shift the weight of Tory hegemony. In 1914, taken by surprise, Labour had committed itself to the war effort while asking virtually nothing in return. This time they were determined to strike a harder bargain. From the spring of 1939, as Chamberlain shuffled reluctantly into war, the Labour Party offered to collaborate in the construction of a new war economy, but only on condition that Labour be admitted to positions of real power. The appeasers believed that a new world war would destroy the containment of labour engineered by Stanley Baldwin in the 1920s. This only served to reinforce their refusal to plan seriously for war. And they were right. When Chamberlain was ousted in May 1940 the Baldwinite solution to the 'rise of labour' finally disintegrated.

Notes

1   M. Foot, *Aneurin Bevan*, London 1966, p. 135.
2   E. Barry, *Nationalisation in British Politics*, London 1965, p. 341.
3   W. Citrine, *Men and Work*, London 1964, p. 300.
4   Barry, *op. cit*, p. 321.
5   R.P. Shay, *British Rearmament in the Thirties, Politics and Profits*, Princeton 1977, p. 260.
6   G. Orwell, review in *New English Weekly*, 17 February 1938, reprinted in S. Orwell and I. Angus (ed), *The Collected Essays, Journalism and Letters of George Orwell*, vol. 1, Harmondsworth 1970, p. 339.

10

Labour and the nation, 1939–51

The Second World War opened up new possibilities for the labour movement. In 1940 Labour was brought into the Coalition Government. In 1945 a landslide electoral victory put the first majority Labour Government in power. Full employment stimulated trade union growth, the density of union organisation rising from around 30 per cent in 1938 to 45 per cent ten years later. The proportion of wage-earning women in trade unions doubled during the war, but fell back again after 1945. After the war a sizeable slice of British industry was taken into public ownership, and significant advances in social welfare provision, which had been improvised or promised during the war, were established on a permanent basis by the Labour Government. There was little reason to doubt – before the re-emergence of mass unemployment in the 1970s – that the events of the 1940s had given rise to an irreversible change for the better in the position of the working class in Britain.

But there were limits. Those who in 1945 thought they were on the threshold of a gradual transition to socialism were to be sadly disappointed. Part of the explanation for this is to be found in international events. From the outset the Labour Government, caught up in the profound economic, imperial and diplomatic crisis created for British capitalism by the Second World War, acted from hand to mouth with little overall sense of direction. Just as important, though perhaps more difficult to pin down precisely, were the weaknesses in the popular mobilisation underlying Labour's victory in 1945. The curious political conditions of 'People's War', of the war against Fascism, made possible a major shift to the left in popular attitudes, but at the same time involved tensions and ambiguities which served to undermine the capacity of the forces of the left to sustain and exploit the opportunities which had seemed to be opening up towards the end of the war.

I

For nine months after the declaration of war nothing much changed. Believing the country to be secure from direct attack, Chamberlain proceeded unhurriedly with rearmament, and continued to hope for a negotiated settlement with Germany. The parties declared an electoral truce, but Labour declined the offer of participation in a coalition government. The unions renounced strikes, and Whitehall showed a greater readiness to accept union representation on advisory boards. But there were still a million unemployed in the spring of 1940, and little had been done towards the construction of a war economy. Then Hitler put an end to the 'phoney war'. During April and May 1940 Nazi armies overran Norway, Denmark and Holland, Belgium and Northern France. By 3 June the evacuation of the British Expeditionary Force from Dunkirk was complete. On 17 June France surrendered. In August the Luftwaffe began its battle for Britain in earnest. Chamberlain was an early victim of the German offensive. Following a backbench Tory revolt over the loss of Norway, Churchill emerged as Prime Minster in a Coalition Government on the day the Germans invaded the Low Countries. Clement Atlee and Anthony Greenwood represented Labour in the five-man War Cabinet. Ernest Bevin moved direct from the TGWU to the Ministry of Labour – a decisive recognition of the key role organised labour must play in the war effort.

The new Government responded to the emergency with a mass of improvisations which, between them, laid the basis for the building of an integrated war economy. As in the First World War, the attempt to plan a private capitalist economy necessitated a large measure of business participation in the machinery of control. Trade associations were authorised to act as state agencies in rationing materials, fixing output, laying down prices and allocating markets. Nevertheless, centralisation went a good deal further than on the previous occasion. By the early months of 1941 Keynes and other outside recruits to the civil service had pioneered the first official statistics of national income and expenditure. This provided the basis for the 1941 Budget which marked the substitution of Keynesian management of overall demand for the Treasury's traditional narrow approach to fiscal policy merely as a means of financing government expenditure. But most important was the extension of labour controls that provided the Government with the means of direct, physical allocation of resources between the various sectors of the war economy. Manpower planning meant that relations between trade union organisation and the state, mediated through the dominating person of Bevin, were even more critical to the war effort than had been the case in 1914–18.

Bevin deflected Treasury pressure for statutory wage controls, which the trade union leaders saw as the most dangerous threat to their power. Instead the Government contented itself with 'Order 1305' which gave statutory back-up to the no-strike agreement between the TUC and the British Employers Federation and established a National Arbitration Tribunal to handle disputes that could not be settled within existing collective bargaining procedures. The Government looked, not without result, to the trade union leaders to use their influence to moderate wage demands. In return food subsidies, price controls and rationing were used to hold down the cost of living. Over the war as a whole there was a marked egalitarian shift in the distribution of income, both as between classes and within the working class itself. Property incomes and salaries were squeezed, while many lower paid sections of the working class improved their standard of living. This was, in part, a spontaneous result of full employment, of the shift of workers from the low-paid service sector into manufacturing industry, and of the influx of married women into the labour force. But it also reflected deliberate government action of prices and taxation.

In the Essential Works Order (March 1941) Bevin took power to prevent workers leaving their jobs and to fine workers for absenteeism and indiscipline. Following the thorough registration of the labour force, both male and female, during 1941, Bevin made increasing use of powers to direct labour where it was most needed – into the mines, onto isolated construction sites, and so on. These extensive measures of industrial conscription were acceptable partly because Bevin linked them with the vigorous promotion of collective bargaining and trade union recognition. Employers not conforming to trade union conditions were denied the protection of the Essential Works Order. Statutory intervention to fix minimum wages and conditions in poorly organised industries was extended rapidly during the war. One such intervention, the Catering Wages Act of 1943, became a test case of Labour influence in the Coalition when 116 Tory back-benchers broke ranks in protest against what they saw as the advancing dictatorship of Bevin.

Working-class co-operation in the war effort was further buttressed by advances in welfare provisions, many of them improvised to meet the immediate necessities of war. Cheap school meals for all children replaced the pauper provision available previously, partly to facilitate the entry of women into war industry. Day nurseries were provided for the same reason. A new concern with national efficiency and military potential eased the path to improvements in pre-natal and infant welfare services. The Blitz promoted the development of universal emergency housing and health provision. 1941 saw the abolition of the most hated instrument of public economy – the household means test. In 1943 the Cabinet indicated its acceptance of the main principles of the Beveridge Report, which outlined a major extension of social security, and assumed the creation of full employment, family allowance and a National Health Service. The permanance, in one form or another, of the quasi-corporatist alliance of state, business and labour, was accepted both by important sections of business opinion, and by the TUC. The TUC's 1944 Report on Reconstruction sought to revive the Whitleyist project of 1917–18 – advocating the establishment of representative joint councils to determine general policy in private industry. Most trade union leaders, at the end of the war, would have been happy to accept the definition of their situation offered by Political and Economic Planning:

> Organised labour is no longer a force in opposition to a social system controlled by and in the interest of the employing class; it is an integral part of a new social system. . . . Instead of fighting against the political and economic machine, organised labour is now in a position to exert over the machine an ever-increasing degree of influence.[1]

Organised labour collaborated in the war effort believing not only that a war against Fascism must be a just war, but also that national mobilisation involved the established ruling class in a genuine surrender of traditional privileges and powers. The real advances made towards a more egalitarian distribution of income, and in the provision of state welfare services, lent plausibility to this view. Ernest Bevin observed that:

> civilisation cannot survive if it rests upon a propertyless proletariat. That is why I have urged that if our country is not big enough to solve our problems by means of the land, like the peasant countries can, you have got to find a substitute, and

the substitute is the vested interest of social security within
your own state in which all shall participate.[2]

Bevin's expectation of the growth of a new sense of working-class
citizenship, of working-class participation in the nation, was not
disappointed. Public opinion polls and Home Office surveys of
popular morale revealed a readiness to accept the burdens of war
which resulted not only from patriotism or anti-fascism but also
from the belief that something approaching equality of sacrifice –
'fair shares for all' – was in fact being achieved.

Yet the ideology of the 'People's War' cannot be seen as an
unambiguous legitimation of wartime corporatism, or merely as a
solvent of class antagonism. 'Nation' and 'class' were related in
more complex ways than that. The 'Dunkirk spirit', beloved of
corporatist politicians of all parties in the 1960s and 1970s, was
double-edged. It combined a determination to defend Britain
against Nazi attack with a bitter resentment of the incompetence in
high places revealed by the military débacle on the Continent. Following Dunkirk, workers put in grotesque hours to produce aircraft for the coming Battle of Brtain. But at the same time *Guilty
Men*, a leftist tract issued at the height of the crisis, found a mass
audience because it put into print the hatred felt by soldiers return-
ing from France for the Establishment which had led them to disaster. George Orwell was not alone in perceiving a revolutionary
spirit in Britain. During the autumn the Communist Party, over-
coming the unpopularity caused by its opposition to the war, was
able to focus working-class unrest in the factories, and over inadequate air-raid precautions around a sizeable campaign – culminating in the People's Convention of January 1941.

Undoubtedly, the mass of working people supported the war,
especially after Hitler invaded the Soviet Union in June 1941.
Nevertheless, industrial unrest increased. The numbers of strikes
grew steadily over the years, exceeding the previous peak year
(1920) in 1943. Most of these strikes were small and short, demonstration strikes rather than pitched battles. Even so the average
number of days lost per year over the war as a whole was well
above the level of the 1930s. The main trouble spot was mining,
where large-scale strike action in 1942 and again in 1944 reflected,
beyond the immediate wage issues involved, a rapid increase in the
accident rate, and the frustrations of a workforce tied to the pits by
the Essential Works Order and incensed by the refusal of the Coali-

tion Government to move beyond a half-hearted and ineffective system of state control of the industry to outright nationalisation. The miners were determined to use their wartime strength to prevent any return to the desperate conditions created by private ownership in the industry between the wars.

In engineering, the other main locus of strike activity, it was the re-emergence of shop steward organisation that held the centre of the stage. In the upheavals of wartime, shop stewards played an important part as unofficial social workers, helping with income tax forms, housing and transport problems, as well as representing workers in the factories. In many instances they gained a high degree of control on the shop floor. 'We ran the place' is a common memory of wartime shop stewards, especially in the aircraft industry.

There was resistance to the introduction of women into male preserves, but in general dilution proceeded smoothly. From 1943 women were finally admitted to the Engineering union. Much of the strike activity arose not, as in the First World War, from the defence of craft practices, but from the relatively unorganised militancy of new entrants into the industry – apprentices demanding better pay and a more secure status; teenage girls drafted into munitions production and resentful of the imposition of industrial discipline.

After the Russians came into the war, the Communist Party, the strongest organised force among the shop stewards, swung around to a passionate advocacy of war production and opposition to strikes. During the next 15 months around 50,000 people joined the Communist Party. This growth reflected both the immense popularity of the Soviet war effort, and the Communists' success in combining support for the war effort with a continuing commitment to class struggle at home. Their campaign for increased production was accompanied by an offensive against managerial prerogative. In striking contrast to more recent times, opinion polls in the autumn of 1941 showed that the public were inclined to blame production hold-ups, not on the unions, but on managerial malpractice. The Communist Party proclaimed its support for the Churchill Government. But, at a time when Labour saw its membership of the Government as ruling out any public agitation on war strategy, the Communists put themselves at the head of the campaign for the opening of a Second Front in Europe – one of the largest political agitations ever seen in Britain. Communist success was, however, shortlived. As the end of the war came in sight thoughts of reconstruction began to predominate over anti-fascism in the popular mind. The Communist Party, reluctant to risk national anti-fascist unity by raising demands for a socialist recon- struction policy, found its politics increasingly diverging from the tide of working-class opinion.

The publication of the Beveridge Report in December 1942, fol- lowed immediately on the news of the British victory at El Alamein. It now began to seem possible that the war would be won, and the Report served to crystallise popular demands for a new social order when it was. Before the end of the month opinion polls revealed that 95 per cent of the population had heard of the Report, and 90 per cent approved of it. After two months of silence – the Tories fought hard against any firm commitment to implementing Beveridge's proposals – the Cabinet finally announced its grudging and partial acceptance of the Report. Ninety-seven Labour MPs voted against the Government in an unprecedented display of frust- ration with the timidity and deference shown by Labour Ministers to Churchillian dictation. The Beveridge debate gave notice that the party truce would eventually collapse under pressure from back- bench Labour opinion. For the time being however the revolt was an isolated event and the Parliamentary Party soon settled back into its habitual loyalty. A small band of leftists led by Bevan kept running fire of criticism against the Government. But the party as a whole was trapped by the political truce. With local organisation weak through disuse, and depleted by conscription and the mobil- isation of women for war production, the Labour Party could do little to accommodate the emerging radicalism of the latter years of the war. One result of this was the temporary prominence of Com- mon Wealth, a new political party predominantly composed of idealistic middle-class socialists which achieved a series of startling bye-election successes toppling Conservative candidates who would otherwise have been returned unopposed. Commonwealth had no future as a political party. Its success depended entirely on the continued existence of the truce between the major parties. But it pointed the way forward to 1945.

After the Normandy landings in June 1944 the defeat of Hitler was clearly in sight. In December armed conflict broke out between the Greek resistance movement and British troops occupying Athens. This precipitated the biggest crisis in the House of Com- mons since the Beveridge debate. For British socialists – apart from that large section tragically cut off from the realities of the international situation by the ideological constructions of Stalinism – it was becoming inescapably clear that the purpose served by coalition was less and less the maintenance of national unity in the war against Hitler, more and more the silencing of left-wing opposition to Churchill's plans for the restoration of reactionary regimes in liberated Europe. The new militancy of Labour's rank and file was clearly revealed in the Party Conference in December 1944 which returned the strongest critic of the Labour Ministers, Nye Bevan, to the constituency party section of the National Executive. This same conference overwhelmingly rejected the proposals of the leadership for post-war reconstruction, proposals which omitted any specific commitment to nationalisation. Instead they voted for a composite motion moved by Ian Mikado which called for 'the transfer to public ownership of land, large-scale building, heavy industry, and all forms of banking, transport and fuel and power.'[3] The nationalisation proposals of Labour's 1945 election programme stemmed from this resolution, though they fell a long way short of it.

The experience of Coalition Government captivated Atlee, Bevin and other Labour leaders. Despite the clear evidence of militancy in the party and of anti-Tory feeling in the country, these leaders continued to believe that it would be impossible for Labour to win a post-war election against the national saviour, Churchill. Right to the end they were planning for a continuation of Coalition Government during a period of reconstruction to follow the end of the war in Europe. When Churchill offered such an arrangement after the German surrender in May, Atlee and Bevin wanted to accept. They were overruled by the National Executive. Dragged unwillingly out of Coalition, they entered the election campaign in the summer of 1945 with some trepidation. In fact there was a landslide. Labour gained nearly 48 per cent of the total poll; the Conservatives less than 40 per cent. Bastions of reaction in the London suburbs, in agricultural East Anglia, and in the working-class Tory strongholds of the West Midlands fell to Labour. Atlee went to Downing Street as Prime Minister of the first majority Labour Government, with a massive lead of 147 seats over all other parties. A moment of euphoria was understandable. But the difficulty Labour's rank and file had experienced in persuading their leaders to enter the fight at all should have alerted them to the dangers that lay ahead.

II

In 1944 a Treasury report remarked: 'The time and energy and thought which we are all giving to the Brave New World, is wildly disproportionate to what is being given to the Cruel Real World.'[4] If the war generated the social optimism which swept Labour to power in 1945, it also presented the new Government with a gigantic economic problem. Invisible income had fallen due to the selling off of foreign investments and the destruction of British merchant shipping. Wartime borrowings had hugely increased Britain's indebtedness. During the war American financial aid had made it possible for British industry to abandon exports in favour of armament production. Consequently by 1945 the volume of British exports was only one-third of the pre-war total. Less than 2 per cent of the labour force was engaged in export industry, compared with nearly 10 per cent in 1939. Cruelest of all was the sudden and unexpected ending of American 'lend-lease' aid in August 1945. In the long term the lending objective of the Government had to be the export drive. Nothing took priority over this. Controls inherited from wartime were used to hold back domestic consumption and to ensure high levels of capital investment. 'Austerity' was successful in laying the basis for British participation in the long boom of the 1950s. Meanwhile, however, the Government faced a series of acute balance of payments crises.

In 1945 there seemed little alternative to soliciting a new loan on whatever terms the Americans might see fit to offer. The terms, negotiated by Maynard Keynes, were harsh. The interests of American capitalism, which had emerged from the world war with an industrial dominance equal to Britain's in the mid-nineteenth century, lay in the liberalisation of the world economy. While Britain was allowed to retain measures of import control and bulk purchase arrangements, her freedom to bargain on tariffs was severely restricted. More important, the Americans insisted on a commitment to remove exchange controls and to make sterling freely convertible within twelve months of the take-up of the loan. This left the Government an impossibly short period in which to solve the basic economic weaknesses underlying the balance of payments problem.

Despite these inauspicious circumstances, the Government proceeded during its first two years in office to put through a major programme of social reforms. In 1946 legislation on National

Insurance and on the National Health Service gave concrete form to the reconstruction promises of the wartime Coalition. Compared with the situation in the 1930s these were major advances. Compared with what a Conservative Government might have been expected to do to redeem wartime pledges had one been returned in 1945 they were significant achievements. But judged against the expectations of many socialists and some Labour voters, both measures left a good deal to be desired. The National Insurance Act failed to achieve Beveridge's objective of providing non-means tested benefits as of right, since benefit rates were set substantially below the real value that Beveridge, estimating susbsistence needs, had recommended during the war. As a result, large numbers of claimants were forced into dependence on means tested National Assistance benefits – the old poor law in a new guise.

The National Health Service was widely seen as a victory for socialist principle. In the mind of its creator, Aneurin Bevan, the establishment of a free and comprehensive health service, based on the principle of need, not on ability to pay, was a milestone in the progressive articulation of the Socialist Commonwealth within the shell of a capitalist society. In practice, however, the scheme did not go significantly beyond what had been accepted in principle by all parties during the war. The introduction of the National Health Service was the occasion of much political sound and fury. But this had more to do with the collective hysteria of the doctors, and the opportunism of the Tories – who had identified Bevan as the socialist Achilles heel of the Government and were determined to break him – than with any merits or demerits of the Act. The doctors convinced themselves that they were fighting the introduction of a full-time salaried service. In reality Bevan had never proposed this, despite the fact that it had long been Labour Party policy. Similarly he appeased the consultants by allowing pay-beds in National Health hospitals. Bevan displayed both nerve and skill in his war with the British Medical Association. It was only at the eleventh hour that the doctors capitulated, agreeing not to strangle the Health Service at birth by a general boycott. It seems likely that Bevan was not too distressed by all this noisy resistance, since it provided a useful cover for his own strategic retreat from the party's policy of a salaried service. His achievement, one Labour MP remarked, lay in 'the way he applied the anaesthetic to supporters on his own side, making them believe things they had opposed almost all their lives.'[5]

Bevan's decision not to arouse further opposition by including provision for birth control under the Health Service was symptomatic of a general weakness in Labour's social policy – its failure to make inroads into the subordinate and dependent position of women. The new social security provision assumed such dependency and tended to reinforce it. The important advances in state provision for children's needs which had been made during the war – school milk and meals, provision of baby and infant foods – were continued. And family allowances had been introduced just before the 1945 election. But the Labour Government, despite its concern to increase production, shared trade union prejudice against accepting the permanence of married women in the workforce. Consequently it neglected the needs of working mothers and allowed the whole war-time apparatus of day nursery and creche provision for pre-school children to lapse. Another key area of weakness in the Government's social policy was housing. Almost all the houses built under the Labour Government were in the public sector. But faced with the legacy of wartime destruction, a seriously run-down building industry, shortages of vital materials, and a post-war boom in marriages, babies and expectations about housing standards, it is not surprising that the Government fell far short of meeting demand. Housing had been the leading issue in the 1945 election. The Government's failure here led to bitterness which, at one moment in late 1946, seemed likely to erupt in a rash of popular direct action, squatting.

In the field of nationalisation the Government fulfilled its pledges, and quickly. Acts nationalising the Bank of England and the mines were passed in 1946. The railways, road haulage and inland waterways followed in 1947. Only iron and steel, the subject of a major row within the Cabinet in 1947, was delayed. To many in the Labour Party, as well as to some of its opponents, it seemed as though the basis for a gradual transition to socialism was being laid. The nationalisation of 20 per cent of productive industry represented the first step towards bringing the commanding heights of the economy under public control. In fact no such denouement was intended by most of those responsible for carrying through the programme. The degree of public ownership undertaken by the Labour Government was not significantly greater than in several other Western European countries after the war. Most of the industries taken over were run-down and in need of reorganisation and major injections of capital from the state. Compensation was paid

at a generous rate for these decaying assets, saddling the nationalised industries from the start with a huge burden of debt. The main
effect of nationalisation was to shift responsibility for loss-making
industries to the state, while releasing private capital for reinvest-
ment in profitable and expanding sectors of industry.

The Government make no attempt to operate the new public
sector as a lever to control the economy as a whole. Specific
demands for nationalisation had accumulated on the Labour
Party's shopping list piecemeal – in response to this union's pressure, or that industry's notorious inefficiency. The programme
therefore had no overall coherence. The failure to nationalise joint
stock banking rendered the nationalisation of the Bank of England
largely irrelevant to securing Government control over finance. The
failure to nationalise any export industries left the Government
entirely dependent on the private sector for the fulfilment of its
most important objective, the export drive. In deciding the form of
nationalisation no provision was made for the ongoing involvement
of organised workers in the control of public industry. Rather, with
the full support of the trade union leadership whose own authority
would have been threatened by real measures of workers' control,
the Government appointed representatives of the business and
managerial class to the Boards of nationalised industries, together
with a sprinkling of retired trade union officials. Moreover the
Boards, so composed, were given a large measure of autonomy
from direct ministerial control. Had the Government been attempting to fashion, in the nationalised industries, a weapon capable of
breaking capitalist resistance to its economic plans, it could hardly
have devised a less suitable instrument. But this was never its purpose.

There was some serious thinking, particularly in those unions
where the Communist Party was influential, about the implications
of economic planning in a mixed economy. But, most trade union
leaders were more concerned to defend free collective bargaining
than to promote socialism, and the Government made no serious
attempt at planning. The maintenance of wartime physical controls
helped the Government to contain inflationary pressures without
resorting to the monetary restrictions which would have threatened
full employment and the general level of economic activity. But
wartime controls had been designed to ration scarce supplies on an
ad hoc basis, rather than to allocate resources in conformity with a
long-term, integrated economic plan. The Labour Government

took over this machinery unchanged, merely substituting the export drive for arms production as the key goal of the system. Nothing was done to overcome the fragmentation of 'planning' between rival government departments or to establish an economic general staff. Moreover, the machinery of control itself was left in the hands of business and the traditional civil service: men who viewed the controls as an unavoidable, but happily temporary evil, to be dismantled as soon as normal trading conditions were restored. There is little doubt that the majority of the Labour Cabinet shared this view.

III

The inadequacies of economic planning contributed to a succession of crises during 1947 which marked the turning point for the Government. An exceptionally severe winter, together with a chronic coal shortage and bad planning produced an alarming economic collapse. Transport broke down, factories closed, unemployment shot up to nearly two million. The fuel crisis, together with a sharp rise in American price levels which reduced the value of Britain's borrowed dollars, made it virtually certain that the removal of exchange controls – set for July in the terms agreed for the American loan – would be a disaster. The Cabinet, following Treasury advice, decided nevertheless to meet the July deadline. Disaster followed, and the Government, humiliated, had no option but to reintroduce exchange controls.

The anxiety of the Labour left about the general direction of Government policy first came to a head in November 1946 when fifty-three Labour MPs put down an amendment to the King's Speech calling for a recasting of foreign policy in order to promote 'a democratic and constructive Socialist alternative to an otherwise inevitable conflict between American capitalism and Soviet Communism.'[6] At the end of the war prospects had seemed bright for the emergence of a socialist Europe as a third force between the two super-powers. But in foreign affairs the Labour leadership proved quite impervious to demands for a break from Churchillian policies. Instead the Government declared the continuity of its policy with that of the wartime coalition, and, in the name of anti-communism, lent its weight to the repression of socialist possibilities in liberated Europe. Ernest Bevin, now Foreign Secretary, was, beyond all reason, obsessed with the Russian menace. The organising principle of his diplomacy was the twin nightmare of the Red Army attacking the Middle East oilfields or even the channel ports, accompanied by an American return to its pre-war isolation from European affairs. Grossly exaggerating both possibilities, Bevin cast British policy in a Cold War mould from the start, thus helping to accelerate the breakdown of the wartime Grand Alliance. At the same time, as the left pointed out, his baseless anxiety about American isolation greatly restricted the room for manoeuvre in the critical negotiations with the Americans over economic aid. Without a fundamental break from Bevin's foreign policy there could be no prospect of a sustained socialist offensive at home.

In November 1946 the left challenge fizzled out without even being put to the vote. But in March 1947 a revolt of seventy-two Labour MPs achieved a short-lived victory, reducing the period proposed for military conscription from 18 to 12 months. (This cut was restored before the Act actually came into effect, following a threat of collective resignation by the Chiefs of Staff.) In April the 'Keep Left' group was formed – the nearest the Labour left came in this period to establishing an organised presence in the Parliamentary Party. Government strategy was attacked for its anti-communism and deferrence to the Americans; for the failure to tackle the balance of payments problem directly by a much more rapid withdrawal of British troops from Europe and the Empire; and, on the domestic front, for the absence of any attempt to construct the machinery necessary for economic planning. But no general campaign for an alternative socialist strategy developed from this initiative.

Instead, over the critical summer of 1947, the energies of the left were fully engaged in a campaign to prevent Atlee and Herbert Morrison from abandoning the Government's commitment to nationalise the steel industry. It had always been apparent that there would be more capitalist resistance to the public ownership of steel than to any of the other nationalisation measures proposed by the Government. Keeping steel nationalisation in the programme was, therefore, a real victory for the left. But, as later events were to show, success on this single issue could in no way compensate for the failure of the left to mount an effective challenge to the overall direction of government policy.

Underlying this failure was the uncritical loyalty to the Labour

Government displayed by the mass of organised labour after the war. The TUC accepted the continued illegality of strikes, and although unofficial strikes continued there was no post-war upsurge as after 1918. The peak year for working days lost through strike action in the 1940s remained 1944. It seems that the euphoria of 1945, sustained by the vigorous legislative programme pursued by the Government during its first two years in office, blinded the left to the need to organise. Bevan, during the war the pre-eminent leader of the left, was now silenced as a voice in opposition. The National Health Service kept him imprisoned within the Government, first by the opportunity to create it, then by the need to defend it against attacks from within the Cabinet. He was neither able, nor inclined, to give a lead to factional activity by his back-bench supporters against the overall strategy of the Government. In 1945 G.D.H. Cole was one of the very few British socialists who clearly perceived the incompatibility between accepting the terms of the Keynes loan and any policy of socialist reconstruction in Europe. Even the Communists, in line with the agreement on spheres of influence in Europe, supported the loan. In advocating rejection of American aid on the terms offered Cole found himself completely isolated, a voice in the wilderness. Eighteen months later, when the Keep Left group was organised, it was too late. Whatever opportunities had existed for a socialist reconstruction in the disturbed conditions of post-war Europe by 1947, these were fast vanishing in the hardening division of the continent between East and West. The Government's desperate need for further dollar credits was eventually met in the European Recovery Programme negotiated following General Marshall's offer of massive American aid to Europe in June 1947. Marshall Aid was clearly designed as a weapon in the Cold War and it put a sharp end to any lingering prospect of the emergence of a third force, democratic socialist, Europe.

From 1947 the Government turned increasingly towards management of the economy by monetary methods rather than by physical controls: these were abandoned as quickly as continuing shortages would permit. The one innovation attempted in the machinery of control was the setting up of Development Councils – tripartite consultative bodies on an industry basis intended to foster productivity, innovation and co-operation between business, trade unionism and the state. The councils, which had minimal powers of intervention in their industries, had more to do with realising the corporatist dream of 'industrial self-government' than with facilitating effective economic planning by the state. In fact hardly any Councils were established because businessmen refused to co-operate. Meanwhile Treasury influence in economic policy reasserted itself, with a deflationary budget in the autumn of 1947 and a cut back in the housing programme. In March 1948, in line with the new emphasis on the danger of inflation, the Government gained acceptance for a policy of voluntary wage restraint – though only at the price of a continuation of food subsidies at a substantially higher level than they had originally intended. There were many loopholes in the policy, and it led to a rapid widening of the gap between nationally negotiated wage rates and actual earnings. Nevertheless, for the next two years, it appears to have had some effect in holding down wage rises. The net result of Labour's retreat after 1947 was to halt the trend towards greater equality in the distribution of income that had emerged during the war. From 1948 the share of wages in the national income began to fall.

Opposition to wage restraint within the unions was led by the Communist Party, which had reversed its pro-Government position (in line with international developments) towards the end of 1947. The Labour machine was quick to react, expelling the so-called 'crypto-communist' MPs in April 1948. These expulsions, and the atmosphere of witch-hunt which they promoted, helped to silence the non-communist left in the Labour Party. In October 1948 Arthur Deakin, Bevin's successor at the TGWU, launched a major attack on Communist influence in the unions. The General Council called on affiliated bodies to exclude Communists from office. Some unions, like the NUGMW already did so. In others – notably the AEU and the NUM – the political balance was too close to permit such a manoeuvre. But the TGWU sacked nine Communist full-time officials, including Bert Papworth, the busmen's leader, who also lost his seat on the General Council. Full-time officials were vulnerable; but Deakin was unable to crush the unofficial dockers' movement which conducted a major series of strikes during the late 1940s.

The crisis year of 1947 was also the turning point in Conservative and business attitudes to the Labour Government. Cabinet disagreements over steel helped the opposition to present the decision to go ahead with nationalisation as a capitulation to the doctrinaire left. At the same time the Government's decision to delay the implementation of nationalisation until after the next General

Election, gave time for the steelmasters to organise anti-nationalisation propaganda on a very large scale, and encouraged other threatened groups to do likewise. In face of growing business hostility, the Government accelerated decontrol, while the Labour Party Executive protested its desire, after steel, to 'consolidate'. Labour's next term of office, they promised, would see no further significant extension of the public sector. Despite Marshall Aid, wage restraint, and a substantial growth of exports, the persistent weakness of the balance of payments led to another sterling crisis in the autumn of 1949. The Government overreacted, devaluing sterling by a massive 30 per cent. The effect of this on domestic prices undermined wage restraint – though the prospect of an imminent General Election enabled the General Council to hold the line on an even more restrictive policy for a few more months. The results of the election, held in February 1950, came as a shock to the Government. Although, in a very heavy poll, Labour won more votes than in 1945, the Conservatives increased their turn out a good deal more. Labour lost seats particularly in the residential suburbs of Southern England – a reflection of the frustration felt by middle-income groups squeezed by the egalitarian trend of the 1940s, and mobilised by the anti-statist demagogy of Churchill and his followers. Labour was returned, but with an overall majority of only six seats.

Over the next eighteen months a thoroughly demoralised Government slid towards defeat in an atmosphere of growing disunity within the movement. Steel nationalisation, though it went through, was emasculated by the resistance of steelmasters confident that a Conservative Government would shortly be able to return the industry to private ownership. At the TUC in the autumn of 1950 the General Council was defeated over wage restraint. Underlying this was a growing rank-and-file resentment at the degree to which the trade union establishment had placed loyalty to the Labour Government before the pursuit of their members' interests. Relations between organised labour and the Government were further worsened by the use of Order 1305 – which had been little employed since its introduction in 1940 – first against striking London Gasworkers, and then, in February 1951, against the leaders of the unofficial Port Workers' Committee. In a context of seething unrest in the docks, an Old Bailey jury refused to convict. A few months later the Order was dropped.

The outbreak of the Korean War in June 1950, and the consequent huge increase in armament spending, set the scene for a showdown between left and right within the Government. In his 1951 budget Hugh Gaitskell insisted on imposing charges on teeth and spectacles, despite Bevan's clear warning that he would regard this as a resigning issue. The saving – a mere £25 million – was insignificant compared with the inflated rearmament programme. But Gaitskell's purpose seems to have been served. Bevan, accompanied by Harold Wilson and John Freeman, resigned. This final purge of the left did nothing to improve Labour's electoral appeal. Faced with the prospect of a stormy Labour Party conference and a new balance of payments crisis, Atlee called a new General Election for October 1951. Despite everything, popular fears that a Conservative victory would mean a return to mass unemployment was sufficient to give Labour more votes and a higher percentage of the poll than ever before – or since. Nevertheless, the Conservatives were returned, due to changes in constituency boundaries which discriminated against Labour and a sharp reduction in the number of Liberal candidates.

In 1951 a senior civil servant summed up the record of the Atlee Government: '. . . it puts me in mind of nothing so much as the voyage of Columbus in 1492. You will recall that when Columbus set out he didn't know where he was going; when he arrived he didn't know where he was; and when he returned he didn't know where he had been.'[7] Much of the history of the Labour Party during the next ten years revolved around attempts to make sense of the record of the Atlee Government. Not the least of Labour's problems was to understand why it was that the Conservatives, most unexpectedly, proved both ready and able to run the new social order bequeathed to them from the upheavals of the 1940s.

Notes

1 Political and Economic Planning, *British Trade Unionism,* London 1948, p. 148.
2 Alan Bullock, *The Life and Times of Ernest Bevin,* vol. 2, London 1960, p. 71.
3 R. Miliband, *Parliamentary Socialism,* London 1972, p. 277.
4 W.K. Hancock and M.M. Gowing, *British War Economy,* London 1949, p. 542.
5 P. Addison, *The Road to 1945: British Politics and the Second World War,* London 1975, p. 273.
6 House of Commons, *Debates,* 18 November 1946, Col. 526.
7 A.A. Rogow and P. Shore, *The Labour Government and British Industry, 1945–1951,* Oxford 1955, p. 173.

11

The labour movement in crisis, 1951–74

After 1951 the labour movement entered into a long drawn out and, as yet, unresolved crisis. The number of Labour Party voters, which had increased in every General Election since 1910 (except 1931), fell from its peak of 14 million in 1951 to 11.5 million by 1979. Individual membership of the Labour Party fell from a high point of just over 1 million in 1952 to 630,000 by 1981. Trade union organisation, after twenty years of stagnation, resumed its growth in the 1970s. In 1974, for the first time, more than half of the occupied population belonged to trade unions. But whether this growth can be sustained in the 1980s, in the conditions of mass unemployment which seem likely to persist for some time, remains to be seen. Labour's crisis was not simply one of numbers. Underlying the long-term decline of the Labour Party was its failure to resolve the conflicts set up within working-class politics by the experience of Labour Governments administering the decline of British capitalism. On two occasions, in 1970 and 1979, these conflicts precipitated a sharp lurch to the right in British politics. In the early 1980s it seems clear that the construction of a socialist politics capable of taking on the crisis of British capitalism will require a fundamental rupture with many of the established structures and practices of the labour movement.

I

In the absence of a sustained working-class offensive, the reforms of the post-war Labour Government were quickly assimilated into the logic of a capitalist economy. But it was a much altered capitalism. Labour's reforms and, more important, the war itself had greatly accelerated the decline of the free-market economy. Apart from the denationalisation of steel and road transport, Conservative Governments made little attempt to undo the mixed economy, dismantle the social services or restore *laissez-faire*. Indeed, from the later

1950s the size of the public sector tended to grow regardless of which party was in power. During the 1940s business leaders, at least in the larger firms, had fully accepted the extension of state intervention which, in many ways was functional to their own drive towards large-scale integrated and planned production. They had little reason to fear that the growth of the state would seriously weaken their power. A state machine whose personnel – in the civil service, on the boards of nationalised industries, on innumerable advisory and consultative committees – was effectively merged with the financial and managerial elites represented no threat to the collective power of capital. Any possibility that it might do so was undermined further by the rapid development of multinational companies the scale of whose international dealings placed them well beyond the scope of effective Government regulation.

During the 1940s there had been a significant redistribution of post-tax incomes. But this did not continue, despite the greatly enhanced bargaining power of organised labour during the years of near full employment. Because they understood that the ability of strong trade unions to eat into the rate of profit threatened the central dynamic of economic growth in a capitalist economy, Governments set themselves to maintain profit levels rather than to pursue equality. The impact of taxation became steadily less progressive. Confronted with a long-term fall in the rate of profit, capital used its political leverage to compensate for declining pre-tax profits by reduced taxation on corporate income. The nationalised industries were run as a service to the private sector, providing an indirect subsidy to profits via cheap fuel and transport, and the Government subsidised private industry directly with cash grants, investment allowances, employment premiums etc. By 1971 these direct subsidies accounted for about 6.5 per cent of total Government expenditure — rather more than was spent on housing and about two-thirds of Health Service expenditure. In addition nearly 40 per cent of research and development costs in the private sector were financed by the Government. By the late 1960s nearly half the capital investment undertaken by private industry was being paid for by the state.

For all the state's interventions, however, British industry remained chronically inefficient. Between 1950 and the early 1980s industrial output in Britain has grown at approximately half the rate of her major competitors. One major cause of this failure was the 'stop-go' cycle. Recurrent balance of payments crises were met

with deflationary measures which restricted manufacturing investment and disrupted forward planning by business. The memory of
past glories hung heavy on successive British Governments, who
were reluctant to cut defence expenditure. Equally damaging was
the priority given by Governments to maintaining the value of sterling and its role as a reserve currency, a priority which reflected the
continuing predominance of financial over manufacturing interests
in the formation of economic policy. The root cause of recurrent
balance of payments crises was stagnating productivity and chronic
undercapitalisation in British manufacturing industry. Between
1960 and 1976 Britain's share of world manufacturing exports was
nearly halved. The British economy appeared to be caught in a
vicious circle which led from recurrent financial crises, to deflation,
to slow growth, to undercapitalisation, to export weakness, and so
back to crisis again. By the early 1980s both devaluation and the
Common Market had been found wanting as solutions to the British disease. If North Sea oil remained a panacea, it seemed probable
that headlong disindustrialisation under the Thatcher Government
would create more problems than could conceivably be solved by
even the most productive use of the oil revenues.

In the 1960s Harold Wilson boasted that Labour had become
'the natural party of government'. This was the root cause of the
movement's crisis. The experience of Labour Governments whose
leaders aimed not to transform, but to manage, the existing social
order, broke the basis of the traditional partnership between party
and unions. The crisis was intensified by the fact that, faced with
progressive economic decline, Labour Governments were unable
even to defend existing welfare provisions, let alone extend them. It
was, however, the pursuit of incomes policies by Labour Governments that set up the most insidious tensions within the labour
movement. Time and again the collapse of incomes policies
revealed the impossibility of transcending class conflict in pursuit of
supposedly 'national' economic goals. In a society still marked by
profound inequalities of wealth and income, the rhetoric of
national unity and purpose could never long withstand exposure to
the realities of the basic economic conflict over wages. Cabinet
ministers attempted to rationalise their managerial roles in the language of equality. Workers, in the absence of any coherent alternative notion of the general interest, justified their sectional militancy
by the cynical and angry assertion that in the capitalist jungle it was
every man for himself and the devil take the hindmost. It was these

confrontations which, above all, registered the collapse of any sense of a larger socialist purpose that might once have been embodied in the partnership of unions and political party.

II

This, however, is to anticipate. In the 1950s the Labour Party's problem was not that it had become the natural party of government, but that it seemed incapable of presenting a sufficiently coherent face to the electorate to recapture power at all. Bevan's resignation from the Cabinet in the spring of 1951 provided a focus for opposition within the party. The fall of the Government was followed by a resurgence of left-wing pressure to commit the Party Conference to specific further measures of nationalisation, and, with rather less success, to a foreign policy more independent of the United States. Alarmed by Bevanite advances in National Executive elections, the right organised to prevent any recurrence of the lurch to the left that had followed the 1931 debacle. The core of the right's power in the early 1950s lay in the 'triumverate' of trade union leaders – Deakin (TGWU), Williamson (NUGMW) and Lawther (NUM) – who had established their authority in defending Bevin's anti-communist foreign policy and the Labour Government's wage freeze in the late 1940s. Distrusting Atlee's 'soft' handling of the Bevanites, Deakin threw his weight behind the younger middle-class intellectuals in the Parliamentary Party whose leading personality, Hugh Gaitskell, had precipitated the confrontation with Bevan in 1951.

In the spring of 1954 Bevan resigned from the Shadow Cabinet in order to oppose German rearmament, an issue on which he could expect support from a much wider spectrum of opinion in the party than just the traditional left. At the same time he challenged the right for the succession to Atlee, abandoning his secure place as a constituency party representative on the party executive in order to stand for the Treasurership – a post elected by the whole Conference and regarded as a trial run for the leadership. The 'triumvirate' responded by putting up Gaitskell for the Treasurership, and ensuring a (very narrow) victory for German rearmament by a quite scandalous manipulation of union block votes. Defeated in the leadership struggle (Gaitskell succeeded Atlee after the 1955 election), and deserted by some of his more important followers (Wilson had been quick to step into Bevan's place in the Shadow Cabinet), Bevan saw little alternative but to come to terms. Gaitskell accepted him back as spokesman on foreign affairs, in return for his silence on domestic issues. In 1957 Bevan came out in favour of the British nuclear deterrent.

Bevanism never strayed far from the politics of manoeuvre in the central apparatus of the labour movement. At this level Bevan sensed that he was fighting a losing battle. In 1949, early in his struggle on the National Executive he remarked with weary humour: 'It is a form of torture unknown to the ancients . . . to be compelled on the last Wednesday of every month to convert the leaders of the Labour Party afresh to the most elementary principles of the party.'[1] Bevanism secured considerable support within the trade union movement – it was far from being confined to the Constituency Labour Parties. Nevertheless, beyond denouncing those trade union leaders who cast their block votes with scant regard for the expressed political opinions of their members, Bevan could see no way of effectively mobilising rank-and-file trade unionists to break the right-wing stranglehold. For the Bevanites 'politics' remained separate from the industrial concerns of trade unions, and, apart from a brief flirtation with the breakaway 'Blue Union' on the docks in 1955, they never carried their attack on the right into the every-day affairs of trade unionism. The Bevanites were caught in the same trap as crushed the Socialist League in the 1930s – their lack of a mass base made them susceptible to party discipline. But party discipline made it impossible for them to take the steps necessary to build a mass base.

During the later 1950s the ideas of the revisionist 'new thinkers' – Crossland, Strachey, Jenkins and others – were written into the Labour Party's policy statements. Drawing out the logic of the last years of the Atlee Government, the revisionists accepted the permanency of the mixed economy. They argued that the Keynsian revolution in economic policy, together with the managerial revolution within business, had transformed the nature of capitalism – indeed the word 'capitalism' disappeared altogether from Labour Party policy documents during the 1950s. Socialism no longer meant the common ownership of the means of production – Keynsian techniques of economic management rendered nationalisation obsolete as a means of public control over economic decision making. The capitalist class no longer held power – if indeed it still existed. The key task of the Labour Party in future would be to step up levels of social expenditure in order to eliminate the inequalities left over from old-style capitalism.

Left-wing resistance to the spread of revisionism was muted in the later 1950s, not least because Bevan had opted out of the struggle in order to concentrate on foreign policy issues. But Gaitskell and the revisionist intellectuals were not content with this easy victory. In the aftermath of the 1959 election – when Labour lost for the third consecutive time and by an increased margin – Gaitskell convinced himself that only a dramatic change in the image of the party could reverse the electoral tide. It was insufficient quietly to change the substance of party policy. In his attempt to amend the symbol of Labour's socialism, Clause Four, Gaitskell intended to provoke a set-piece confrontation with the left, to stage a dramatic and well-publicised disassociation of the party from its (supposedly) socialist past.

But Gaitskell had misjudged the line-up of forces within the party, and, in particular, the attitude of the trade union leaders. The right-wing leaders, whose control was already seriously weakened by Frank Cousins' accession to the leadership of the TGWU in 1956, saw little purpose in risking a confrontation with the basic loyalties of trade union activists among whom the arguments of revisionist intellectuals carried little weight. At successive union conferences during 1960 the delegates demonstrated their loyalty to Clause Four and this persuaded the union leaders to insist that Gaitskell drop his amendment. In the event a compromise formula, drawn up by Wilson, was sufficiently ambiguous to prevent the successful defence of Clause Four from having any visible effect on the party's domestic policy. Nevertheless, the revisionists had suffered a clear rebuff on the battlefield of their own choosing, and this shook the apparatus of control in the party sufficiently to allow a unique, if shortlived, victory for the left in the field of defence policy.

When the Campaign for Nuclear Disarmament (CND) was established in 1958 to demand unilateral nuclear disarmament by Britain its leaders thought the conversion of the Labour Party would be quite a straightforward matter. It was not until 1960 that unilateralism made decisive gains in the unions, and it did so then partly because the cancellation of the Blue Streak missile exposed the economic absurdity of the British aspiration to nuclear independence, but mainly because Gaitskell's blunder over Clause Four had weakened the restraints normally felt by delegates about attacking the leadership. The other crucial development was that the Communist Party, seeing the way things were going, abandoned its long-standing opposition to unilateralism in the interests of left unity. The victory of the unilateralist resolution at the Scarborough Conference in 1960, in the face of Gaitskell's pledge to 'fight, fight and fight again' to reverse the decision, was the occasion for much jubilation on the left. But no-one had much idea how to translate one successful resolution into a new direction for Labour politics.

Gaitskell's success in reversing the Scarborough decision a year later resulted not so much from the activities of the newly organised Campaign for Democratic Socialism, as from the inability of the left to broaden its challenge sufficiently to make it stick. Much of CND's success as a mass movement rested on its concentration on the single issue of nuclear disarmament. But the simple moral imperative – Ban the Bomb – which appealed so effectively to the disproportionately young and middle-class supporters of CND on the streets, could not, by itself, carry the left very far in the argument about foreign policy in the Labour Party. CND had failed to prepare the ground ideologically for this wider argument. New Left attempts to develop a programme for 'positive neutralism' during 1960–1 came too late to prevent *Tribune* and the established Labour left from being drawn into acceptance of a compromise plan that involved acceptance of NATO and the abandonment of unilateralism. Gaitskell, determined to gain on this issue the symbolic victory he had been denied on Clause Four, would accept no compromises and staked his leadership on total victory. In the absence of any credible alternative policy or leadership on the left, Gaitskell's obstinacy won the argument. In 1960 delegates at a number of crucial union conferences had voted against the Bomb partly in order to reinforce their message that Clause Four should not be tampered with. A year later these same delegates backed away from reaffirming a clear unilateralist stance, not because they had changed their minds on the defence issue itself, but because the question remained too narrow to justify a split in the party which, given Gaitskell's position, now appeared to be the real issue at stake.

Despite the crisis in the internal affairs of the party, Labour's electoral prospects took a sudden turn for the better during 1961. The boom which won Macmillan the election in 1959 gave way to a new 'stop' phase. Subsequent events conspired to undermine the Conservative hegemony – severe unemployment in the winter of

1962–3, the humiliating rejection of the Government's application for Common Market membership in January 1963, and the much publicised sexual peccadilloes of Profumo, the Defence Minister, in the following summer. When illness forced Macmillan to resign, and the 14th Earl of Home took over the premiership in the autumn, the decay of the Tory regime seemed complete. The Labour Party was quick to seize its opportunities. Shortly before he died, Gaitskell reunited the party around a nationalistic platform of opposition to the Common Market. Harold Wilson was well-fitted to consolidate the new mood of unity when he succeeded to the leadership in 1963. Despite his sympathy with much revisionist thinking, he still retained some credibility with the Labour Left, and he abhorred the bull-in-a-china-shop tactics of the Gaitskellites. The policy on which Labour fought the 1964 election followed revisionist prescriptions, though with some significant changes of emphasis. While Crossland, in the mid-1950s, had assumed that economic expansion was unproblematic, Wilson placed the slow-growth, 'stop-go' syndrome at the heart of his campaign against the Tories. He gave a radical twist to the theory of managerial revolution, stressing its incompleteness, and placing the Labour Party at the head of an offensive of professional managers, technicians, scientists and workers – all anxious to 'serve the nation' – against upper-class deadwood in the boardrooms and the aristocratic amateurism that characterised the British elite and was so conveniently symbolised in the Fourteenth Earl himself. Building on the Conservatives' initiative in indicative planning – the establishment of the National Economic Development Council in 1961–2 – Wilson was able to overcome TUC hostility to incomes policy sufficiently to secure a well-publicised agreement to trade union co-operation in the development of a national plan for economic growth. In this way the special relationship between Labour and the unions could be transformed from the electoral liability which Gaitskell had believed it to be into a positive electoral advantage. Cousins' support for incomes policy at the 1963 TUC set the seal on a degree of unity between left and right seldom attained previously in the party's history. The Labour left was happy to fall into line, and all too ready to interpret Wilson's version of managerialism as a declaration of war on capitalist power. In fact, Wilson's rhetoric made socialism synonymous not with public ownership or with equality but with the achievement of a high-growth capitalist economy. When, after 1964, the growth failed to materialise, the contradictions between Wilson's managerialism and the aspirations of either trade unions or socialists became painfully apparent.

III

The sharp clashes between left and right which dominated the public history of the Labour Party in the 1950s create a misleading impression of political vigour in the movement. In reality the period saw a decline not only in the number of people voting Labour, but also in the individual membership of the party, which fell by a quarter in the ten years following 1952. At the same time the growth of trade union membership, rapid during the 1940s, virtually ceased; and the percentage of the total occupied population organised in trade unions actually fell from 45 per cent in 1951 to 42 per cent by the mid-1960s.

This decline in the size of the organised labour movement was, in part, a result of structural shifts in the composition of the labour force. Some of the best organised industries declined rapidly – between them coal, cotton and the railways lost nearly half a million workers between 1948 and 1964 – while badly organised industries like distribution, food manufacturing and chemicals expanded. Crucially important was the expansion of women's employment. Apart from the temporary influxes of wartime, the proportion of women in the labour force had changed little since the 1850s. Between 1951 and 1966 it grew from 31 to 35.6 per cent – accounting for almost all the net increase in the workforce during those years. So long as women were organised so much less effectively than men (there was no improvement before the mid-1960s) this increase in the female section of the workforce was bound to weaken the labour movement as a whole. A further cause of falling trade union density was the accelerating shift from manual to white-collar employment. Despite rapid growth of the white-collar unions, in the early 1960s a manual worker was still twice as likely to be a member of a trade union as a white-collar worker.

The Labour Party's difficulties also owed something to a process of working-class depoliticisation. When they fell from power in 1951 Labour politicians had predicted a return to mass unemployment and savage attacks on the welfare state under Tory rule. Instead near full employment was maintained, welfare services improved, and real wages rose by over 2 per cent each year. Between 1951 and 1964 the number of cars in Britain increased from

2.5 million to 8 million; the number of television sets from 1 million to 13 million. The fridge and the washing machine reduced domestic drudgery in many working-class homes. A large number of working-class families were, for the first time, able to buy their own houses. Between 1947 and 1966 the proportion of the total housing stock held under owner-occupation grew from 27 to 47 per cent – a remarkable success for the Tory ideal of a 'property-owning democracy'. Not surprisingly, in these circumstances, many working-class electors concluded that there was now little need for a Labour Government to defend their economic position.*

The decline in the Labour vote after 1951 was largely a result of abstentions in solidly working-class seats, rather than of any substantial switching of Labour voters to the Conservatives. Low turn-out was accompanied by a great increase in the proportion of electors who, according to opinion polls, saw little significant difference between the parties. National politics, it seemed, was ceasing to have much relevance to a large number of working-class people. Neither left nor right of the Labour Party had much to offer in this situation. Bevanite fundamentalism, in particular the stress on nationalisation, ran foul of widespread popular disapproval of public ownership, at least as implemented by the post-war Labour Government. The revisionist panacea of a social-democratic party detached from the traditional working-class image of the Labour Party, had little relevance to the problems of mobilising electors who, in so far as they were interested in politics at all, continued to conceive of them as essentially a matter of class interest. The increasing proportion of Labour MPs – and, perhaps, also of local Labour activists – from middle-class backgrounds also tended to inhibit the articulation of working-class concerns within the Labour Party.

Working-class interest in the Labour Party was further undermined by a shift among better-paid workers from the broader concern with welfare that had been at the heart of the socialist appeal after the war, to a narrow concentration on wage struggles at factory level. Shop steward organisation, operating largely independently of official trade unionism and established collective bargaining procedures, grew rapidly. As renewed foreign competition began to exert pressure on employers to keep down costs from the

* But it is easy to overdraw the picture of the 'affluent' 1950s: during the decade the proportion of the population living in poverty, below National Assistance scales, roughly doubled.

mid-1950s, employer resistance to wage drift generated an upsurge of shop floor organisation and militancy. Outside coalmining, where pit-closures and the abolition of piece work led to a drastic reduction in strike activity, the number of strikes per year more than doubled between 1957 and 1964. These strikes were typically small, shortlived and unofficial. They also reflected a militant sectionalism which, while a major obstacle to subsequent attempts to enlist trade union support for policies of wage restraint, did nothing to bridge the gulf between everyday industrial activity and anything that might be understood as socialist politics.

IV

Labour came to power in October 1964 with a very small majority and a very large balance of payments deficit. At first the Cabinet resisted pressure for deflation and pressed ahead with significant increases in pensions and other benefits, the abolition of health service charges, and new capital gains and corporation taxes. But the much-heralded strategy for growth, the National Plan, was stillborn, its targets sabotaged six weeks before they were published by an emergency deflationary package in June 1965. George Brown's Department of Economic Affairs was not capable of withstanding the power of finance and the Treasury, despite the close links it had formed with the new Confederation of British Industries and the TUC. The Cabinet, under strong American pressure, decided to accompany deflation with a statutory incomes policy. Already it was becoming clear that a Labour Government which refused to tackle capitalist power would be forced, instead, to take on organised labour.

For the time being both sides held back from confrontation. The TUC had already accepted the principle of voluntary wage restraint, and, in the autumn of 1965, Congress established its own machinery for vetting wage claims on the understanding that the Government would refrain from implementing statutory restraint. The Government stuck by its part of the bargain, despite the fact that TUC declarations were having no noticeable effect on the rate of wage inflation. In March 1966 Wilson went to the country, rallying the movement behind him. Despite the disappointing record of the previous eighteen months, *Tribune* proclaimed its belief that only the lack of a solid parliamentary majority was preventing the Government from initiating socialist reforms. Frank

Cousins was assured by Wilson that an improved majority would enable the Government to withstand financial pressure for a statutory incomes policy. Disillusion followed rapidly. Reassured by a greatly increased majority, Wilson demonstrated his determination to stand up to the unions by a reds-under-the-beds campaign against a seamen's strike, and, in June, he precipitated Cousins' resignation by going ahead with prices and incomes legislation.

All this, however, proved insufficient to prevent a renewal of the financial crisis. Overriding opposition from both left and right in the Cabinet, Wilson and Callaghan rejected devaluation and opted for further, and massive, cuts in public expenditure, together with a statutory wage freeze. There was little determined opposition from the left in the Parliamentary Party, mainly because the General Council, whipped into line by threats of mass unemployment if the policy did not hold, managed to secure TUC acceptance of the freeze. George Brown was fatuously contented: 'The TUC, not for the first time, is ahead in saying "We will surrender for the good of the country". This is what this party and this movement is always doing.'[2] Over the next year the freeze, and the period of severe restraint that followed it, held well – earnings rose by a mere 1.7 per cent, considerably less than the rise in the cost of living. This was probably as much a result of unemployment, caused by the Government's deflationary policy, as of rank-and-file loyalty to the Government.

From the summer of 1967 events moved rapidly towards the collapse of Wilson's economic strategy, and of the ability of his Government and its allies in the trade union leadership to hold the line against an upsurge of militancy. Reflationary measures in the summer of 1967 secured TUC acquiescence in a further year of statutory incomes policy, but horrified foreign sterling holders. The resulting run on the pound finally forced Wilson to devalue sterling in November 1967. Devaluation was accompanied by a new round of public spending cuts, including the ending of free milk for secondary schools and – the final nail in the coffin of Wilson's Bevanism – the reimposition of prescription charges. Wilson's claim on trade union loyalty was now wearing very thin. His Government had not only failed to initiate any significant redistribution of income (indeed its taxation policies had a decidedly regressive effect), it had also failed to stimulate the economic growth that was a precondition of expanded welfare services. During the whole term of office welfare expenditure hardly kept pace with increased need resulting from the rise in unemployment and the growing proportion of those age-groups in the population which made the greatest demands on the services. The Government made a number of inroads into the principle of universality in the social services the effect of which – as with the Health Service and school meal charges and council house rent increases – was to expand the petty bureaucratic tyrannies associated with means tested benefits in the lives of the poor.

With such a record it is not surprising that the Government's popularity sank rapidly. In the autumn of 1968 the Government's economic policies were overwhelmingly rejected at both TUC and Labour Party Conferences.

Within the TUC ideas about drastically widening the area of bargaining with the Government to embrace not just wages and prices, but the whole range of economic and social policy were gaining ground. The institution of an annual Economic Review from 1967–8 was intended to provide the General Council with an independent economic policy as a basis for negotiating terms with the Government. More important, for the time being, was a growing clamour for an end to Government interference with collective bargaining. All this reflected disillusion in the trade union movement with Wilson's corporatism. There were limits beyond which the trade union leadership could not be induced to place nation before class. The shift to the left also reflected longer term changes in the trade union movement. The election of Hugh Scanlon to the leadership of the AEU in 1967, on the basis of a Broad Left alliance of Communist and Labour left activists, symbolised the emergence of a new generation of full-time union officials whose experience in wartime and post-war shop steward activism encouraged them to take a more democratic approach than had their predecessors. These men saw their jobs less as helping the Government to manage the economy, more as removing obstacles to the free conduct of shop-floor bargaining. Together with the growing strength of some white-collar unions, whose opposition to incomes policy was facilitated by their members' lack of traditional political loyalty to the Labour Party, these developments swung the balance of power in the TUC more decisively away from the right than at any time since the 1920s.

In 1965 the Government had established a Royal Commission to examine the law affecting industrial relations. The Donovan Report, published in June 1968, provided the occasion for Barbara

Castle's attempt to introduce legislation which would have included provision for compulsory strike ballots and a cooling-off period in unofficial strikes, although the Donovan Commission itself had poured cold water on both proposals. Barbara Castle's White Paper, *In Place of Strife*, unleashed a storm of protest at all levels in the labour movement. The General Council was almost unanimous in its opposition; fifty-three Labour MPs voted against the White Paper; the National Executive opposed it. A significant minority in the Cabinet led by Callaghan, were opposed from the outset. A Liaison Committee for the Defence of Trade Unions, established by the Communist Party in 1967 to fight the renewal of the Prices and Incomes Act, organised unofficial strikes in February and again in May 1969 as part of a campaign for a Special TUC and a general strike against the proposed legislation. More important was a strike of Ford workers early in 1969 against an officially negotiated package deal which, in line with the policy urged on car industry leaders by Barbara Castle, included penalty clauses for workers involved in unconstitutional stoppages. Though the outcome of the strike fell a long way short of complete victory for the strikers, it nevertheless served to remind trade union leaders how easily any restrictions on their freedom of action could leave them isolated, overtaken by rank-and-file militancy. The decision of both major unions involved, the TGWU and the AEU, to support the strikers revealed clearly that the Government could no longer rely on trade union leaders to act as policemen against their own membership.

Impressed by the evidence of discontent, and by the knowledge that support for the Bill from the Parliamentary Party was unlikely so long as the General Council remained opposed, the Government finally backed down in June, abandoning the legislation in return for vague guarantees from the TUC leadership that they would do something about the problem of unofficial strikes. This compromise prevented a confrontation, but it did nothing to resolve the cause of friction between the Government and the labour movement. In the run-up to the 1970 election the Government abandoned any attempt to enforce their incomes policy. But they had discovered no means of securing rapid and sustained economic growth without first confronting the power either of organised labour or of capital.

V

While the Wilson Government struggled on to defeat in 1970, reviving militancy within the trade unions halted the decline in membership and sparked off a major new upsurge of trade union growth. Between 1968 and 1974 the number of trade union members rose by 15 per cent. Most of this growth occurred in the two years 1969–70. This was not a spectacular increase by the standards of previous trade union explosions, but it marked a radical break from the stagnation of the previous twenty years. Trade union density increased from 42.5 per cent in 1968 to 54.9 per cent in 1976, an achievement largely explained by a rapid extension of trade unionism among women and white-collar workers. It seemed that the movement was, at last, beginning to respond effectively to the change in the structure of the labour force which had been the main cause of its stagnation since the 1940s. Rapid trade union growth was accompanied, and in part caused, by a strike wave on a scale that dwarfed anything that had occurred since the early 1920s. As the pattern of short, small strikes characteristic of the 1950s and 1960s gave way to an increasir.g number of larger and longer strikes, the number of working days lost rose from around three million a year in the 1960s to nearly twelve million a year between 1968 and 1974. A higher proportion of strikes were made official as trade union leaders ran to keep pace with their members: 'We find out what the members are planning to do anyway, and instruct them to do it.'[3] The right-wing NUGMW paid the price for its bureaucratic inflexibility during 1969–70, stagnating while the rival TGWU lent its support to unofficial strikes and boomed. While the traditionally militant sectors of the workforce – carworkers, miners, dockers, etc. – played a large part in this explosion, much of the strike activity occurred among groups of workers with little previous record of militancy, the women clothing workers of Leeds, the St Helen's glassworkers, and such diverse groups of public employees as teachers, dustmen, postmen and hospital ancillary workers.

Behind the trade union explosion lay the combined effect of price rises and increased taxation on real wages. The average increase in post-tax real income levels, running at about 2 per cent a year during the 1950s, fell back to 1 per cent during the 1960s. Moreover the Labour Government's attempts at incomes policy disrupted the established system of wage determination, in particular disallowing the principle of 'comparability' by which many workers in the public sector and elsewhere had kept their earnings in line with those achieved by more strongly organised workers in high-productivity industries like motor cars. These pressures, together with the effect of the downward extension of income tax liability, ensured an actual decline in real living standards for many groups of workers between 1965 and 1969. In view of the Labour Government's record there is a delightful pathetic irony in George Brown's indignant response to the London dustmen's strike of 1969: 'They will destroy us all and all that we stand for and all that we were invented for. We were invented to look after the poorer people.'[4] The strike wave was evidence that 'the poorer people' had decided that it was time they looked after themselves.

Faced with a wages explosion in full swing, and pledged against any attempt to revive Labour's corporatism, the new Conservative Government attempted instead to force down the level of pay settlements by taking a firm stand in the public sector. Early in 1971, in a six-week confrontation with the postmen, which involved the loss of more working days than any strike since the 1920s, the Government successfully showed its determination. Simultaneously, in the biggest strike involving a single private employer in British history, the Ford workers were defeated in their demand for parity with other car firms. The threat by Henry Ford II to withdraw his investment from Britain persuaded Jack Jones and Hugh Scanlon to settle the dispute over the heads not only of the shop stewards but also of the full-time officials responsible. Encouraged by these successes, the Government pressed ahead with its Industrial Relations Bill, despite furious trade union opposition. A campaign by the Liaison Committee for the Defence of Trade Unions for a general strike against the legislation met with the support of several union executives who backed 'Kill the Bill' protest strikes involving the loss of as many working days as had been lost in total in an average year in the 1960s.

The Act sought to restrict legal immunity to 'registered' trade unions, whose rule-books had been approved by the state, thereby exposing unofficial trade union activities to legal controls. It also made provision for legally enforceable contracts, outlawed sympathetic and political strikes, and gave the minister power to impose a sixty-day 'cooling-off period', or to require a pre-strike ballot. Its central purpose was to force union leaderships to tighten their control over rank-and-file militancy. The Act constituted a frontal challenge to trade union autonomy, launched in the middle of a strike wave, and at a time when the trade union leaders were in full reaction against their earlier attempts to discipline the membership on behalf of the Labour Government. Although strike action against the legislation was narrowly defeated at a Special Congress in March 1971, the TUC adopted a policy of non-registration and nonco-operation with the new Industrial Courts when the Act came into force early the next year. By this time wage militancy had revived, and the victory of the miners after a massive and highly visible strike marked by the use of flying pickets to cut off coal supplies to the power stations, helped to generate a mood of euphoric combativity in the ranks of organised labour. In this atmosphere the first attempts to enforce the Industrial Relations Act – which had not been invoked during the miners' strike – led rapidly to the humiliation of the Government.

The NUR, conducting a work to rule in pursuit of its wage claim, complied with an instruction under the Act to hold a ballot. When this showed a 6:1 majority in favour of industrial action the Government had little option but to settle the claim. A good deal more complicated was the attempt of the National Industrial Relations Court (NIRC) to deal with an unofficial dockers' boycott of low-paid container work. Although the TGWU, advised by the General Council, agreed to appear before the NIRC, it could not prevent the dockers from continuing their action. The climax was reached when the Appeal Court ruled that, due to faulty drafting, the Act did not after all make unions answerable for the actions of their members. The NIRC then switched its attention from the TGWU to the dockers themselves, and in July 1972 five of their shop stewards were jailed for contempt of court. 'Arise ye Workers' urged a much-photographed dockers' banner. Within days escalating spontaneous strikes had forced the General Council to threaten a general strike. In short order the Law Lords reversed the decision of the Appeal Court, and the Government sent in the comically convenient Official Solicitor to secure the release of the 'Pentonville Five'.

The events of July 1972 discredited the confrontation policies of the Heath Government. Under pressure from an establishment thoroughly alarmed by these portents of social chaos, Heath made a dramatic about-turn, agreed to put the Industrial Relations Act on ice, and invited employer and TUC leaders to participate in tri-partite talks with a view to launching a new incomes policy. TUC leaders accepted the invitation with some relief. The eventual breakdown of the Chequers' talks was caused partly by the TUC's insistence on rather tougher terms for a policy of voluntary wage restraint than they had demanded of Wilson in the 1960s, and partly by the reluctance of the Government to be tied to any explicit deal with the TUC. Heath had secured the legitimation he needed from the TUC's agreement to discuss incomes policy at all. In November he broke off the talks and introduced a ninety-day freeze, followed by statutory restraint. Union responses to this turn of events were confused. The TUC condemned the non-redistributive character of the Tories' incomes policy, boycotted the Pay Board and the Price Commission, and (following a victory for militancy against the platform at a Special Congress) called a one-day general strike against the policy on 1 May 1973. At the same time, however, none of the more powerful unions attempted to break through the incomes policy, and those who did – hospital workers, gas workers, civil servants – were defeated. Union leaders frightened by the events of the previous summer, did not wish to precipitate another crisis. And the acquiescence of ordinary workers may have owed something to the fact that their own militancy, together with Conservative tax cuts, had resulted in an unprecedented rise of over 7 per cent in real post-tax income during the previous year. Again, however, the lull in militancy proved to be shortlived. During the winter of 1973–4 a new crisis erupted, culminating in the imposition of a three-day week (to save energy supplies), another miners' strike, and the defeat of the Heath Government in the snap General Election of February 1974.

The experience of the Heath Government enabled the two wings of the labour movement to patch up their differences. Wilson led the party in fierce opposition to the terms of British entry into the Common Market, despite the fact that these appeared to differ little from those he himself had been happy to accept two years earlier. Reflecting on the record of the 1960s, Tony Benn declared: 'The crisis that we inherit when we come to power will be the occasion for fundamental change, and not the excuse for postponing it.'[5] To this end, in 1973, the party adopted its most radical programme for forty years, promising a fundamental attack on inequalities of wealth and power, extensive nationalisation with workers' participation, and effective state planning of the economy.

The enhanced strength of the Labour left rested squarely on its alliance with the big guns of the trade union leadership, Jack Jones and Hugh Scanlon. At long last the block votes were being turned against the right. This seemed like a fundamental change. After seventy years of waiting Labour's socialists now began to feel that they were in a position to dictate the terms of the 'labour alliance'. When, in February 1973, negotiations between the TUC and the Labour Party resulted in a measure of agreement on the programme for the next Labour Government, this appeared, to the theorists of the Labour left, to open up the prospect of a series of 'social contracts' between the unions and future Labour Governments, each more socialist than the last, which would gradually, but irreversibly, extend the 'political economy of labour' into the citadels of capitalist power.

VI

Little came of this attractive prospect. Instead Labour's new attempt to administer capitalism proved even more disastrous for the cohesion of the labour movement than the 1960s experience.

For a time after Labour's return to power Government and unions preserved a wary peace. Jack Jones masterminded a 'social contract' of sorts. But, in the absence of any radical socialist offensive by the Cabinet, this had less to do with advancing the political economy of labour than with one more doomed attempt to contract the unions to a Labour-administered capitalism. The upshot, following a new financial crisis and acceptance of draconian terms for an international loan, was entirely predictable. In 1969–70 Barbara Castle's *In Place of Strife* had opened the way for Edward Heath. In 1978–9 Jim Callaghan's attempt to enforce a 5 per cent pay norm set the scene for the election of Margaret Thatcher. In 1979 Labour won fewer votes than at any time since 1931. Nearly one-third of trade unionists voted Conservative. But the defeat was not only electoral. The whole political spectrum had swung sharply to the right. The dismantling of the welfare state and the re-emergence of mass unemployment – both trends originating during the Labour administration – represented the end of the social settlement negotiated in the crisis of the Second World War.

After 1951 the readiness of Conservative Governments to accept full employment and the welfare state began the process of eroding the self-confidence of the labour movement. Thirty years later, when the counter-attack on the gains of the 1940s was open and unashamed, the labour movement no longer had the capacity to resist. What had disintegrated through the intervening years was precisely the sense of a *movement* – the sense that each local and particular struggle, and each part of the institutional structure, was in some way linked to the whole by a common socialist purpose, a commitment, however vague and ambiguous, to the construction of a new social order. Since the 1890s this sense of purpose had been embodied in the notion of a division of labour between the two major institutional components of the movement, the unions and the political party. The precise character of this division of labour was constantly changing and argued over, and a minority challenged the very idea that there could be a meaningful division between economic and political forms of struggle. But it was not until the 1960s and 1970s that the underlying partnership between a trade unionism devoted to the protection of workers' interests on the job and a Labour Party seeking to promote the wider social needs of working people showed signs of terminal crisis.

It may be that the crisis in the old labour movement will open the way for the renewal of mass socialist politics in Britain. The secession of the Social Democrats (SDP) in 1981 was the result of a process by which the traditional right-wing holders of power in the party had been forced into the position of a factional minority. This process began, more than twenty years earlier, with the formation of the Campaign for Democratic Socialism to combat the first victory for unilateral nuclear disarmament. The CND mobilisation in the early 1960s helped to precipitate a major revival of interest in socialism, libertarian politics and direct action. The 1960s and 1970s saw, not only the disastrous experience of Labour Governments, but also an expanding network of extra-parliamentary activism involving shop stewards, student radicalism, the women's movement and a fissiparous revolutionary left. All these things ensured that the new currents within the Labour Party had a far more open attitude to the possibility of supplementing parliamentary with extra-parliamentary campaigns than had characterised the Labour left in any previous period. Struggles to increase the accountability of MPs to the party activists reflected, not only a deep suspicion of the existing parliamentary leadership, but also a sharpened awareness of the limitations of any parliamentary leadership. What was not, however, in evidence was any capacity to carry this new radical politics to the mass of the electorate.

Probably the most important growth points for socialist politics occur at the conjunction between the labour movement and those autonomous mass movements energing outside its traditional areas of concern. Women have not only flooded into the trade union movement, they have also organised themselves independently, thereby forcing feminist issues into the political arena to an unprecedented degree. Labour movement activists have hardly begun to face up to the fundamental challenge posed by feminism to their traditional practices and strategies. Women's experience, like that of an increasing section of the male population which cannot expect to have regular jobs in the foreseeable future, denies that division between the world of wage labour and the rest of life around which men have constructed their economistic trade unions. Similar challenges to the complacent assumption that the labour movement embodies the best interests of all the oppressed have been apparent in the revival of nationalist politics in Scotland and Wales, the self-organisation of the Black minorities in Britain and the ferocious alienation displayed by unemployed youth in the summer of 1981. Any renewal of socialist politics will have to come to terms with these developments. A further key to the possibility of a mass socialist politics lies with the environmental, anti-nuclear and peace campaigns which bring working-class politics together with a significant mobilisation of middle-class radicalism. These issues may help the left to win over sections of the middle-class electorate which would otherwise be lost to the SDP. At the same time the extraordinary growth of the nuclear disarmament movement throughout Europe raises the hope that British socialism may at last find a way out of the debilitating choice between pro-Soviet fellow-travelling, nationalist insularity and capitalist Atlanticism in which it has been trapped since the effective partition of Europe after the Second World War.

There are, then, some potential growth points, some fragments which may yet be put together into the beginnings of a new mass socialist politics. But, at the time of writing (spring 1982), it is far from clear how the left will set about recreating among the mass of the population an alternative, socialist, definition of the general interest, or building the institutional structures necessary to translate such a definition into political practice. Whatever means may eventually be found to do this, one thing at least is clear – there is little prospect of reconstructing a majority for social transformation on the basis of that curious and shifting partnership between an economistic trade unionism and a narrowly electoral politics that lay at the base of the labour movement us it emerged during the last 100 years. Whether this is a matter for regret rather depends on what we put in its place during the coming decades.

Notes

1 M. Foot, *Aneurin Bevan*, vol. 2, London 1975, p. 259.
2 Leo Panitch, *Social Democracy and Industrial Militancy: The Labour Party, the Trade Unions and Incomes Policy, 1945–1974,* Oxford 1976, p. 119.
4 R. Hyman, 'Industrial Conflict and the Political Economy', *Socialist Register*, 1973, p. 109.
5 Panitch, *op. cit.*, p. 211.
6 *Ibid.*, pp. 228–9.

Further Reading

This study is largely based on the very substantial number of books and articles about aspects of labour history which have been published since the 1950s. Of the studies published before that date the most valuable are:

S. and B. Webb, *Industrial Democracy*, London 1902
S. and B. Webb, *History of Trade Unionism*, London 1902
G. D. H. Cole and R. Postgate, *The Common People, 1746–1946*, London 1946

In common with other labour historians I owe a particular debt to E.J. Hobsbawm, some of whose most important essays are reprinted in *Labouring Men*, London 1964. See also, for the best short economic history, Hobsbawm's *Industry and Empire*, London 1968. Two further collections of essays are especially helpful:

A. Briggs and J. Saville (eds), *Essays in Labour History*, 3 vols, London 1967, 1971, 1977
H. Pelling, *Popular Politics and Society in late Victorian Britain*, London 1968.

Most of the statistics quoted in the text derive from:

B.R. Mitchell and P. Deane, *Abstract of British Historical Statistics*, Cambridge 1962
A.H. Halsey (ed), *Trends in British Society since 1900*, London 1972
D. Butler and J. Freeman, *British Political Facts, 1900–1968*, London 1969

For a full bibliography see H. Smith, *The British Labour Movement to 1970: A Bibliography*, London 1981, and the annual listings in the *Bulletin of the Society for the Study of Labour History*. Below I have listed those works which I have found most useful in writing this book. The place of publication is London, unless otherwise noted.

1 Trade Union Histories

R.P. Arnot, *A History of the Miners Federation of Great Britain*, vols 1–3, 1949–61.

P. Bagwell, *The Railwaymen: The History of the National Union of Railwaymen*, 1963.

G. Bain, *White Collar Trade Unionism*, Oxford 1970.

J. Child, *Industrial Relations in the British printing industry: The Quest for Security*, 1967.

H.A. Clegg, *General Union in a Changing Society. A Short History of The National Union of General and Municipal Workers, 1889–1964*, Oxford 1964.

A. Fox, *A History of the National Union of Boot and Shoe Operatives, 1874–1957*, Oxford 1958.

R. Hyman, *The Workers' Union*, Oxford 1971

J.B. Jefferys, *The Story of the Engineers*, 1946.

S. Lewenhak, *Women and Trade Unions*, 1977

J. Lovell, *Stevedores and Dockers; A Study of Trade Unionism in the Port of London, 1870–1914*, 1969

R. Price, *Masters, Unions and Men. Work Control in Building and the Rise of Labour, 1830—1914*, Cambridge 1980.

H.A. Turner, *Trade Union Growth, Structure and Policy*, 1962.

J.E. Williams, *The Derbyshire Miners*, 1962.

2 The mid-Victorian Years

K. Burgess, *The Origins of British Industrial Relations: The Nineteenth-Century Experience*, 1975.

R.V. Clements, 'British Trade Unions and Popular Political Economy, 1850–75', *Economic History Review*, xiv, 1961–62.

H. Collins and C. Abramsky, *Karl Marx and the British Labour Movement*, 1965.

J.D.D. Dunbabin, 'The "Revolt of the Field": The Agricultural Labourers' Movement in the 1870s', *Past and Present*, 26, 1963.

J. Foster, *Class Struggle and the Industrial Revolution: Early Industrial Capitalism in Three English Towns*, 1974.

R.Q. Gray, *The Labour Aristocracy in Victorian Edinburgh*, Oxford 1976.

R.Q. Gray, *The Aristocracy of Labour in Nineteenth-century Britain*, 1981.

R. Harrison, *Before the Socialists*, 1965.

R. Harrison (ed), *The Independent Collier*, Sussex 1978.

H.M. Perkin, *The Origins of Modern English Society, 1780–1880*, 1969

R. Samuel, 'The Workshop of the World', *History Workshop* 3, 1977.

J. Vincent, *The Formation of the British Liberal Party, 1857–1868*, Harmondsworth 1972.

3 1880–1910

F. Bealey and H. Pelling, *Labour and Politics 1900–1906*, 1958.

N. Blewett, *The Peers, The Parties and the People: The General Elections of 1910*, 1972.

K.D. Brown, *Labour and Unemployment, 1900–1914*, Newton Abbot, 1971

J. Burnett, *A Social History of Housing, 1815—1970*, 1978.

P.F. Clarke, *Lancashire and the New Liberalism*, Cambridge 1971.

H.A. Clegg, A. Fox and A.F. Thompson, *A History of British Trade Unions since 1889*, vol 1, Oxford 1964.

M.J. Daunton, *Coal Metropolis, Cardiff 1870–1914*, Leicester 1977.

D.A. Hammer, *Liberal Politics in the Age of Gladstone and Rosebury*, Oxford 1972.

J. Harris, *Unemployment and Politics: A Study in English Social Policy, 1886–1914*, Oxford 1972.

P. Joyce, *Work, Society and Politics: The Culture of the Factory in Later Victorian England*, 1980.

G.S. Jones, *Outcast London*, Oxford 1971.

G.S. Jones, 'Working-class culture and working-class politics in London, 1870–1900. Notes on the remaking of a working class.' *Journal of Social History*, 17, 1974.

J. Liddington and J. Norris, *One Hand Tied Behind Us: The Rise of the Women's Suffrage Movement*, 1978.

H. Mcleod, *Class and religion in the late Victorian City*, 1974.

S. Meacham, *A Life Apart. The English Working Class, 1890–1914*, 1977.

R. Moore, *Pitmen, Preachers and Politics*, Cambridge 1974.

T. Nairn, 'The Nature of the Labour Party' in P. Anderson (ed), *Towards Socialism*, 1965.

T. Olcott, ' "Dead Centre": the women's trade union movement in London, 1874—1914', *London Journal*, 2, 1976.

H.M. Pelling, *The Origins of the Labour Party*, Oxford 1965.

S. Pierson, *Marxism and the Origins of British Socialism. The Struggle for a New Consciousness*, 1973.

F. Reid, *Keir Hardie: The Making of a Socialist*, 1978.

R. Roberts, *The Classic Slum*, Harmondsworth 1973,

J. Saville, 'The ideology of Labourism' in R. Benewick *et al.* (eds), *Knowledge and Belief in Politics*, 1973.

E.P. Thompson, *William Morris: Romantic to Revolutionary*, 1977.

P. Thompson, *Socialist, Liberals and Labour: The Struggle for London, 1885–1914*, 1967.

S. Yeo, 'The Religion of Socialism', *History Workshop* 4, 1977.

4 1910 – 1931

V. L. Allen, *Trade Unions and the Government*, 1960.

E.E. Barry, *Nationalisation in British Politics: The Historical Background*, 1965.

S. Beer, *Modern British Politics*, 1965.

E.H.P. Brown, *The Growth of British Industrial Relations*, 1959.

A. Bullock, *The Life and Times of Ernest Bevin*, 2 vols, 1960–7.

A. Clinton, *The Trade Union Rank and File. Trades Councils in Britain, 1900–40*, Manchester 1977.

M. Cowling, *The Impact of Labour 1920–24: The Beginning of Modern British Politics*, Cambridge 1971.

J.E. Cronin, *Industrial Conflict in Modern Britain*, 1979.

G. Dangerfield, *The Strange Death of Liberal England*, 1936.

R.E. Dowse, *Left in the Centre*, 1966.

B.B. Gilbert, *British Social Policy 1914–1939*, 1970.

J. Hinton, *The First Shop Stewards' Movement*, 1973.

B. Holton, *British Syndicalism 1900–1914: Myths and Realities*, 1976.

W. Kendal, *The Revolutionary Movement in Britain, 1900–21*, 1969.

K.G.J.C. Knowles, *Strikes: A Study in Industrial Conflict*, Oxford 1952.

C.J. MacFarlane, *The British Communist Party: Its Origins and Development until 1929*, 1966.

S. Macintyre, *A Proletarian Science. Marxism in Britain 1917–33*, Cambridge, 1980.

S. Macintyre, *Little Moscows: Communism and Working-class Militancy in Inter-war Britain*, 1980.

A. Mason, *The General Strike in the North East*, Hull 1970

R. McKibbin, *The Evolution of the Labour Party, 1910–1924*, Oxford 1974.

G.A. Phillips, *The General Strike: The Politics of Industrial Conflict*, 1976.

G.A. Phillips, 'The Triple Alliance in 1914', *Economic History Review*, xxiv, 1971.

S. Pollard, *The Development of the British Economy 1914–1950*, 1962.

S. Pollard, 'Trade Unionism and the Depression', *Journal of Contemporary History*, 1969.

G. Routh, *Occupation and Pay in Great Britain, 1906–1960*, Cambridge 1965.

J. Skelley (ed), *1926: The General Strike*, 1976.

R. Skidelsky, *Politicians and the Slump*, Harmonsworth 1970.

J. White, *The Limits of Trade Union Militancy. The Lancashire textile workers 1910–1914*, New York 1978.

5 1931 – 1951

P. Addison, *The Road to 1945. British Politics and the Second World War*, 1975.

V.L. Allen, *Trade Union Leadership*, 1957.

T. Burridge, *British Labour and Hitler's War*, 1976.

A. Calder, *The People's War*, 1971.

D. Coates, *The Labour Party and the Struggle for Socialism*, Cambridge 1975.

R. Eatwell, *The 1945–51 Labour Governments*, 1979.

M. Foot, *Aneurin Bevan*, 2 vols, 1966–73.

J. Harris, 'Social Planning in Wartime', in J. Winter (ed), *War and Economic Development*, Cambridge 1975.

J. Hinton, 'Coventry Communism: a study of factory politics in World War Two', *History Workshop* 10, 1980.

D. Howell, *British Social Democracy: A Study in Development and Decay*, 1976.

H. Land, 'The Introduction of Family Allowances' in P. Hall *et al.* (eds), *Change, Choice and Conflict in Social Policy*, 1975.

I. McLain, *Ministry of Morale: Home Front Morale and the Ministry of Information in World War Two*, 1979.

R. Miliband, *Parliamentary Socialism*, 1961.

H. Pelling, *The British Communist Party. A Historical Profile*, 1958.

B. Pimlott, *Labour and the Left in the 1930s*, Cambridge 1977.

D. Rubinstein, 'Socialism and the Labour Party', in D.E. Martin and D. Rubinstein (eds), *Ideology and the Labour Movement*, 1979.

6 The last thirty years

P. Anderson, 'The Left in the Fifties', *New Left Review* 29, 1965.

H. Beynon, *Working for Fords*, Wakefield 1973.

P. Duff, *Left, left, left: A Personal Account of Six Protest Campaigns, 1945–1965*, 1971.

P. Foot, *The Politics of Harold Wilson*, Harmondsworth 1968.

J. Goldthrope *et al.*, *The Affluent Worker*, 3 vols, Cambridge 1968–9.

N. Harris, *Competition in the Corporate Society: British Conservatives, the State and Industry, 1945–64*, 1972.

B. Hindess, *The Decline of Working-class Politics*, 1971.

S. Holland, *The Socialist Challenge*, 1975.

R. Hyman, 'Industrial Conflict and the Political Economy', *Socialist Register*, 1973.

M. Jacques and F. Mulhern, *The Forward March of Labour Halted?*, 1981

M. Jenkins, *Bevanism: Labour's High Tide. The Cold War and the Democratic Mass Movement*, Nottingham 1979.

Leo Panitch, *Social democracy and Industrial Militancy: The Labour Party, the Trades Unions and Incomes Policy, 1945–74*, Oxford 1976.

F. Parkin, *Middle-class Radicalism: The Social Basis of the British Campaign for Nuclear Disarmament*, Manchester 1968.

H.A. Turner, *et al.*, *Labour Relations in the Motor Industry*, 1967.

J. Westergaard and H. Resler, *Class in a Capitalist Society: A Study of Contemporary Britain*, Harmondsworth 1976.

Index

WITHDRAWN

Cressman Library
Cedar Crest College
Allentown, PA 18104

DATE DUE

322.20942
H666 ℓ

3 1543 50131 7178